Advanced Praise

Jeni takes you on an intimate journey of transformation and liberation. She invites you to join her as she learns to shine the light of grace on all aspects of her life, loosening the chains of perfectionism for the benefit of all people and all living things. Reading Jeni's story, you will be inspired to heal and love from a place of grace, wisdom, and profound acceptance.

 —April Kaiserlian LMSW, Psychotherapist and
  Certified Meditation Teacher

In *The Life That Love Builds*, Jeni Juarez shares her life journey with deep authenticity, vulnerability, and insight. Within this work is a beautiful invitation into the sacred work of living compassionately and consciously, inviting pure love into your life and the lives of your loved ones. Here we find a pathway both for living in connection with the deepest realms of our internal, wonder-filled inner child and for looking outward in awe at the miraculous universe we all share.

 —Benjy Wertheimer, Shantala musician

A journey from trauma to triumph. With raw honesty and deep poignancy, Jeni Juarez takes the reader through her quest for healing. As she navigates painful experiences, she always concludes with her own "Hindsight Wisdom," or wisdom from a mentor, mystic, or spiritual teacher. A must-read for seekers of wholeness and self-healing.

 —Elizabeth Meyette, author of *The Silenced Ones*

The Life That Love Builds tells the story of one woman's journey as she overcomes adversity and heartache. This is a thoughtful and insightful story about the power of light and love as a guiding source for one's life.

 —Cheryl Blackington

In *The Life That Love Builds*, Jeni invites us to share her journey from struggle and pain to healing, authenticity, and transformation. Through her eyes, we can see what is possible when we face our shadows and open to the lessons they can teach. Along the way, we can't help but laugh, cry, and fall in love with her.

—Carol Hendershot, Certified MBSR Teacher,
Co-founder Grand Rapids Center for Mindfulness

The Life
that Love Builds

The Life
that Love Builds

**HOW TO COME HOME TO
YOURSELF BY LETTING GO OF NORMAL**

Jeni Juarez

To my mother. You are my first and greatest spiritual teacher, and your wisdom floods my heart as it does these pages. From the depths of my soul, thank you for giving me life. I love you.

To all the great matriarchs of my family, for your courageous continuation of a wisdom that runs deeper than any written words could convey.

To the Baba in the Blanket, Maharajji. We both know this is your book. Thank you for this life that your love continues to build from unseen realms. Thank you for being there from before the beginning and after the end.

TABLE OF CONTENTS

Preface

"I'm at a point in my life where I need to focus on the material world. I'm going to go to college, get a career, buy a house, make a family, and build my success. Maybe when I'm old and I retire, I'll come back to my spiritual life."

As my mom took in these words—an odd declaration for anyone to make, let alone her sixteen-year-old daughter—an expression of shock and sadness swept over her face. Then came a look of disgust. "So, you're preparing to die?" she asked. I went silent, and we both let the conversation drop.

You see, it hadn't been long since I confided to my mother that my heart was beckoning me toward the depths of mystery that existed beyond modern religious dogma. I told her that I had rediscovered this incredible joy by connecting to nature with a childlike curiosity, appreciating the moon phases, bodies of water, flowers, and herbs; making special teas and lighting candles while taking time for silence and reflection; and praying for goodwill for myself and others.

I had even purchased a unicorn tarot deck. Unicorns were always my favorite animal growing up (they still are), even though so many of my peers, as well as adults, loved to tell me they didn't exist. The readings I did for myself felt more like intimate conversations between myself and my heart than the demonic, evil fortune-telling myth I had been fed at church.

This wasn't new for me; as a child, I was a natural yogini and kitchen witch. I'd lie on the living room floor, moving my body into what I now recognize as *asanas,* or yoga postures. I had a rock collection stored in a unicorn tin, and I'd make natural "weed killer" and other potions at my gramma's house with her giant stash of spices, soaps, and perfumes. I talked to butterflies and bumblebees, and I adamantly believed in angels, fairies, and mermaids. I sang made-up songs in an operatic voice, and I believed my canned chicken noodle soup contained magical healing powers.

When I told my mom that I was turning away from this—my intuitive, wonder-filled nature—toward a materialistic, achievement-driven ideology, she equated that to a sort of death. It would take me many years and painful experiences to realize what she was alluding to.

Introduction

"Always tell the truth and you will never be afraid."
—Neem Karoli Baba

I've known for a long time that this book needed to be written. It has been begging to come through me since my childhood when I first wrote out a timeline of notable life events as well as a scathingly judgmental introductory paragraph. Oh, that pre-teen angst!

The subtle tugging to write a book stayed with me throughout my older teen years and early twenties. I saved all of my journals and poetry from those respective periods until I put down the pen for a decade of noise and distraction, focusing instead on my outer life at the expense of my inner life. Even then, I remember making a few comments while I worked at a bookstore, saying things like, "I can't decide if my future book will be shelved as humor, a memoir, or a self-improvement title," and, "I'll probably write a book someday, but I'll have to wait until my parents die."

Well, now that I'm walking into my forties, I can no longer ignore that little voice inside beckoning me to "live out loud." To be clear, I don't find my life to be particularly extraordinary. I don't have an impressive resume or education, I don't have a brand or a technique to sell you, and I'm not the leader of a non-profit or some amazing humanitarian effort.

Actually, I've spent my life desperately trying to fit in and be normal. Perhaps the most remarkable thing I've done is to survive. But something magical happens when we're brave enough to share our stories: we inspire others to share theirs, too. And as we each find our voice and our power, so too will we find our collective freedom from all the limiting beliefs we've adopted since our youth.

But first, there are a few things I'd like to be upfront with you on:

- I am a work in progress. I am not all-knowing or saintly; I fuck up a lot (and swear a lot), and I definitely get things wrong. But you can count on me to call it like I see it. After all that I've been through, I refuse to put on any more masks. You'll only get the truth from here on out, no matter how uncomfortable it is.

- I did not write this book to tell you how to radically change your story and live your best life. I wrote this book to tell you that you *can*. That *we* can, together. (And it *might* look totally different from what you're envisioning right now.)

- While I do think it's important for us to draw lines in the sand when it comes to our values, I'll be the first to admit that I have changed my mind countless times in my life already. By the time this book is printed, it's likely I will have widened and refined my perspective again. And I think that's a *good thing*. May we *all* endeavor to continue learning, growing, and evolving, no matter our age or circumstance.

- I share stories from my life experience as an offering of love to you. My prayer is that my willingness to be vulnerable might make you feel less alone, less impotent, less unworthy. I know for a fact that you are powerful, brave, and deserving of all the love, joy, and peace you could imagine in your wildest dreams.

A Broad Stroke

My life has not been an easy road to travel. I am a child of a nasty, highly contested divorce. I have been obese since I was eight years old, and I was a lonely, only child until I was ten. I was relentlessly bullied for my weight and social class by my peers and adults throughout my adolescence. I possess a history of debilitating anxiety and bouts of depression, along with suicidal thoughts and attempts. I've been the patient of almost a dozen different psychologists, and I spent two weeks of my sophomore year of high school participating in a voluntary outpatient stay at a mental hospital. I have a history of alcohol addiction, substance abuse, and disordered eating. I've experienced countless instances of unreported sexual harassment, assault, and abuse. And perhaps most painfully, I have suffered mental and emotional abuse from the people who were charged with ensuring I felt safe, loved, and accepted.

I am also a truth-teller. A survivor. A mother. A spiritual warrior. An intuitive. A contemplative. A yoga instructor. A writer. A confidant. And an unrelenting optimist. I possess an insatiable curiosity, a hunger for wisdom, and a longing for community. And I am dedicated to self-realization and liberation-while-living. I have a ceaseless drive to empower others to take charge of their own healing journey because, as I have been known to say, *If I can do it, anyone can do it.*

I spent the first thirty years of my life doing what I thought I was "supposed" to do to be a *good girl* worthy of love and praise; to fit in and be accepted. I achieved honors in college and graduated with a business degree because it seemed like the most practical choice. I worked my way up the retail corporate ladder from seasonal help to assistant store director over the course of fifteen years. I got married, had children, and bought a house before I turned twenty-five. And yet I carried on with a tortured and agonizing interior life ever since I was a young child. I was the epitome of "high functioning."

As is the case with many stories of transformation, mine occurred because of a traumatic loss. When my grandmother died in 2014, whoever I was until that point died along with her. I faced the choice of giving up or rebuilding, and I chose to rebuild.

Over time, I found the courage to confess the pain of my inner landscape and to seek the help of mentors, teachers, and friends as I navigated the new territory of intentional self-care and healing. I embarked upon a 200-hour yoga teacher training program in pursuit of this new passion of radical self-love. I began to reevaluate my interests and hobbies, choosing to redefine and align myself with life-enhancing communities and experiences. I abandoned my career path in favor of more time and space for myself and for what *really* mattered to me. I discovered the richness and freedom of living life out loud by coming out from my own shadow and boldly sharing my story and my feelings. And by doing so, I discovered that I am not alone on this path, although feeling alone is a very common sentiment shared by trauma survivors.

How to Approach This Book

What follows is a collection of stories from my life from my point of view—the only perspective that I can speak to with any amount of definitive confidence. I offer a keyhole glimpse into my inner world, and I share with you some of the most practical yet significant practices (including meditation, yoga, mindfulness techniques, and other healing methods) that have supported me along the way.

You may at times resonate with me, and perhaps at others, want to throw this book across the room. Some stories may evoke warm feelings while others bore you or make you feel sad. My invitation to you is to walk beside me in this vulnerable exploration of the most poignant experiences of my life and bear witness to a perspective that may be different from your own. Invite yourself to take part in this practice of inner exploration and become like a scientist investigating your own experience.

I do not recommend that you sit with the intention of reading this book front to back in one or a few sittings. Instead, let it unfold in bits and pieces, maybe selecting a story to read at random or flipping through until you are drawn to something. My intention is not to "share my life with you" but to share experiences that culminated in new layers of understanding—of deeper compassion, integrity, and wisdom—as a support to you.

A lot of what happens in our lives is beyond our control. However, on a fundamental level, we have a choice: fear or love. I spent many years building a life from fear: fear of failure, fear of looking foolish, and fear of abandonment. In doing so, I abandoned myself. Now, let me show you the kind of life that love can build.

I offer this book with a profound and inarticulable amount of gratitude for the teachers, guides, and loved ones who've walked this path before me and who have offered up their Light so that I could find (and continue to find) my own. My personal definition of Grace is an intelligent unfolding of unfathomable love. It is through Grace alone that I am still here today to tell my story, and it is through Grace alone that this book will come from my heart, through my fingers, out to you. My prayer is that you will accept what is useful, discard what is not, and ultimately conclude that your intuition—your own deepest knowing—is and will always be the final arbiter of Truth.

PART I

The Separation

A Slow Day in Eden

Standing at sunrise,
       Contemplating intentions.
I've sought memories
       In meanings hidden and
Found chaos.
My grasp is slipping –
       My mind is sleeping.
           I've misplaced motivation,
       But the longing still exists.
Reckless words hold power to bind
       My ankles uncomfortably to the ground.
Head tilted slightly back
       To see in the sky
       What on earth
       I cannot find.
This garden once inspired
       now lies fallow.
Darkness steals color from life and
       suffocates hope.
But I,
       I breathe possibility,
           Awakened by curiosity,
       No longer in a haze.
Upon the death of those false expectations
       Shall I create a mountain of poetry.

1

The (not so) Great Before

As I grew older, the adults in my life began to teach me what they thought was right and wrong, good and bad, appropriate and inappropriate according to the unspoken agreements and rules for participating in "civilized society" in the eighties and nineties. And so began my feelings of not-good-enoughness, of trying to be a good girl and making everyone proud so I could feel loved and accepted.

I have yet to meet someone who has come out of their childhood in one piece. While many of us eventually conclude that our parents did the best they could, the truth is a lot of them did some real harm, both physical and psychological, while struggling through the work of raising us. Most of them carried a lot of unresolved childhood wounds—wounds passed on generationally—into their own adulthood and parenting style. And my parents were no exception.

I don't know much about my parents, grandparents, or extended family. We never talked about it. Except for my grandpa on my dad's side, who talked about himself so much that I started tuning him out. I regret that now; I wish I had taken the time to hear his story then. But when it comes to my parents' lives, all I have are the soundbites of stories often told when they were under the influence and feeling a little less armored.

My dad is the oldest of five siblings. He was an average student and a great baseball player. He had an excellent work ethic and ruthless determination to get what he wanted. Although he came from a financially modest family, he earned and saved enough money to buy himself a brand new Z28 Camaro when he turned eighteen. He still owns that car, and I'm pretty sure he considers it his oldest child.

Despite his work ethic and his playful personality, my dad was continually criticized by my grandfather. His hair was too long, his music too loud, his grades too low. I don't doubt that my grandfather loved his firstborn son and felt that his "tough love" approach was in my dad's best interest. However, all it seemed to do was instill a pervasive sense of unworthiness in my dad. A stern disciplinarian, my grandfather convinced my dad that he was a bad kid who deserved the spankings, groundings, and struggles that he's had to endure to get to where he is in life.

Although my dad never laid a finger on me out of anger, he most certainly took up my grandfather's habit of criticism as motivation. If I got an A- on my report card, my dad would ask what I could have done to make it an A. If I got an A, what did I need for an A+? If I said, "This sucks," he'd ask, "Is that Christlike behavior?" It was as if I were a dog or a machine that he was constantly trying to program for perfection. When I achieved momentary perfection, the ecstatic adoration I received was intoxicating. When I came up short, the shame and subsequent self-loathing were catastrophic.

I know even less about my mom's childhood, except for some rather significant traumatic memories replayed again and again by her. Her mother was a fiercely independent and brilliant woman who lacked warmth and patience for children. And her dad was a tortured genius and an alcoholic. My grandmother left my grandfather, my mom, and my two uncles to save herself when my mother was very young.

I don't know if my mom ever fully recovered from the wound of abandonment by her mother. And it was made all the worse when my grandfather died before her eyes when she was seventeen years old. She had miscarried just before his death, and the grief she felt after his passing was beyond anything she could make sense of. One month later, she walked the stage with her graduating class, and just two months after that, she found out she was pregnant with me.

Having only recently begun dating my dad, I don't know that her pregnancy was planned, easy, or even wanted. And all of that anxiety, grief, and traumatic pain settled deep into my developing body as I shared my mother's inner agony from within the womb.

My early childhood memories of my mother are few. My inner snapshot of her at that time is of a woman with adamantine determination to prove her worth to a world hell-bent on dismissing it. She took some night classes at college for computer science while working as a waitress at a nearby bowling alley and later at her uncle's restaurant. After reconnecting with her mother, who was now working in hotel finance, my mom endeavored to break into the misogynistic IT industry of the 1980s. When it came to her professional life, my mother was brilliant, intense, and took no bullshit. Her natural beauty and charisma made men love her and women envy her. But in her personal life, she was aching.

I remember my mom sleeping a lot when I was young. It seemed she was so weighed down with grief and depression that, at times, she could not even stand. This was not the life she had imagined. She had dreams of finishing her degree and making a name for herself in the fields of psychology and philosophy. She wanted to help children thrive, travel the world, and own a beautiful home with a pool and a closet the size of a bedroom. Instead, she got married at eighteen at the justice of the peace while two months pregnant with me.

When I was about preschool-aged, my dad played softball for two different pub-sponsored leagues. After working long days as a truck driver, he would go play ball with his buddies and then head to the bar afterward. My mom and I would sit in the stands to watch him play for what felt like hours until she'd take me home to wait for him. At other times, she'd take me along to the bar, leaving me to play under the tables and mess with the tabletop poker game or the pool sticks while they both drank.

Although not evident by his weeknight choices, my dad tried to shake my mom loose from her deep sadness. He'd cajole her into a game of golf or a trip to the beach, and occasionally, a weekend getaway. But no matter where they went or what they did, the connection didn't last long, and they'd eventually devolve into screaming matches or resentful silence. My mother's grief over the loss of her father and her own abruptly ended youth was a heavy load that my dad was not equipped to support her through. They loved each other deeply, but their unhealed wounds made it impossible for them to see or hear each other.

Around that same time, my mom accepted a job at a hotel with her mother in a city that was forty-five minutes away. Instead of commuting daily, she began staying the entire week at the hotel. I didn't find out until much later that it was during those weeklong stays that my grandmother would beg my mom to leave my dad and instead move in with her. My grandma couldn't stand my dad, and she no doubt believed she could offer her daughter what she thought would be a better life.

The deep loneliness I felt in my little body became all the worse during those periods of separation from my mother, punctuated by embittered arguments on the weekends. I have heart-wrenching memories of holding my arms out to the sides like a V as I stood between my parents, crying and begging for them to stop fighting.

Overwhelmed by the energy, I would lock myself in the basement bathroom, howling out loud that it felt like my heart was breaking. I still recall the sensations of my emotional heart feeling stabbed and ripped apart as I sat on the cold, tiled floor. My nights were filled with recurring nightmares of falling endlessly into a black void, never hearing anyone, never seeing anyone, never reaching the bottom, feeling lost, alone, and afraid.

Hindsight Wisdom

I can already hear the defensive responses that some of you may have toward this. "...good intentions, ... came from a good place, ...didn't mean harm." And I get it! The truth is, I didn't even realize how much this constant beratement negatively affected me until I began using the same language on my own children. And then I began to notice their perfectionistic tendencies and the accompanied anxiety that it causes, too.

Whether it was because my dad was concerned for me, concerned for his reputation, or a little bit of both, his behavior was a repetition of what he internalized as a child, and his unconscious motivation was fear. But let's be clear: this is a subtle form of mental abuse, rooted in intergenerational trauma, and it *has. to. stop.* And the cycle can only be changed if it is first interrupted. That work starts with *us*.

"The child is very open and can feel the pain and suffering going on in its immediate environment. The child is aware of its own body and can also feel the tension, rigidity, and pain in the mother's body or anyone else it is with. If the parents are suffering, the child feels it. If the mother is suffering, the baby suffers too. The pain never gets discharged."

—A.H. Almaas

The Slow Death of a Family

I wanted nothing more than to be with my mother. So, when she sat me down one night in our living room, I was eager to be near her and hear her secret. She told me that someday soon, I might need to decide which parent I wanted to live with. She hoped I would choose her, but she assured me that she'd love me no matter what. I was eight years old.

Not long after that scary conversation, I woke up one morning to "catching" her trying to pack a TV into the back of her gray Oldsmobile while my dad pleaded with her in the kitchen not to leave. My mind filled with fear and confusion as I watched them, but no one stopped to even look at me, let alone speak to or reassure me. They were like children themselves, frantic and lost in a sea of emotion.

After an overwhelming exchange that my frightened mind could not understand, a memory was created that would never go away: me sitting in a recliner in that same living room, now with my dad's head in my lap, crying and repeating, "Jeni, what are we going to do?" Any boogeymen in the basement or Bloody Marys in the bathroom mirror didn't hold a candle to the terror and sense of helplessness that took hold in my heart that day.

> "Trauma is not what happens to you; trauma is what happens inside you as a result of what happens to you."
> —Dr. Gabor Maté

The divorce was ugly and unfriendly, spanning the course of five years. It essentially amounted to a half-decade-long custody battle over me. As their attorneys argued on each of their behalf about who was and was not fit to raise me, I spent most of my days and nights at my grandparents' house. I maintain that if it were not for the unwavering love and tenderness of my grandmother, I would not have been able to keep afloat enough in my formative years to be the contributing member of society that I am today.

Those blurry years of the divorce changed me from the playful, imaginative child that I was to a shy, awkward, anxious little girl.

My grandparents kept their house stocked with sweets, so I began to soothe myself with food. By the time I was in fifth grade, I wore a men's 42 waist in jeans, and I had sized out of the girls and even juniors' clothing sections. I was isolated from school friends and cousins because of the stigma attached to broken families in the Catholic community at the time, not to mention my parents' fear of outsiders seeing our "dirty laundry." Disconnected from my friends, my family, and myself, I began in earnest to fill the unfillable hole inside with food and TV.

During the years of the divorce settlement, my mom reconnected with an old boyfriend—her first true love—and moved into a townhouse with him. He was passionate and playful in a way that seemed to spark her back to life, but he was also a belligerent alcoholic and rebellious, continually getting into legal problems from the time he was a teen. Still, their chaotic love story swept them both off their feet and had them believing in fresh starts.

When I was ten, they moved into a rental home so we could have enough space to welcome my soon-to-be-born sister, Alyssa. Alyssa's dad also had a son from a previous relationship who was my age, extraordinarily kind, and quickly became one of my closest friends, even though we only saw each other every other weekend. Because of the limited time they got with us "older kids," the weekends that we were all together became like mini celebrations. We'd play sports in the yard, rent piles of movies from the video rental store, and make an event out of grocery trips to purchase all of our favorite snacks and foods.

Despite this respite, my mom was longing for more; she wanted a house that she could call her own. It was anything but easy, no doubt, for my mom to purchase a house on her own income while co-parenting a pre-teen, caring for a baby, and navigating the profound mental and emotional challenges of postpartum and post-marital healing. But eventually, we moved into a beautiful home in the same neighborhood in which she had been raised. When she looked out at our backyard, she could see her childhood backyard butted up against the property line. She had rebuilt her life from scratch and was celebrating her successes in her job and her hard-won freedom to finally be herself.

Meanwhile, my dad started dating an awful woman whom he worked with. She was fat-phobic, openly racist, and overtly disgusted with my body. Although she loved to make butter-rich pastries, pasta, and other comfort foods, she constantly remarked about my food choices while simultaneously glorifying her two younger daughters and their athletic, slim builds. Not only would she degrade my dad's intelligence by calling him a stupid Polack, but I would also hear her call my mom crazy and a bitch while she'd complain to my dad about their messy divorce. Hearing her talk about my parents like that filled me with rage that I wasn't allowed to express.

My mom purchased a journal for me and encouraged me to write about everything that I was feeling and experiencing. I had never journaled before, but it was such a relief to pour my big emotions out all over the page each night. I filled the journal with everything from curse-laden tirades about how much I hated my dad and his girlfriend to how much it hurt to see the boys and girls begin taking notice of each other at school while I continued to be the receiver of fat joke after fat joke.

Feeling like an outsider at my dad's house made it much more attractive to spend time at my mom's. My mom talked to me like an adult, and we'd do sister-like things, like staying up late playing dominoes by candlelight, going shopping, watching movies, and taking drives to the beach. She wanted so badly for us to be friends, and I was so eager to drink up any time I could get with her.

By the time my parents settled their divorce, I was thirteen years old and thoroughly jaded. Both of my parents were too self-absorbed to notice how dark my inner life was becoming. I still preferred to be at my mom's house, but that slowly changed, too, as my mom's relationship with her boyfriend became more chaotic and violent. Eventually, I didn't want to be with either of my parents. I felt very alone; it seemed that even God had abandoned me during those darkest days of my life. Incoherent memories of unsettling sensations, smells, and snippets of screaming, fighting, alcohol, and police clutter my mind to this day.

Hindsight Wisdom

When we experience trauma, whether a single instance like a car crash or a repeated trauma like child abuse or neglect, our prefrontal cortex (the most evolved part of the brain) goes offline. This temporarily blocks our ability to use logic or reasoning. Meanwhile, the primal part of the brain, the amygdala, goes online instead, initiating the fight-flight-freeze response. In the case of persistent/pervasive trauma, the continual activation of the amygdala and deactivation of the prefrontal cortex leads to a hypervigilance that makes it difficult to construct "firm" long-term memories.

What we end up with is a mishmash bundle of fragmented memories of sight, sound, smell, touch, taste, and stories that aren't remembered in a beginning-middle-end sequence. This repression of memories is only one symptom of complex post-traumatic stress disorder (C-PTSD), which is the emerging diagnostic term for individuals who have experienced repetitive, inescapable, relational trauma. It has been very relieving to learn this as an adult, finally understanding why I have so many holes in my memory from my youth.

A Window of Hope

Although it was an incredibly dark and scary time for me, certain activities kept the light of hope flickering within my heart. My grandparents took me to different parks, museums, and sometimes even plays or musicals. They kept a stash of art and baking supplies so I could create and express myself during the long days I spent at their house. We'd listen to opera and classical music, and they even purchased a used piano when my parents signed me up for lessons.

Another source of joy was the near-weekly trips to the bookstore that my dad and his girlfriend took us on. Those two or three hours were sacred to me. I'd collect an armful of books about dreams and poetry, and my favorite go-to anthologies—*Garfield* and *Chicken Soup for the Soul*—before locating an oversized comfy chair to bury myself in. My love of reading books and writing poetry carried me through many lonely days.

It was through Grace that I returned to my natural sense of childlike wonder for a fleeting moment in my early teens. During this time, I found some of what would become my longest-lasting friendships. Meg and Anna both had their own stories of heartache from their formative years, and this mutual vulnerability was part of what bonded us so closely to each other during our freshman year of high school.

Together we talked about life like ancient mystics and sages, writing and performing poetry at coffee bars and contemplating the purpose of life and the nature of reality. We would do full moon rituals and honor the solstices and equinoxes, and we learned together some of the medicinal benefits of plants and herbs. We didn't realize it at the time, but we were planting seeds for a future awakening: a remembering of sacred practices long forgotten by our blood-and-bone ancestors.

Falling Back to Sleep

But just as easily as I had remembered my essential nature as one in the web of many, I quickly forgot again as I grew closer to adulthood. That fateful conversation with my mother in which I told her I intended to "shelve my spirituality" until old age marked the emergence of my success-driven false self (ego) and the forgetting of my intuitive wisdom.

As the layers upon layers of painful life experiences piled on, so too did my attempts to numb the agony I was in as a result of them. By the end of my freshman year of high school, I was smoking cigarettes, drinking liquor, and putting myself in risky situations on the weekends with some new friends from school. AOL (America Online) had recently been introduced, so I began spending a lot of my weeknights flirting and making friends with strangers in chat rooms and through instant messenger. I suffered terribly from insomnia and developed a mild (self-diagnosed) case of obsessive-compulsive disorder (OCD). But despite all of these attributes of complex post-traumatic stress, my strongest and most pervasive survival strategy was perfectionism.

Feeling so out of control for so much of my young life, my mind sought to control any and everything it possibly could. I adopted the false belief that if I did everything exactly perfectly, I would be invulnerable to pain and disappointment. I created detailed charts for recording my weight, measurements, food intake, and daily exercise goals. When my fixation on my body's size didn't work, I turned my focus toward developing strict beauty routines with the goal of having perfect skin, hair, and nails. I also strived for perfection at school, obsessing over my grades, taking as many advanced placement courses as I could, and aiming for straight As in all subjects.

Although I was maintaining my fragile exterior of achievement and put-togetherness, inside, I was living a tortured existence.

I would pray not to wake up the next morning; living felt like an unbearable burden. I began to experience suicidal ideation and even attempted to take my life in bizarre and unsuccessful ways, like trying to drink bleach in my coffee and eat broken glass mixed into my oatmeal. I started cutting myself and putting matches out on my skin as a way to release some of the deep psychological pain I was feeling. Eventually, the incessant panicking and catastrophizing took their toll, and I asked my dad to be admitted to an outpatient therapy program in a mental hospital.

For two weeks of my sophomore year, my grandparents drove me to the hospital instead of school, where I'd spend seven hours rotating between individual and group therapy and alone time. We did worksheets on alternative ways to process difficult emotions, and I was asked over and over if I was currently a danger to myself. I made some "friends in suffering" who would encourage me to answer "Yes" to the recurring question, so I could stay the night with them, a request I'm relieved to say that I turned down.

After two weeks of assessment, it was determined that I had "situational depression" and a generalized anxiety disorder. I was prescribed Prozac and sent back to school. There wasn't the language or understanding of a highly sensitive person or complex developmental trauma. There was no inquiry into the root causes of my neuroses; only some pills to dull my strong emotions enough to let me get through the day.

I remember a friend at school remarking, "You don't seem sad anymore, but you don't seem to feel anything." I spent that evening contemplating swallowing the entire bottle along with the muscle relaxers my pediatrician had prescribed for my back pain. The next morning, I gave my dad a large bottle filled with various prescription pills and told him I didn't trust myself with them.

Hindsight Wisdom

Life can be really hard sometimes. If you're feeling overwhelmed by emotional distress and are not sure of what
to do next, you may find it supportive to reach out to the
National Suicide and Crisis Lifeline by calling or texting
988.

I first encountered the Adverse Childhood Experiences (ACE)
study when I read about it in *The Deepest Well: Healing the Long-
Term Effects of Childhood Adversity* by Dr. Nadine Burke Harris (I
highly recommend it). The study found a direct link between childhood trauma and adult onset of chronic disease, incarceration, and
employment challenges. Although the study had been conducted
in the nineties, it wouldn't enter even the fringe of medicine until I
was well into my thirties. At that time, there was no reliable framework for recognizing or understanding what was happening to my
brain and immune system as I encountered the repetitive traumas
of emotional and verbal abuse, feeling unsafe in my home and in my
body, and eventually, experiencing sexual harassment and assault.
And western medicine had nothing to offer me except band-aids to
cover up the pain.

I spent a month that winter living with my long-time and dear
friend, Julie. I couldn't handle being near either of my parents without having an anxiety attack, and Julie's parents had known my
family since Julie and I were in first grade. They were tender-hearted
educators who volunteered and went to church and didn't have a
single liquor bottle in their house. It felt so foreign that I remember thinking to myself, "Her parents don't drink? That's weird." And
then the very next thought crept in… "Or is my family weird?" It
was an eye-opening experience for me to notice a different way for a
family to "be" together. It gave me a glimpse of the kind of parent I
could choose to be someday.

Julie (right) and me at her house

The same year as my outpatient stint, my mom began to have what I understood as a nervous breakdown. Although she was now engaged to my sister's father, their drinking and past wounds made their precarious relationship more unstable and destructive. As he had done many times in his life, he eventually cycled back into the carceral system, leaving my mother once again to take on the difficult task of maintaining a home and caring for a young child all alone.

My mom seemed stuck in a mental health crisis for an extended period, hardly eating or sleeping. Inspired to renovate our home, she asked me to help her demolish the cement stairs leading from a door off the kitchen in the back of the house. She envisioned a slider off the back of the house, too, so she knocked the entire back wall out of the spare room, leaving our home protected from the world and the elements by nothing but a plastic sheet. Then she decided she didn't like how the stairs leading to the basement and second story were set, so she had a contractor rip both staircases out, temporarily replacing them with ladders.

I was so afraid to use the ladder to go down to the basement with my laundry. One day, while talking to Anna on the phone, the ladder slipped out from under me, causing me to fall on my back on the ladder as I hit my head on a cement uprising on the floor. I was knocked unconscious, and the phone cut out, triggering Anna to call her dad who called 911 and made the forty-minute drive in twenty minutes to my house where I was alone.

Meanwhile, I had somehow put the ladder back, climbed up, and went to the couch, only to go unconscious again. I awoke confused and, feeling a patch of warmth on my head, reached to touch my crown only to discover so much fresh blood matted to my hair. I called Anna immediately to tell her that I had been attacked while sleeping. Knowing better than filling me in on the forgotten details, she told me to stay put and that help was on the way. After an ambulance trip and some stitches in my scalp, I was sent back home, where things continued to get worse.

My mom had racked up a considerable amount of debt over the course of the renovations, but they were never completed. Having been abandoned by the contractors who did the demolition but would not complete the work, our once beautiful and cherished home was like an abused and neglected woman who could no longer safely hold our family together. Not long after, my mom had no choice but to forfeit our home to the bank. Suddenly, we were packing her and my sister up to move to Florida to stay with her mom.

She asked if I wanted to go with her, but I was terrified at the thought. We had endured almost a full year of not speaking to each other after an argument that ended with her slapping me across my face and me walking out the door and to my dad's. Her drinking and dysregulated nervous system were both triggers of my anxiety and depression, and our interactions were often at risk for volatile emotional eruptions from either or both of us.

I also knew that the circumstances in Florida would not be joyful or stable. Not only was the relationship between my grandma and mother fraught with dysfunction and old trauma wounds, but also my grandmother had been so cruel and unloving toward me the last time I had seen my her that I came home and considered suicide again. My mental health was in crisis, and I couldn't imagine walking away from what little familiarity and stability I had in my life, so I made the heartbreaking decision to stay.

I will never forget how it felt to watch my mom drive away from me again. Only this time she had my then-six-year-old sister and one of my best friends in the car with her. My friend was having a tough time at home and decided to take advantage of the opportunity to move in with my mom and sister. She ended up coming back not long after, but the feeling of being replaced remained with me for years. Our friendship was never the same again.

I kept coming back to the house for a couple of weeks even though it was now bank-owned and in foreclosure. I would wander around the empty house, screaming between loud sobs as I tried to make sense of what was happening. I still didn't like being at my dad's, even though he had broken up with his wretched girlfriend, and now with my mom gone, I felt abandoned and alone all over again.

Toxic Love and Hard-Learned Lessons

By my junior year of high school, I was sleeping over at one of my girlfriends' houses most evenings. My dad started dating the woman who would later become my stepmother. After working 8 a.m. to 8 p.m. all week, he would make the forty-five-minute drive to stay at her house on the weekends. With no real reason or desire to stay home, I started regularly going out to parties after school and on the weekends.

I met my first serious boyfriend at one of our after-school parties. Beau was two years older, handsome, and kind of mischievous in an alluring way. After a long night of talking and making out, I was totally infatuated. A mutual friend convinced him to go to Homecoming with me, so we started spending more time together. I'd hang out with him and his friends after school, and we'd smoke weed, listen to music, drink beer, and play cribbage. Our group and all of their parents became like family to me, and it wasn't long before I started packing a duffel bag and spending the weekends at his mom's house with him.

Beau and I had a lot of fun together; we'd take drives, go golfing, shoot pool, and party. He was my first chosen intimate relationship, and I was pretty head-over-heels for him. I didn't notice the toxic traits of our relationship for a long time. But looking back, I can see how, whether intentionally or not, he was starting to influence how I looked and what I wore.

He'd mock me by calling me "Face" because it was common for people to comment on "what a pretty face" I had, implicitly detaching my fat body from the compliment, and he'd tease my large eyes by calling me "alien eyes." Beau put a lot of emphasis on how we looked together, so we'd often match our outfits and work out for fun. I remember feeling so special when he and two of his friends took me to the mall to help me pick out some new sneakers. Slowly but surely, my whole look was changing.

I got introduced to Mini-Thins through one of his friends—a "caffeine" pill that was just legal speed meant for adults and truckers. It gave me the energy to get through all my AP classes, homework, and work, and it also conveniently suppressed my appetite. I started running and doing cardio after school, and I lost fifty pounds in about three months. I'd also pop them for fun when we'd go drinking on the weekends so I could have the energy to go all night.

Hindsight Wisdom

In a fat-phobic culture that fetishizes extreme weight loss, eating disorders are often overlooked or even celebrated if it means you're achieving a more "normal" body. Adolescents and adults alike continue to be subjected to this abuse via toxic beauty culture because of the false belief that a fat body is an unhealthy body and a thin body is a healthy one, completely ignoring the dangerous methods oftentimes used to achieve a lower weight.

If you are suffering from the harms of disordered eating, please know that you are not alone. It is not a personal failure, and you deserve support as you begin your healing journey. For support, resources, and treatment options, consider reaching out to the National Eating Disorders Association (NEDA) online (nationaleatingdisorders. org) or by phone call or text at (800)-931-2237.

Depression followed me like a shadow those first couple of years after my mom and sister moved. Alyssa would send me cards filled with artwork and her newly learned handwriting, and my mother would send me cards with flowers and kittens on the cover, with the insides completely covered in her words of love and encouragement. She knew how hard the separation was on me, so she would plead with me to stay strong and remember who I was and how much she loved me.

But the words weren't enough. I was languishing in my mind, completely cut off from my body and the world around me. I lived in my head all day, telling stories of fear and abandonment and worthlessness. So as soon as I was done with work and school, my only goal was to drown out the incessant thought streams that assaulted me. I spent my entire senior year in a haze of drugs and alcohol, sometimes mixing them as a personal form of Russian roulette.

A year into my and Beau's relationship, I went to Florida for Christmas to visit my mom and sister at my grandma's house. When I came back home, things began to change. He started calling me his "Sunday-through-Thursday Girl," and he'd tell me that he needed space from me to hang out with the guys on the weekends. Some nights I'd stay at his mom's house, sitting in his room by myself, looking out the window and wondering when he'd come home. And the more I pressed him about what he was doing, the more he'd accuse me of suffocating him and being too needy.

What unfolded in those following months would teach me more about self-respect, trust, and integrity than I could ever want to learn. I discovered that he had cheated on me with more than one girl, but even that wasn't enough for me to break up with him and move on. I wanted him for myself because I believed that no one else would ever love someone like me. And out of that desperation and fear of being alone, I humiliated myself again and again.

Couch Surfing My Way into Love

Right before my high school graduation, my mom met a man named Martin through an internet group about mediumship and hypnotherapy. She boldly decided to take a solo trip across the ocean to meet him and a group of like-minded individuals. And while there, she fell in love with him. Martin asked her to marry him, and after coming to the States to meet our family, Martin brought my mom and sister back to England with him.

Not long after, my dad proposed to and married my stepmom, sold my childhood home, and moved twenty minutes outside of the city. The new house was a charming one-story ranch sitting a little back from the road, and it was surrounded by trees. Having grown up near downtown Grand Rapids my whole life, this move was a drastic change that I was not okay with. All the darkness and eerie quiet provoked my anxiety so much that my stepmom would tease me about how easy it was to find the house at night since I had every single light on.

It was an hour-long commute to college and the bookstore I was now working at, so the extra gas money and the inconvenience put upon my robust social life were a huge drag. I started packing overnight bags again and stayed the night with friends. I reconnected with Anna, who had recently moved into a one-bedroom apartment with her new boyfriend, Felix. It was like a dream come true to hang out together, drinking and smoking, laughing and listening to music.

But the truth was, I was pretty messed up from my relationship with Beau. By that time, I was drinking a fifth of liquor every two days. It was to the point that I'd ask my buyer to get me two bottles at a time, so I wouldn't have to ask so often. Anna and Felix's apartment became a landing place for many of our friends and Felix's family. We would sleep in chairs, on couches, and on the floor, making trips to McDonald's for food and the gas station for mixers and snacks.

It was at Anna and Felix's apartment that I met my future husband, Paulo. He was Felix's younger brother, and he was going through a particularly difficult time. He was experiencing homelessness after leaving his grandfather's house and refusing to stay with his dad. Felix offered to let his brother stay at the apartment until he figured out his next move.

Paulo was charismatic and funny. I don't think I have ever met someone who made me laugh so much! We met in May, and we hung out together, along with his cousin, that entire summer. Paulo and I considered each other only friends; I was still going back and forth with Beau, and Paulo was ending a long-term relationship, too. We weren't interested in each other romantically, anyway. I had a lot of judgment about his background and vagrancy, and he thought I was an aggressive and bossy alcoholic. But by the end of the summer, we were inseparable. When I wasn't with him, I thought about being with him or plotted how to talk to or see him.

The way Paulo treated me was so entirely different from Beau's; I felt respected, valued, and seen. He was so patient with my awkwardness and my completely dysfunctional view of what an intimate relationship looked like. I would frequently punch him in the shoulder or chest when I got frustrated, and he would calmly say, "Jeni, I don't put my hands on you, please don't put your hands on me." I can't even tell you how many times he had to repeat that mantra, gently redirecting my inappropriate, habitual behavior like he would a difficult child.

I remember the night we decided to officially become a couple. It was late in the evening, and we ran up to 7-Eleven for some pop and snacks. We sat in the car for what seemed like forever and talked about how our feelings for each other had changed over the summer. He asked me if I was done with my ex, to which I replied with an emphatic *yes*, so we agreed to become exclusive.

That was in September of 2003. We had a twin-sized bed in Anna and Felix's would-be dining room, and we pinned sheets to the ceiling with thumbtacks as makeshift walls. I had a plastic tote with some clothes and personal items in the corner. Without even asking, we started playing house at our friend's and brother's place. I still feel a twinge of embarrassment over how presumptuous we were, but I am so grateful for the space that my friends (now family) gave us at that time because it completely changed the trajectory of our lives.

Making a Nest of Our Own

It all changed rather quickly, actually. Two months after we officially started dating, I received a promotion to cafe manager at the bookstore. I had only been in the lead barista position for six months before that, so it was a sudden and unexpected blessing to be recognized for my leadership and to receive a sixty percent pay increase. The job change was fortuitous because a month later, Anna and Felix told us they were expecting a sweet baby in the coming months and they wanted to start creating their nest, alone.

Never in my life had I been so brave or impulsive, but I decided that since I had recently gotten a raise and we were so in love, we should get an apartment together. Paulo was working as a cook at a restaurant and donating plasma at the time. He told me that whatever money he made would go to our place. That was enough for me! We grabbed a newspaper and looked through the classifieds, circling potential options in our price range. When I told my dad our decision, he wasn't so sure about it.

"Why don't you just live at home until you finish college? You won't have to pay rent or utilities, and you can focus on school," he said.

"Because Dad, I already pay for my phone bill, my car insurance, my gas money, and my personal items, clothing, and food away from home. I may as well add rent to the list and have my own space and live closer to school."

That was part of it, but a bigger part of the truth was that I had a place to return to from Anna and Felix's, but Paulo didn't. And that uncertainty made me sick. I *loved* this man, and I couldn't think of a more logical decision than to move in together. It proved to be the start of such a sweet and devotional, frustrating, and emotional love story of two souls who, in the words of our oldest daughter, "probably find each other in every lifetime."

It still kind of catches me and makes me smile when I think about how young and impulsive we were to jump into the decision to move in together. Until I met Paulo, my "life plan" was to open a sports bar in a quiet town nearby where a college was soon to be built. I imagined myself staying up all night drinking and talking shit to employees while schmoozing with customers, living alone, and sleeping all day. I had told my mom long ago that, thanks to my sister being born after ten selfish years of only-childness, I had experienced the "birth control" necessary to know that I did *not* want to be a mother.

Boy, was I wrong! Once Anna and Felix's baby girl was born, my heart started to yearn for the family bond that I always felt was missing from my own life. I knew as soon as we moved in together that my heart belonged to Paulo; there was simply never any question for either of us. Living together felt so natural and comfortable. We were in sync, and we loved each other's company.

So when, after a year and a half of dating, my mom invited Paulo and me to England for a seventeen-day visit, we started talking a little bit more seriously about getting engaged. I remember teasing him, saying, "Ya know, if we know we want to get married someday, it'd be pretty cool to say we got engaged in England..." He smiled because he knew I was right, but he wanted to play it cool so we could pretend that it was more spontaneous than it was.

My mom, Alyssa, and Martin lived in a little town called Stoke-on-Trent near Manchester. While we were visiting, my mom attended a two-day hypnotherapy course in London. When she was in class, my stepdad took us kids on a tour of the city.

As Paulo and I explored the subway station, we checked out the small shops that lined the waiting area. We saw a jewelry store that had big signs advertising, "Going Out of Business! Everything 50% off." Accepting it as a symbol of good fortune, we quickly ducked inside while the rest of my family waited for our scheduled departure.

I immediately found two rings that I loved, and Paulo shooed me out of the storefront so he could decide which one would be *the* one.

That night, Paulo asked my mom for permission to ask for my hand in marriage. I love that about him—that he decided to ask the parent whom we were with, even if it wasn't "traditional" according to Western culture to ask the mother. It felt so special that he'd honor and respect the mother of his bride-to-be in that way. He got on one knee in the middle of our room at the bed & breakfast and declared his love for me as he asked me to marry him. And even though we had imagined and planned and shopped together, it was nonetheless one of the most special and unforgettable memories of my entire life.

It was not long after we returned from England that my eleven-year-old sister reached out to confess that she wanted to come home to the United States. She told me that Mom and Martin's marriage had taken a bad turn, and it was wearing on her. Of course, there was no question that she could come to stay with us, even though that meant we would need to play the role of guardians to her. Paulo and I were prepared to make sure she got to and from school, ate, and had all that she reasonably needed. Although we agreed to jump headfirst into this big responsibility, fate had other plans.

My mom and I were struggling to get the power of attorney documents sorted out, so I couldn't enroll Alyssa in school. At risk for truancy, my mom had no choice but to abruptly walk away from her marriage to make sure her youngest child was registered for middle school. They both stayed with us long enough for my mom to get a job and secure an apartment. Who knows what might have been if that situation had played out differently? But with our space back to ourselves once again, we started to plan our wedding.

A lot happened in the five years after my mom and sister came back from England. Paulo and I got married in the tropical climate atrium of a beautiful garden and sculpture park, and we honeymooned in Vegas. Not long after, we packed all of our freshly opened wedding gifts into my dad's basement, cut our belongings by one-half, and moved into a 600-square-foot apartment while Paulo worked two full-time jobs so we could hurry up and pay off the wedding debt we had accumulated.

Our first dance as husband and wife

I was promoted to district cafe trainer at the bookstore, which meant I was charged with training newly hired or promoted cafe managers throughout western Michigan in addition to managing my own store's cafe. Between eating at restaurants, enjoying happy hour with my coworkers, and paying off our wedding debt, we were making the most money of our lives but not seeing much of it.

Despite my childless declarations to my mother a few years back, Paulo and I started trying to get pregnant immediately after our wedding. We knew we wanted to start a family, and we really wanted to have our children while we were young. It was what our parents had done, and we liked how they were in their forties and still had a lot of energy for life, with most of their kids grown and out of the house. On Mother's Day in 2007, our dreams came true. I was pregnant!

Elaina Breathes Meaning into Our Lives

My pregnancy with Elaina was fraught with mental and physical stress. Anxiety hijacked my brain, and I spent a great deal of the time worrying that I was somehow harming my unborn child without knowing it. I was already fat when I got pregnant, so it didn't take long for the excess weight to affect my back and neck. My posture was poor from standing all day on hard tile in the cafe, and eventually, my hips and knees were aching, too. With Paulo working third- and first-shift, I was alone most nights. It was pretty lonely in our tiny apartment by myself, so I slept for most of the time that I wasn't at work.

There was a lot I didn't know about pregnancy and childbirth. My Catholic middle school had ripped the section about human reproduction out of our Christian morality textbooks and gave them to our parents to teach. So, of course, this meant that I didn't learn what was involved in making a baby until I was a grown woman trying to get pregnant. The fearful perfectionist in me obsessively checked day-by-day fetal growth websites and books, frantically checking *What to Expect When You're Expecting* to look up any weird feeling I experienced. I was so convinced that I might have Elaina in the car on the way to the hospital that I went to the ER three different times during my third trimester, thinking that I was in labor when I wasn't.

The third time though, I begged them to keep me. My cervix was dilated five centimeters, and I was getting closer to active labor. I probably would've lasted a few more days at home, but I didn't yet understand the importance of patience during the childbirth process. It was ten days before my due date, and the hospital gave me one hour to cross the 6cm dilation threshold for them to admit me. After an hour of squats and lunges during and in between contractions, I got my wish. Had I known what was going to come next,

I probably would've gone home to wait it out and let nature take her course.

My labor stalled shortly after I got settled into my room, so they put me on Pitocin. The pain of the artificially stimulated contractions quickly escalated beyond what I had ever imagined, and with a dysregulated nervous system and no coping skills, I panicked and immediately requested the epidural. As scary as that giant needle and the "potential for death" waivers were, it was lovely to be able to take a nap after being awake for over twenty-four hours.

I learned some tough lessons about consent during my labor and delivery with Elaina. First and most importantly, *know what you're consenting to if asked whether med students can participate in your labor and delivery.* Each time I was checked for dilation, at least two or three individuals were putting their hands up in my vagina and rooting around to measure my cervix.

No one ever asked whether I had a sexual trauma history; no one ever checked in to see if I was still comfortable with the agreement. And I was too deep in the process to appreciate how entirely inappropriate the whole thing was, considering my history and that this was my first child. I felt like a lot of choices were taken away from me, either by not informing me ahead of time or by talking over me without asking for my input.

Worse yet, by the time I was ready to push, the epidural had worn off on the right side of my body. With half of my lower body numb and half alert, I pushed for forty-five minutes before our sweet girl came into the world. Having been in labor from midnight until 11 p.m., I was exhausted. The bright lights turned off, and the overly full room dissipated. As the doctor, nurses, and students, as well as my mom and sister, slowly exited, we began to take in the full measure of what had happened.

There was this precious and fragile little being who was now our responsibility to care for and keep alive. It was both awe-inspiring and horrifying at the same time; I felt waves of joy and protective-ness crash over me while I silently battled back intrusive thoughts of dropping or hurting her by accident. Lord, parenthood is not for the faint of heart. It was clear to me right away that Paulo's experience with his twelve brothers and sisters was going to be a crucial support to my panicky and paranoid handling of our newborn.

I tried in earnest to breastfeed, sitting in bed with our baby girl, humming to her as she sucked away. But after our first full day home, her demeanor started to change. Paulo was back to work, and I was trying to console her in any way I could imagine. I vividly remember holding Elaina close to me as I rocked her in the bathroom while sitting on the toilet with the light off, door closed, and water faucet running. I was trying to mimic the environment of the womb, gently singing as I rocked her to the backdrop of falling water. It was not enough; she was inconsolable, and my anxiety started to race.

I called Paulo and asked him to come home from work. His boss wasn't happy, but he immediately dropped everything and drove the five-minute commute home to us. My mom came over the next day because Elaina started running a fever. She recommended we give her formula, so I tried to feed her with a little medicine cup. But she was too upset to drink. Off to the emergency room we went.

What happened next would leave a deep trauma wound in all four of us. Because she was only three days old, the hospital's pro-tocol was to do a spinal tap to rule out meningitis. Not grasping my rights as a patient, I quickly acquiesced to the procedure even though my mom kept repeating that perhaps she was hungry and needed a bottle. I angrily shushed my mom's wisdom, fearing that if we seemed combative, they might decide not to treat our daughter. So, Paulo summoned up the bravery that my mom and I lacked and went into the procedure room to observe.

It would take hearing the story dozens of times over ten years later to fully register the gravity of what happened next. Because

Elaina was dehydrated, the doctor couldn't extract any spinal fluid on his first attempt, so he tried again. Paulo's body tensed as he carefully watched this man before him, sweat beading on his forehead, as he hesitantly said, "If I can't get anything on this third try, I'll go get the doctor."

Shocked, Paulo asked, "Wait, what do you mean you'll go get the doctor? Aren't you the doctor?"

"Well, actually, I'm a medical student," he replied.

Paulo was livid. "No, we're done here. We're going to try something else. You're not stabbing my daughter with that needle again."

So, with the spinal tap test off the table, the next thing they did was hook up an IV to get some fluids pumping into her. I still remember her tiny little naked body, with her arm taped to a stiff brace to prevent her from bending it. She kept fighting against the brace because, as a newborn, all she wanted to do was curl up into a warm ball. But here she was, naked in a glass bassinet, away from my arms, with a needle pumping fluid into her veins. I don't even know where my mind was that night as we sat in the room staring at her. I think my heart hurt so much that I numbed out to the whole experience.

After twenty-four hours of IV fluids, Elaina was perked up and ready to be discharged. Traumatized by the story in my head that I had nearly starved my daughter to death, I refused to try to put her to the breast anymore. If I couldn't see it physically going into her mouth, I wasn't about it.

I pumped and cried for two weeks, supplementing her formula with two ounces of breastmilk per day before I gave up trying to give her breast milk completely. That hospital stay changed me. I didn't feel qualified to parent this child, so I did something I never could have anticipated: I asked Paulo to quit his job.

Paulo did not bat an eye. He told his boss he was quitting without notice because his wife and daughter needed him to be home. Since I was a manager, I was getting paid 100% of my salary during my maternity leave. It was barely enough to keep us afloat, but it would work. We spent the rest of my six weeks off together, immersed in the sleepless haze of newborn life and loving every moment of it.

Me and my little Elaina Bear

When it came time for me to go back to work, Paulo regularly brought Elaina to the bookstore to visit me. She became known as the "bookstore baby," and all of my coworkers and regulars would fuss over her during their visits. Although my schedule wasn't ideal, I felt at ease knowing our daughter was being well cared for by her daddy. In fact, once she turned a year old, we started talking about trying for another baby. We knew we wanted our children to be born somewhat close together, and Elaina was getting to such a fun age of running and babbling and playing that we felt confident we could do it all over again.

Hindsight Wisdom

First of all, my mom was right. Had I known better and had I not been so trapped by fear, I would have advocated differently for Elaina. Perhaps I wouldn't have even gone to the hospital in the first place.

There are so many non-medical resources available to birthing people these days. Lactation consultants can make home visits, as can doulas, midwives, and other supports. Most insurances cover the cost of an in-home breast pump, and there are local community groups online that can even provide donated breast milk as new moms navigate the natural-but-not-easy practice of breastfeeding.

The First Signs of Burnout

Sometimes I look back, and I wonder, how the hell did I do that?! There I was: twenty-four years old, married, and a mother to an infant, working full-time, and in my sixth year of college. My bachelor's degree was taking *forever* to complete. After my first full semester of a twelve-credit course load on top of full-time employment nearly pushed me to a nervous breakdown, I switched to two classes per semester, three semesters per year.

It was frustrating to work retail hours *and* not have summer vacation off from school. I had almost no free time, but I was damned determined to finish what I had started. And I was still holding onto the belief that my business degree would be a golden ticket leading me to a fifty-thousand-dollar-per-year income, until I discovered that I was pregnant with Nolani exactly one month before the end of my final semester, that is.

While Paulo and I had been planning to have another baby soon, I expected that it wouldn't happen until after I graduated, got a new job, and bought a house. Going off-script felt like a failure.

I knew that no company was going to hire a pregnant woman for a leadership position. And as excited as I was for this second baby, it was discouraging to have worked so hard to climb the corporate ladder while finishing my degree, only to accept that I'd continue wearing a hat and an apron, serving coffee to folks at the mall.

My hopes of stepping away from the cafe into a higher-paying position were briefly reignited when I found out my store was transferring our location to the mall across the street. Everyone had to be reinterviewed for their position, and I heard whispers that an assistant store manager position might be opening up. So, I seized the opportunity to throw my name in the hat.

When I was interviewed and then passed over for that promotion in favor of an outside candidate with more experience, I was deflated. We were now a year beyond the financial crisis of 2008, and the recession meant a wage and hiring freeze the very same year I graduated. Many companies started filing for bankruptcy, and middle management positions were being eliminated everywhere. I felt trapped in my position, reliant on my employer for my family's survival.

By the time Nolani was born, the income that once had us feeling free to do what we wanted when we wanted now barely covered the bills. With two young children, an increasing inflation rate, and rising food and gas prices, we were struggling. I watched as the same $125 that used to fill our grocery cart to the brim began to cover only a small handful of items. Soon, I was applying for WIC and food stamps to make it week-to-week despite being a college graduate and a manager.

Now with a two-year-old and an infant in the house, Paulo going back to work was off the table; none of our parents were retired, and daycare was outrageously expensive. Thankfully, if there was one thing that Paulo and I had each learned growing up, it was how to adapt and be resourceful. With our two creative minds, we made it work for a little over another year on only my income. It broke my heart to work so much; I missed a lot of "firsts" with the girls. But Paulo's patient attention to the girls was much better than my overwhelmed, panicky self, so the division of labor worked for us.

The Haze

If I could describe in one word what that first year of having two babies, twenty-three months apart, was like, it would be *frenetic*. It was wild and intense and very disorienting to have two babies in diapers, on two different nap schedules, both competing for my attention. Not only that, but we were also quickly outgrowing our two-bedroom apartment.

We were considering moving into a three-bedroom apartment in a complex down the road where my friend and her family had recently moved. It had in-apartment laundry, which was desperately needed, but the rent was going to be almost $1,000 per month, which was $300 more than what we were already paying. When I told my mom this, she nearly had a heart attack. Having closed on her own home a few months prior, she had been (not so subtly) encouraging us to look at buying a house instead of renting, too. Plus, there was an incentive that President Obama had created in response to the recession that was giving first-time homebuyers an $8,000 tax credit if they closed on their house by June 2010.

At that time, we had seven weeks until the deadline. So, we figured, what was the harm? We may as well see what kind of mortgage we'd qualify for. And if we couldn't find something before the deadline, we'd go with the super expensive apartment.

I am not kidding when I say that we looked at forty-five houses in about four weeks. I was up late at night, texting my realtor home listings that I wanted to line up for the next day. Houses were selling fast because of the incentive, and we were only qualified for an $80,000 mortgage.

Most of the houses we looked at in our preferred neighborhoods and limited budget were dilapidated or gutted, with scary basements or crumbling foundations. Then one day our realtor texted me and said, "Jeni, I know you feel strongly about this area of town, but I am telling you this house is a gem, and I really want you to consider it."

Now, it's not that I was trying to move into a rich, white suburbia neighborhood where all the houses looked the same. Both Paulo and I came from poorer backgrounds and sketchy neighborhoods, so that wasn't what turned me off to this area. It was that it was only two blocks away from a major highway and four blocks down from one of the busiest intersections of Grand Rapids. This wasn't exactly a walkable neighborhood. I was resistant, but I agreed to humor her.

As we pulled up, Paulo jumped out of the car to peek through the oversized front window. He smiled big at me and said, "We're going to put an offer on this house."

I rolled my eyes and smiled back, thinking, "There's no way in hell we're putting an offer on this house."

Boy, did I change my tune when we got inside. The front rooms were giant and open, and the kitchen had more cupboard space than I knew what to do with. All the bedrooms had hardwood floors, and the master bedroom upstairs was enormous. Intoxicated by Paulo's enthusiasm, I didn't immediately notice the lack of outlets in the rooms or the very ugly and outdated bathrooms (carpet in the upstairs bathroom!), and I had no idea what I was getting myself into with the wallpaper hiding the plaster walls with deep cracks in them due to the natural shifting of the house.

But it was meant to be because even though the house was $5,000 over our initial budget, I received a surprise bonus check of a little over $5,000 at work. So, with a few extra documents proving the legality of our sudden cash injection, our offer was accepted, and we were set to close. Adding to the synchronicity, our closing date was set for the day after Mother's Day.

We had six weeks to move before our lease was up on our apartment, so we took the $8,000 tax credit and put it to work on updating the house. We made some plumbing repairs, updated the breaker box, swapped out all the outlets in the house from two-prong to three-prong, and gutted and redid the hideous upstairs bathroom with its god-knows-what's-on-it blue carpeting. We even ripped the three layers of wallpaper and wainscoting off the dining room walls before Paulo and his buddy spent several days mudding and sanding and mudding and sanding to fix the crumbling plaster we had exposed.

I finished repainting the final room, our bedroom, the night before we were set to move. Nolani was five months old, and it was a very exciting occasion indeed. We even got to retrieve all of our wedding gifts from my dad's basement after four years of not being able to enjoy and use them, along with many other boxes of our belongings we had to pack away when we first moved into that cramped apartment only a few years ago.

Starting to Sink

It took me quite a while to adjust to our new house. Even though we had blown through the tax credit trying to get it cleaned up and move-in ready, it still needed a lot of work. Now we were broke, and Paulo was still a stay-at-home dad. I would cycle between loving all the space and being thrilled to know it belonged to *us*, to feeling suffocated in a crappy house in a crappy neighborhood. Still very much recovering from giving birth only five months earlier, I wanted nothing to do with meeting the neighbors or even hanging out outside in our yard.

Another struggle I was facing was my body image. Although I had lost an unhealthy amount of weight in a short period of time in high school, those first few years of living with Paulo and learning how to cook for us caused me to put all the weight back on and then some. By the time we got married, I weighed over 240 pounds, and I peaked at 270 pounds when I went into labor with Elaina. On my 5'2" frame, that was a lot to carry on top of my children.

My doctor recommended a medical weight loss program through the local hospital that was used as a pre-bariatric surgery program. I went to an informational meeting where they explained that, for sixteen weeks, I would agree to consume only their soy-based, pre-packaged protein sources, and nothing else. No fruits, no veggies, no nothing. It was called a Very Low Calorie or VLC Diet.

For four months straight, I ate 800-900 calories per day in the form of what I called "astronaut food," and I attended weekly meetings where we would be weighed, get bloodwork done to check our health stats, learn about nutrition, and participate in group exercise. It was expensive and the food was horrible, but the self-deprivation was oddly familiar and comforting.

Besides the medical weight loss program, Paulo and I had also purchased a membership at the YMCA. We started taking the girls to their daycare (which Nolani hated), and he and I would work out together and separately for up to two hours most days after work. I was laser-focused on being skinnier than I had ever been because I was *certain* that if I was smaller, I would feel more comfortable in my body and stop hating myself so much.

The thing is, even though I was losing weight, we weren't healthier. I was still drinking a lot, I was working inconsistent shifts and I had nothing resembling a normal sleep schedule. There was very little enjoyment or appreciation of what was going on in my life. I was so overly focused on *taking care* of my girls and the house that I rarely, if ever, stopped to look them in the eyes. It felt like I was constantly busy, running toward a finish line that kept getting pushed further away from me.

Hindsight Wisdom

The fact that I needed to have bloodwork done to ensure that I wasn't internally dying should have given me pause. Instead, I did this sixteen-week self-abuse program not once, but TWICE. I did not yet know that a diet over-saturated in soy-based foods could increase the possibility of breast cancer due to too much estrogen, nor did I appreciate the very frustrating reality that no matter how strict the diet protocol, if it was short-term, the results would be short-term, too.

My First Big Goodbye

That achievement-driven, obsessive momentum toward an impossible perfection was tragically derailed a few months later when, only a month before Nolani turned a year old, my grandfather went to a routine checkup and ended up being sent to the hospital instead.

He had been diagnosed with Myelodysplasia or preleukemia. His blood counts were dangerously off, so he was given a transfusion. But for whatever reason, he wasn't given proper Lasix between bags, so his lungs flooded, and he had to be intubated. For the next ten days, he remained heavily sedated on a cocktail of opiates and muscle relaxers.

My grandpa used to love hearing me sing, and we would frequently have singing contests in the car where we'd both sing nonsense words in operatic voices. My gramma was always the judge, and I was always the winner. He especially loved it when I agreed to cantor at the Cathedral downtown; he was my biggest fan as I led the songs during Saturday night mass. Remembering this when we had a quiet moment alone in his room, I softly sang to his weakened and dying body. I sang the song that first came to mind; the one that I sang to my daughters every night at bedtime: *A Dream Is a Wish Your Heart Makes* from Disney's *Cinderella*.

I promised him that I would take care of Gramma when he was gone. I promised him that she wouldn't be alone and that we were going to be okay.

A couple of days later, my grandmother had to make the difficult choice to remove him from life support. I remember that time so clearly. My grandmother, a diabetic, refused to leave his side to eat or even to go to the bathroom. She was determined to be there for his final breath. Many times, we would watch his body heave as if it were about to take its final breath, only for him to take in another. This went on for a torturous four hours.

Suddenly, a flash of insight came to me. I was so nervous to speak it aloud because it felt insensitive, but my body knew what needed to be done. I leaned over to my grandmother and quietly asked, "Gramma, is his pacemaker still on?" A flash of shock and horror spread across her face as she realized what was happening. She immediately paged the nurse, who came in with a magnet in his hand. His face contorted with embarrassment and pain as he explained that as soon as he placed the magnet on Grandpa's chest, the pacemaker would stop functioning, and he would pass. Minutes later, he was gone.

My grandfather's passing was a painful first true experience with death. I had attended my great-grandmother's funeral as a middle schooler, but this was very different. Watching the life force leave his body shocked me as if someone had dumped a bucket of ice-cold water over my head.

As I began to navigate this new territory of grief, I felt compelled to look at how I was living my life. I could no longer escape the reality that I, too, would someday die. It was time to wonder what, in the words of poet Mary Oliver, I planned to do with my "one wild and precious life."

2

When Your Path No Longer Fits

Shortly after Nolani's first birthday, Paulo was offered a first-shift job in manufacturing, and the girls were babysat by a few different angels disguised as family members. But over time, there were competing needs or conflicting schedules, so we made the difficult choice to put the girls in a daycare center. It was good for them to play with other kids and go on field trips, but it cost us $100 a day, which was almost exactly what I earned in a day's work. Since I wrote the schedule for the cafe, I shifted my work hours to mostly nights and weekends to reduce the cost burden of daycare.

It really sucked; Paulo and I felt more like single parents as we tagged in and out of watching the girls while the other parent worked. We did our best, but there were many arguments over who worked harder and what the other person was or wasn't doing or appreciating. And the daycare center was so damn expensive! We weren't even remarkably better off than we were when living on one income. I had to climb higher up the professional ladder. I may not have gotten the assistant store manager position at my new store, but with the high employee turnover rates in retail, I believed that another chance would come my way and this time I was not going to be overlooked.

I had already been fairly vocal about my interest in moving to the book side for a promotion, but now I was in full-on personal advocate mode. Every single time my district manager would come for an operations walkthrough or a store visit, I would drop it casually into the conversation that I'm still "very, very interested in moving up in the company." When our store's payroll budget was cut, I offered to take over some administrative responsibilities and become a temporary keyholder, both without a pay increase. I upped my game, built relationships, and took every opportunity to prove how capable I was. I probably don't need to tell you that as a younger, overweight woman working in food service for the past decade, it was an uphill battle to be taken seriously, no matter *how* many promotions I had accrued over the years, even with my college degree.

I became so discouraged by how many times I had been told that I was being "groomed" for the position and that I "just needed to wait for the right time." I started applying for new jobs outside of the bookstore. I interviewed for a supervisor position at a distribution warehouse (which would've had me commuting over an hour in one direction) and at a wholesale tire dealership. I made it through three interview rounds for a store manager position at a children's clothing store before it was determined that my wage demands were unrealistically high. As it turns out, small-volume retail stores couldn't compete with my slowly but steadily increasing pay after a decade in management.

My frustration with being continually overlooked and underappreciated for my talents kept growing, as did my stress levels. Anyone who has worked retail knows that not only do you regularly get verbally "beat up" by customers but that the higher-ups relentlessly demand that you make more and more profit every year with less and less payroll.

Time and again, the bookstore demanded that the business come before my family. There was little to no regard for my free time, and I would often get calls or texts on my days off. Mandatory weekends, mandatory December overtime, and shifts that started as early as 6 a.m. and ran as late as midnight (or later on those dreaded monthly inventory nights) meant that I had no opportunity to establish a healthy sleep schedule, or any kind of schedule, for that matter.

I was feeling trapped on the hamster wheel and my body paid the toll. Being in the cafe provided easy access to sweets and coffee to numb my depression and anxiety. And the camaraderie among my fellow baristas and booksellers over the crappy customers and oppressive corporate management led to many nights of pilgrimage to the bar next door. We'd bitch, laugh, and cry about our shared experiences over late-night happy-hour cocktails, cheap burgers, and fried food.

I often got out of work so late that everyone at home was asleep. I told myself that I wasn't hurting anyone by staying up and out all night since they didn't know anyway. I'd joke that my method was: coffee and sugar to wake up, vodka and weed to fall asleep. My days and nights off were spent obsessively cleaning the house, running errands, and making up for lost time with my daughters and husband. There was no time for friends or extended family gatherings, and I had zero concept of personal time or self-care.

My depression and weight grew in lockstep with my drinking. I felt like the Wizard of Oz in the scene where Dorothy pulled back the curtain to discover that it was only a man operating all the levers and pulleys to make things look more impressive than they were. I was behind the curtain of my life, pulling all the strings to make it look perfect, but never participating in it.

Work became a reliable excuse to dodge everything from invitations from friends to dreams about the future. With no discernible weekend, I floated through endless weeks, always living several months ahead of reality as we would rush to tear down displays the day after a holiday, only to immediately switch gears to the next future season or holiday. Wake up, work, tend to the kids, eat, numb out, sleep, repeat.

All that changed (or so I thought) when I got the news that an assistant store manager position was opening in a store that was a forty-five-minute commute away. I felt like this was my big chance.

I visited my alma mater and asked for assistance with my resume, bought a fancy blouse and suit jacket, and delved into financial reports and interview guides in preparation for my interview. I nailed my first interview and then the next. And finally, five years after my first try, I got the promotion I had been waiting for.

My new store was a whole new demographic. It was near the lakeshore of Lake Michigan and served a much older, much more conservative crowd. The store did about a quarter of the sales volume that I was used to, and with much less square footage than the shiny "new" store from which I had come. I didn't care; I finally got the promotion that I knew I deserved, and I was eager to help my new store get back on track with its metrics and prove that I belonged here.

Much wiser than the first time I had switched to a new store culture, I started by keeping my mouth shut and listening. I learned about the people who worked there, what interested them, and how they worked together as a small team. I found it much easier to assimilate into the bookseller staff than I did the management team. Once again, as the youngest manager on the team, I had to work extra hard to prove my right to sit at the table.

Things seemed to be going pretty okay until my gramma's health began taking a turn. She had been cyclically ill ever since my grandfather's death a little less than four years earlier, but that still didn't prepare me for what was to come.

Unconditional Love

I recall a comment that I had made to my best friend at the time: "When my gramma dies, you'll want to keep an eye on me because it might break me."

She was my favorite person. My sunshine. My heart. We had spent countless days together when I was younger, but nothing compared to our closeness after Grandpa died. We were spiritually connected. Paulo and I made every effort to include her in our travels with the girls. We'd take her to parks, to the bookstore, out to dinner, to the gardens we'd gotten married at ... We would bring her to our house for dinner or visit her little independent living apartment for coffee while the girls played with her walking canes and jewelry collection.

My gramma and me

It was effortless and joyful to spend time with her. No matter where our conversations went, she never made me feel unloved. Gramma became increasingly candid with me, sharing how she'd battled with anxiety and depression for many years and how my grandpa had secretly been drinking quite a lot of wine near the end of his life. Our relationship felt safe and authentic, and it was a profound experience of feeling seen and heard. Every time I would get into an argument with my parents, I knew I could count on my gramma to listen to me sob on the phone. And she always gave me wise and calm advice.

Toward the end of 2014, my grandmother was consistently rotating between home, hospital, and rehab. I began to visit her nearly daily, trying to shine some love and light on her whenever I could. One day, I brought all my nail care tools up to the hospital to give her a manicure. I gently held her hand in mine, feeling her paper-thin skin beneath my fingers. She loved having brightly colored nails, and it was a pleasure to fuss over her. I even painted her toenails on one foot; she had lost the other to amputation two years prior.

Hindsight Wisdom

Through my experience, I maintain that if a child has even *one* person in their life who provides them the space to just *be* without the expectation of being a "good" boy or girl, that child can thrive despite nearly any trauma or obstacle. For me, that person was my gramma. Never discount the potentially significant impact that even one moment of loving attention can have on a child.

Breaking the Taboo

That November, on what would have been her and Grandpa's anniversary, I went to the store for some daisies (her favorite) and Starbucks (also her favorite). I had planned to surprise her at the rehab facility and see if she wanted to go out on a date. When I got to her room, it was empty and disheveled. My heart skipped a beat, and I started to panic. I rushed down to the nurse's station and asked where she was.

Looking concerned, the nurse replied, "She just left in an ambulance; she's headed to the hospital." I grabbed my gifts and drove straight there.

She was still in triage when I arrived. They weren't sure what was going on yet, but she had had a bad episode of neuropathy, and she was in a long-term battle against MRSA, gangrene, and sepsis following her amputation. Her kidneys were starting to fail. She had already gone through several open-heart surgeries, and she had cataracts in both eyes. The woman was in terrible physical and emotional pain, but she never let on.

I remember sitting next to her bed in triage when these words surfaced out of the silence: "Gramma, what are you waiting for? It seems as though your body is ready to die... what are you afraid of? Are you afraid of what will happen to us? What will happen to me? Because, I mean, of course, it will hurt. The grief will be painful... but we will be okay. We'll have to be..."

I paused for a moment, feeling the full weight of what I had said. And then I continued, "You know if you ever want to talk about what your final wishes are, you can talk to me. I'll make sure it happens how you want it to."

As these words tumbled from my mouth, I felt a surge of surprise within. No one talks like this; at least, no one I know. When discussing the health challenges of others, statements are so often framed in terms of "getting better," as though death is some kind of error or personal failing.

After a long pause, she began to speak. "I don't want to wear anything fancy. Something simple and bright. And no shoes. That's silly and not necessary..."

As I realized what was happening, I quickly rooted around in my purse and found an old receipt and a pen. I began to write a list.

She continued, "...and I want all the male cousins and Paulo to be the pallbearers. And I want them to play *Amazing Grace* and *On Eagle's Wings* at the service. I want my funeral to be a celebration, not a sad day. Eat good food and be with each other."

Once I had written all her wishes down, I folded the receipt and put it in my wallet. After initially feeling audacious and a bit uncomfortable speaking so bluntly to her, now there was this sense of sacredness and an energetic sigh of relief between us as we acknowledged the reality of her predicament. I sat in silence with her until she was admitted and moved to her room.

Treasured Last Moments

It wasn't but a couple of weeks later that it became evident Gramma was not bouncing back this time. While at work, I got a call from my dad telling me I had better get up to the hospital because it didn't seem like she would be around for much longer. I drove through the disorienting darkness of falling snow with tear-soaked eyes that night.

When I got to her room, my dad, my aunt, and one of my uncles were all sitting around her bed. They had been there for a while, so they were quietly chatting, filling up the space with sweet stories and memories of their childhoods. I pulled a chair over to my gramma's bedside and stroked her dry, rough cheek. She was worn out but still mustered a smile for me. The lights in the room were dimmed, and my intuition once again began to guide me.

"My gramma loves opera. Can I play music on the computer for her?"

"Sure," the nurse replied.

As she watched me open up a Dove chocolate I had pulled out of my pocket, the nurse gave me a stern look and said, "She can't eat that. She's on a heart-healthy diet right now."

"Okay," I replied. But as soon as she left, I secretly popped the chocolate into my gramma's mouth. She smiled conspiringly at me and eased back, listening to the elegant voice of Andrea Bocelli as I stroked her hair.

The next day, I decided not to visit. My gut told me that her five kids would be up to see her, and I felt like my presence would be intrusive. Later in the day, I got a very hopeful text from my dad saying Gramma had turned a corner, was energetic, and was in good spirits. "That's wonderful," I thought. I'm glad they had that experience with her.

The following morning, I was up early and getting ready for work when I got a call from my dad. "You might want to come down here," he said.

I started moving quickly through the house, dialing Paulo's warehouse as his workday had already started an hour ago. As I was leaving a message, I walked into the living room to see Paulo sleeping on the couch. His intuition had told him to call in sick to work. A rush of relief fell over me. He agreed to take the girls to school and meet me at the hospital.

On my way there, I stopped at a nearby bagel and coffee shop. I walked to the counter with tears in my eyes and blurted out, "My gramma's going to die today, and everyone is going to forget to eat breakfast." I ordered a dozen bagels and a giant to-go pot of coffee with all the accompaniments.

Once at the hospital, I set the bagels and coffee down on a side table, and my family brought me up to speed. The doctors had put my gramma under a cooling blanket to lower the temperature of her body and to conserve her energy until we had made a decision. My aunt, a registered nurse like my grandmother, held medical power of attorney. Now justifiably over-identified with the role of daughter rather than RN, she struggled for a couple of hours, gathering the courage to make the impossible decision to let her mother go.

Once again, I found myself in my family's company, this time surrounding the matriarch of the family as she prepared to transition. While not as dramatic as my grandpa's passing, it was no less disorienting. After she passed, it was like we were waking up from a bad dream. Suddenly, everyone was ravenous, and we all took in the bagels and coffee as welcomed nourishment.

A flash of remembrance came upon me, and I reached into my wallet, pulling out the folded-up receipt with my grandmother's dying wishes. I handed it to my aunt, and gesturing toward it, said, "Here are Gramma's final requests. We talked about it a few weeks ago, and I held onto it for her." It seemed at that moment that Grace had worked through me to ensure my grandmother's peaceful transition from this world to the next, and I was so grateful to have witnessed it all.

Hindsight Wisdom

Considering our culture's disconnected and avoidant relationship to death and the dying process, I actually think it's rather auspicious that I found myself in a position to witness both of my grandparents' passing. The experience is more visceral than cognitive, so it's hard to put into words when you see the animating force exit a body. It's more like a felt understanding that whatever the core of our being is, it is both within and distinct from our human form. Understanding that "to our bones" changes everything about how we view death and, consequently, life.

If ever you have the privileged opportunity to hold space for someone who is nearing the end of their life, I would encourage you to accept that gift for what it is—an intuitive experience of the thin veil that separates the form and the formless.

Waves of Grief

The foreboding words I had uttered to my friend not long ago couldn't have been truer. When my grandmother died, it did break me. Whoever I had been up until that point had died along with her.

I was lost in the dark. I barely staggered through the birthdays of both my daughters and of my husband as well as Christmas in the month that followed. I owe Paulo a great deal of gratitude for the gracious, loving, and patient way he cared for me during that time.

I was only beginning to consider acknowledging my grief when, just five weeks after my gramma had died, I received news that my other grandmother, my last living grandparent, was severely ill with pneumonia. It was too much. When my sister and I flew out to be with my mom and uncles after my grandma Abbie passed, it was as though my life had been destroyed by a great cataclysm.

When I returned home, I was a ghost in the shell of my former self. I let go of my workout routine and fell solidly into a sugar-caffeine-alcohol diet. My will to live was at an all-time low. So much of that time is still a haze for me, but I do know that if it weren't for Paulo's patient love and willingness to take over caring for our girls as I floundered helplessly in my grief, things would have been much, much worse for us all.

There were many evenings when I would come home from work only to go upstairs and hide in my bedroom, rocking in my rocking chair and crying. I was in such a state of despair, and I had no clue what I was going to do. I slept like shit, had constant headaches and back pain, and vacillated between bursts of tears and rage. Once again, I was overcome with a deep heartache that made me wish for mornings to stop coming.

3

Turning the Page

One day, while I was having a crying session in my rocking chair, my mom came over. She took stock of me and asked me how I was doing. Through tears, I told her that I wanted to talk to my gramma again... to see her and hear her voice. My mom softly said, "Jeni, she's still here. You can talk to her anytime you want now." She guided me in a meditation and left me once she saw that I was settled in. Slowly, I began to fall into a kind of trance or daydream.

I pictured myself up in the woods behind my grandparents' old house. I grew up playing in those woods all by myself. It was very common for me to pack up a little sack with a journal or book, water, and some snacks, and climb up the initial, steep slope by grasping the smaller tree trunks and pulling myself up, leaning against the bases of the trees as I made my slow incline.

Once I got past the initial slope, there was a network of narrow paths carved out by many pilgrimages from children exploring or sledding, teens making out or drinking beer, and some unhoused folks looking for a safe place to rest. I knew exactly which path to take to go to the highest part of the hill. From up there, I could see a few blocks worth of houses and even the tops of some buildings downtown. There was an abandoned, broken-down car at the bottom of the steep drop-off, and oftentimes you could see deer and other critters looking for food and a reprieve from the noise of the city. To my childlike mind, it was like a hidden forest in the middle of the city.

At the top of this hill, right before the drop-off, lay a fallen tree, the perfect makeshift seat. In this meditative trance, I sensed my grandmother sitting next to me on the trunk. I could feel the warmth of her arm near mine, but I didn't turn to look at her. My gaze was forward and down, heavy under the weight of my grief.

"I wish I could hug you again and feel your cheek against my lips as I kiss you hello or goodbye. I know you're with me, but I want to see and touch and hear and smell you," I said.

As I began to cry, she turned to look at me and replied, "Whenever you want to hug me, go hug your girls. Go hug Paulo. I am a part of them. I'm a part of everyone you love. So, when you want to hug me, go hug your family. And we will be together."

As that vision began to dissipate, I recognized myself back in my room, still sitting in my rocking chair. With puffy red eyes and cheeks, and tears streaming down my face, I walked downstairs and saw both of my daughters standing in the kitchen. I collected them in a hug as they cautiously took in the sight of me. "Are you okay, Mommy?"

"Yes, girls. I'm okay. I'm grieving... I really, really miss Great Gramma. I was crying while I was thinking about her. But then she visited me in my daydream. And do you know what she said?"

"What?" they asked.

"She said that anytime I'm missing her, I should give you girls a hug. So that's what I'm doing."

They melted into me, and I knew at that moment that I had a choice to make. I could let this grief destroy me, or I could heal and transform it into something powerful and beautiful: unconditional love. For my precious family who never gave up on me, who patiently held vigil for me as I wept and rocked and hid away from the world, I would choose to grow from this.

I didn't have the words to articulate it yet, but from that moment on, I no longer considered my life my own; my life was now a gift—an offering of love and service to the divine Grace that had been saving my ass and guiding me every step of my life, even though I didn't have the eyes to see it or the ears to hear it.

"It was as if I had been told a secret twenty years too early," I'd say to folks trying to comprehend my choices following my grandmothers' deaths. When my gramma died, it felt like the loss of a parent. It shook the foundation of the carefully curated storylines of who I thought I was. Without her steady stream of unconditional love, I had no choice but to accept that no one was going to save me. It was time to love *myself* the way that she always had.

> "What you are is God's gift to you; what you make of it is your gift to God."
>
> —Anthony Dalla Villa

The Gift of Foresight

I remember sitting in the breakroom at work, reading an article in a healthy living magazine. It was an interview with some guy who had experienced corporate burnout, quit his job, followed his passion, and was now living his best life. As I read the interview, a particular quote jumped off the page at me: *"If you want to change your life, it's very likely that you're going to have to change your life."*

The quote stood out like a bolded cosmic joke from the universe. It hit me like a belly laugh/punch to the gut. I was embarrassed and emboldened at the same time.

At that time, our management team was pretty divided, and the gossip and manipulation were getting ugly. I saw that my store manager, recently promoted to a store with failing metrics and poor employee retention, was breaking her back trying to get some traction in literally any area of her store. She was working six to seven days a week, both in-store and at home, all hours of the day and night, and still, she was getting her ass handed to her during district meetings with the higher-ups.

I remember observing her one day as she unloaded all her winter gear, laptop, and files upon files of financial documents. She had just made a ninety-minute commute in lake effect snow, and she was sharing how she was experimenting with different natural remedies for stress and immunity, trying to get back into running after an injury, and looking to buy a house with her new husband.

She was talking and moving a million miles a minute, and in the chaos of all this, I was struck with a barrage of inner questions: "I'm aspiring to *this*? Look at how hard she's working! She's giving every last ounce of herself to this store, and for what? To be demoralized during weekly district conference calls? To work twice as hard as her male peers for less money? To regularly push her mental and physical health to their limits for some unseen governing body of shareholders?"

It's as if I were instantaneously reviewing the past six years since I graduated from college all at once. Flashes of late nights doing inventory and high-intensity holiday shopping seasons and the *constant.fucking.training* of new hires and strings of interviews followed by rejection calls and missed birthday parties and family gatherings and a shit diet and alcoholism and going sometimes up to seventy-two hours without meaningful interaction with my children, now six and eight goddamned years old and *OH MY GOD WHAT THE FUCK AM I DOING HERE?!*

Whole30 and the Seeds of Mindfulness

As the days passed, that quote continued to pop into my mind: *"If you want to change your life, it's very likely that you're going to have to change your life."* In my gut, I knew without a doubt that the path I was on was no longer directing me toward something I wanted. A change was going to be necessary, but what?

I needed clarity—an intuitive message guiding my next step. This longing for courage and inner guidance spurred a memory about the Whole30 program I had done the summer before my gramma died. A simple Instagram post made by a friend of mine led me to a couple of Whole30 hashtags, thus igniting my curiosity and leading me to research this Paleo diet-based program.

At first, I thought the "no beans, dairy, and whole grains" rules were absurd. All of the weight loss classes I had taken in my life touted the food pyramid and eventually MyPlate as the gold standard of ideal nutritional guidance. So, before I could buy into this protocol, I needed to understand the foundational basis for it. I decided to pick up the book *It Starts with Food* by Whole30 creators Melissa (Urban) Hartwig and Dallas Hartwig.

In the book, they explained what the Whole30 program was and the "why" behind the rules and parameters. Long gone were the days when I'd use fad diets for weight loss. I finally understood that any progress made through a temporary lifestyle change would never be permanent. *"If you want to change your life, it's very likely that you're going to have to change your life."*

The authors' claims seemed logical to me:
- Eliminate all foods known or believed to potentially cause inflammation and do it for a long enough time that the body's systems can heal a bit.
- Take note of any positive health changes as a result.
- Reintroduce the potentially inflammatory food groups one at a time with space in between, analyzing whether and how they impact your health.
- Adjust your typical diet according to the information you glean from the experience.

I was attracted to the idea of experimenting on myself. What did I have to lose? I was experiencing chronic pain every single day due to my multiple klutz injuries and working on my feet. My energy level was so low that I'd frequently come home from work and lie on the couch, going in and out of sleep until dinner and bedtime. My skin looked like that of a teenager, full of pimples and redness, and my eczema had ravaged my hands to the point that I was constantly scratching and bandaging them. If changing my diet for one month had the potential to help me reduce my weight, increase my energy, *and* improve my health, it would be worth a shot.

There were so many growing pains in my first thirty-day round. I'd never cooked that much fresh food for myself or my family before. No more boxed, bagged, or canned food, and no quick runs for fast food or take-out when I was too tired or lazy to cook. I remember chopping veggies on prep day, wanting to give up and go back to the easy processed food and take-out dinners. But instead, I'd pause and internally repeat this mantra: "I am honoring and nourishing my body with these foods. I deserve to eat like this." It took incredible amounts of willpower at times to overcome my cravings, habits, and inconsistent energy levels.

Hindsight Wisdom

I must confess, I was really angry that first round, and not because I missed sugar, bread, and alcohol (although that was true, too). I was angry from reading all the food labels on things I had previously taken for granted as health food. I'm telling you—big food companies don't give a *damn* about our health. They manipulate the levels of salt, sugar, and fat to light up our taste buds and the pleasure centers in our brains, so we keep coming back for more.

Did you know there are at least sixty-one[1] different forms of sugar used in processed food—things like brown

---

1 https://sugarscience.ucsf.edu/hidden-in-plain-sight/

rice syrup, sucralose, dextrose, stevia, corn syrup solids...
and they put it in *everything*! It's worth getting curious
about the ingredients in your weekly go-to grocery items
because the truth is you can't count on anyone who profits
from your habitual behaviors to truly care about what's for
your greatest good.

My experience with Whole30 during that first round was trans-
formative in the way it helped me strengthen my mind and body.
Although I didn't have to keep a food diary, measure or weigh por-
tions, or track macros, the protocol required me to slow down and
pay attention to every single ingredient I consumed. Preparing and
eating food became a form of meditation. And as each day passed,
my resolve strengthened.

I remembered how, after completing that first Whole30, I
had a level of energy and clarity of mind that I had never experienced before. So, upon my observation of my career aspirations
and the flash realization of the futile trajectory I was on, I decided
that jumping back into the thirty-day elimination diet could be a
supportive way to refocus, clear my head, and seek a new direction
for my life.

Part of the challenge of adapting to a whole food-based diet
is that mindless eating and food addiction are often caused by
emotional and mental stress. And the depression and grief I experienced after my gramma died dragged me right back to my familiar
self-soothing rituals of oversleeping, drinking alcohol, and living
off of sugar and processed food. But now that I knew how good I
could feel when I took good care of myself, the backsliding was even
more intolerable despite its stickiness. So, I started a second round
in February and a third in April.

Each time I completed a Whole30, I discovered new insights
and developed a more nuanced sensitivity of my body. I was treating

my body with kindness and respect for the first time in a long time, if ever. Instead of trying to abuse myself into better health, I was framing it as taking care of my body in a nourishing way. More important than the weight loss that I experienced were the non-scale-related victories. Not only did my eczema slowly heal, but my plantar fasciitis and back pain started going away, too. My adult-onset acne cleared up, and my hair and nails were stronger than ever. My mood was more optimistic, I slept more soundly at night, and my energy remained steady all day long. No more mid-afternoon coffee or naps!

Hindsight Wisdom

Acknowledging my chemical dependence on sugar also shined a light on my chemical dependence on alcohol. It took me an additional six years to unpack and over-write my drinking habits with healthier ones, but I don't know that I ever would've even noticed the habit while immersed in our alcohol-obsessed culture, let alone creating the space to work through it without doing a thirty-day detox. My suggestion to you is, if you think that you *cannot* go thirty days without drinking alcohol, that may be the exact reason why you could benefit from giving it a try.

I'd also like to mention here that the Whole30 program may not be the best choice for everyone. Whole30 co-creator Melissa Urban explicitly states in her revised Whole30 book (published in 2024) that she does not rec-ommend the program for folks with a history of disordered eating. Restrictive diets can become triggering if not done with the proper mindset and appropriate support. I will speak to this more fully later on in the book.

Reframing Self-Care

This newfound capacity for inward attention and self-discipline, and the associated zest for life, guided me toward expanding my repertoire of self-care practices. I would tell people that I was making it a kind of game to see how many different ways I could love myself each day, with activities like drinking water, eating whole foods, and taking a nap or a bath, depending on my needs. It became apparent to me that I was experiencing more success through self-kindness than I *ever* did by talking to and treating myself like a piece of shit.

But what was even better was that my definition of success was evolving away from the narrow and superficial metrics of weight, size, and sex appeal to what really mattered: qualitative factors like the improvement in my confidence, my stress management, my sleep habits, my mood, my participation in life, my strength, my marriage and friendships, my self-worth and self-love, and my enthusiasm and curiosity toward life. My quest toward effortless self-love and optimal health and well-being took me down many different and converging paths.

Over the following months, I started receiving immunotherapy allergy shots to help me better manage my seasonal asthmatic responses. I wanted to start exercising again, but I was too ashamed of my body to consider joining a public gym. Serendipitously, my neighbor offered to sell me her old treadmill. It was a deal too good to pass up, even though I was still working through my back and foot pain and was therefore rather limited to activities beyond work. I decided to make an appointment with my chiropractor. I hadn't been in to see him or my massage therapist since I had completed my shoulder rehab from a nasty, not-so-graceful fall down our wooden staircase the year before.

When I went to their office, I told them each, separately, "I'm in a dark place right now. I want to heal, but I am in so much physical pain, too. I can see that it's going to require multiple angles of therapy, and this is my first step. Tell me what I need to do." They worked with me and gave me exercises to take home. The doctor said my hip alignment was off and that I needed to work on my posture. I began by walking slowly on the treadmill in front of a mirror. I'd watch my feet and my hips, and I'd modify my stance to ensure my toes were pointed straight ahead.

Our family's first 5k

I started getting a chiropractic adjustment and a massage every week, and I got very consistent on the treadmill. I incrementally increased my speed over several months, and four months into my walking, Paulo, our daughters, and I participated in our first 5k.

All these changes in my lifestyle were beginning to shift the kinds of conversations I was having with my family and friends. My experience with Whole30 sent me down a track of curiosity about the ingredients in my beauty products, too. I discovered that I was a late arrival to the natural beauty scene, but my friend Meg was not, and soon we were chatting regularly about the no 'poo method, the benefits of coconut oil and essential oils, and the toxin-laden beauty products that we all use with little to no consideration.

We even started dreaming about creating our own line of natural beauty and self-care products like homemade deodorant, face wash, and bath bombs. It excited and inspired me the way she so confidently explained how straightforward and relatively easy it would be to launch an online business. I wasn't quite ready to make a leap like that, but the seed of confidence would continue to produce fruit in other ways.

That summer, Paulo and I attended a wedding for one of his high school friends. It was a sweet and much-needed opportunity to enjoy a nice drive out of town for an outdoor wedding, where we laughed and danced and reconnected. Later in the evening, we went out for after-party wine and tapas with one of Paulo's buddies and his fiancée.

We used to hang out with Brandon back when we lived in our first apartment and he and Paulo worked at a seafood restaurant near our place. But now Brandon was an up-and-coming entrepreneur in California, having co-created a graphic design company. Still the same fun-loving guy who used to burn us CDs and play beer pong with Paulo, Brandon was now a young millionaire, traveling the world and experiencing things he never imagined could be possible.

As we enjoyed a smorgasbord of wines, cheeses, and desserts, I couldn't help but ask Brandon How did he do it? How did he break out of society's expectations for him to instead create the life of his wildest dreams? He responded to me with a book, *The 4-Hour Work Week* by Timothy Ferriss. We changed topics, but I mentally filed away his recommendation for later.

Nearly five years later, Brandon tragically died in a helicopter ride during one of his adventures. He was a bright and joyful light, gone way too soon. Brandon surely left a lasting impression on me and many others, and I owe a great deal of gratitude to him for the curiosity he sparked in me that night.

Curiosity Growing

Shortly after that fateful conversation with Brandon, I picked up a copy of Ferriss' book to read on my lunch break at work. I never did finish that book, but I read far enough into it to get to a section called "D is for Definition." In it, Ferriss instructs the reader to define their nightmare. If they were to pursue their vision and something went horribly wrong, what would that look like?

Here's what I wrote:

"If I chose to become a teacher, I'd need to become certified and eventually quit my job. I might want to rent our house out and downsize our living space. Maybe someday pull the kids out of traditional school and instead create a half online/ half homeschool model.

My nightmare would be that I can't find a place to work, we don't make enough money, and we lose our house. My fear is that following my dreams will make it hard for me to be the kind of wife and mom that I want to be for Paulo and the girls. I'm scared of crawling back to the bookstore to beg for a lower-level position. I worry that if we choose to travel that I'll lose some very good friends and that my kids will resent me for not giving them a stable upbringing.

I'm scared of going back to eating cheap, processed food because we don't make enough money and going back on financial aid and cutting back on every luxury possible to not lose everything."

Ferriss then asks the reader, "Would these difficulties be permanent? And if not, how could you get things back under control temporarily?"

I wrote,

"It would not mean the end of my life. Aside from potential emotional trauma, none of it would be permanent. We could sell some belongings, and we could cancel cable and switch to a cheaper phone carrier. I could find a part-time job and Paulo could pick up extra hours. We could rent out our house and live with our parents or get a cheap apartment.

We could keep the girls in traditional school but switch from charter to public school for meal- and after-school assistance."

The biggest takeaway from that thought experiment was that imagining different possibilities for our future was not as scary as I thought; that even if things didn't work out how we planned them, we were creative and adaptable enough to figure things out. This was a pivotal moment for me, and it would ultimately guide me toward making some pretty drastic changes in my life.

Paulo and I Try Something New

During our girls' younger years, Paulo and I centered them as best we could. We were both working full-time hours or longer and still volunteering at their school for field trips, class parties, and WatchDOGS dad days. We had after-school picnics in the park, did art and cooking projects, took trips to the zoo and museums, spent afternoons at the bookstore or window shopping at the mall, and enjoyed lots of movie nights, special meals, and snuggles.

Of course, there's only so much time in a day, and the challenges of separate schedules and trying to make up for lost time with our children meant that Paulo and I started to backburner our relationship. Even when we did get a date night, we spent a lot of our time together bickering about how we each felt like single parents or roommates, tagging in and out before and after work shifts.

So, when our seventh wedding anniversary was drawing near, we decided it was time for us to take an extended vacation together, alone. We planned to drive up north and explore Michigan's Upper Peninsula for six long days. We had never taken a nature-focused vacation before, but we were both ready to try something new.

We decided to spend the first three days exploring tourist attractions like Whitefish Point, Tahquamenon Falls, and Pictured Rocks National Park. I think it took me the first full day and a half to settle my nervous system. It can be so challenging to switch from "doing" mode to "being" mode while on vacation; I wonder if that's why it's so common for folks to create itineraries and schedules and reservations, making sure they squeeze out every bit of memory-making possible.

But by that third day, when we were on a six-mile hike around Pictured Rocks, the energy around us started to shift. We started to walk a little slower; more gently. We enjoyed moments of silence and moments of silliness and laughter without trying to. We moved our bodies and filled our lungs and souls with fresh air and sunshine. And somewhere along the way, we both had a sudden realization: We're outdoorsy people!

I know that might sound silly to you, but you need to understand that while I had some experience with traveling and camping as a child, Paulo did not. And this was not how Paulo and I had spent our time together since we first met ten years earlier; this was news to us. And exciting news, too! We felt stuck in a rut with every weekend activity revolving around the same groups of people doing the same things and always involving lots of alcohol.

Don't get me wrong; when we came back to our motel from our hikes, we enjoyed cocktails and beer while watching the sunset from the Lake Superior shoreline. And our final two nights were spent in Traverse City, enjoying a night at the casino and then a four-hour winery tour followed by a pub crawl with our new winery tour friends. Alcohol still very much played a leading role in our ideas of "fun," but now we had a whole new repertoire of possibilities to explore, too.

Mom Follows Her Heart Back to Florida

It had been about eight months since my grandmothers' deaths and about four months since my mom had moved back to Florida to take up residence with my uncles in my grandma Abbie's home. My grandma had become an enabler and caretaker for my uncles in their middle age, and after her death, my mom and uncles held each other close and committed to working things out together in a way that had felt impossible to do before their mom's passing.

While my mom felt she was honoring her responsibility to her brothers and to her mother's dying wishes, my sister and I were both left in the aftermath of this massive shift. Although my mom and I never fully recovered our bond after she had moved to Florida for the first time when I was a teen, it was nonetheless heartbreaking to see her go again. It felt like a wound of grief and abandonment had been cut back open, and the mess it was creating in my life was harder to cover up this time.

Being in that space of deep sadness was breaking me open again, keeping me uncomfortable enough to stay awake to what was unfolding. So, when Paulo and I took our daughters and nephew to visit my mom right before the start of the school year, the ground was fertile for some new seeds to be planted.

One night while sitting under the stars on the lanai, she handed me a book that she had tried showing me once before. It wasn't the right time for me then, because I flatly rejected it. This time, however, I took the well-worn book and started flipping through the crinkled and highlighted pages. My mom had occasional notes scribbled in the margins, and it was clear that she had read at least most of it more than once. She again offered to lend it to me, and this time, I obliged. The book was *Everyday Enlightenment: The Ten Gateways to Personal Growth* by Dan Millman.

I devoured the first chapter that night, but the rest of the book would take me months to process. After the first fifty pages, I realized I needed to get my own copy so that I could highlight my favorite passages and make my notes in the margin. The wisdom in that book had my brain lighting up as I kept nodding, "Yes!" to all the resonance I was feeling. So, when I came to this quote, and I remembered back to that article I had read about needing to change your life in order to change your life, the synchronicity propelled me into an entirely new realm of courage, curiosity, and faith.

> "...life continually returns us to the inescapable reality that the best way to do what you need to do is just to do it. Sometimes it's easy. Sometimes it's tough. But that doesn't change the fact that the only way to get something done is to do it."
>
> —Dan Millman, *Everyday Enlightenment*

Discovering Yoga

Now, with regular physical therapy, consistent exercise, and a clean, whole food-based diet, a paradigm shift occurred. I continued to seek out other opportunities to honor my gramma by loving myself the way that she had loved me—thoroughly and unconditionally. Re-initiated by my mother into the spiritually uplifting literature enthusiast club, a longing was growing in me to pursue the mysterious once again.

I began journaling again, and I adjusted my bedtime to allow for greater consistency and longer rest. I started to reach out to friends whom I had barricaded myself from that previous winter. I strived to get outside as much as I possibly could. But the most beautiful gift of all was the gift of yoga. Yoga unfolded itself to me so elegantly that it's been like a dance.

It started off as a warm-up and cool-down for my cardio workouts, an homage paid to my ex-love of *P90X Yoga X*'s ass-kicking ninety-minute power vinyasa sequence. But slowly, yoga began taking up a greater percentage of my workouts until eventually there were some days that it was all I would do. My practice was always intuitive—a free flow of postures vaguely recalled from *Yoga X* in addition to the natural stretches and shapes I would move into as a child.

I felt so peaceful and yet powerful in my practice. After twenty years of trying to crawl out of my mind and skin, yoga invited me to come back inside. I could sense my awareness of my body, my mind, and my environment sharpening.

Courage showed up regularly on my mat. It was there when I had to honor my limitations in fully expressing a particular asana, and it was there when I would play the edge and knock down yet another seemingly insurmountable barrier in my capabilities. It was a roaring lion when I finally purchased a ten-class pass to a local yoga studio.

I decided it was time; I needed to go. I needed to be for real; to know that what I felt in my heart was true: that I was meant to learn this path, and for confirmation that—yes, actually—my intuitive home practice wasn't half bad.

Oh, I was so scared to go! It took me a couple more weeks to gather the courage needed to finally register for a fundamentals class with an instructor named Katie. She was amazing, so calm and loving. I came alive in that class. So overcome, I stayed after and introduced myself. I told her why I was there (to check my alignment with an actual teacher) and I told her how yoga was transforming me; how it was teaching me that I am in control of my reality and that I'm powerful and beautiful.

Suddenly, I blurted out, "And I think that someday I might become a teacher."

The audacity! My first actual studio class ever! I didn't know where this statement even came from. Something in me felt compelled toward teaching, but yoga? I was a complete novice!

Katie could have given me a million lines: that I needed to take it slow, that it's not good enough income, or that not many people can succeed in it. Instead, she wrote down the names of several yoga teacher training facilities in the area and gave me her email address in case I had questions.

After we finished chatting, I asked if I could hug her, and I thanked her for coming into my life that day. I emailed her later to thank her again for generously offering herself to me as a resource "…as I navigate this new and exciting part of my life. I thoroughly enjoyed your class, and I felt lighter and happier the rest of the day."

She responded in kind and added, "Before Bono was Bono, he sang with U2 and they did a song called, 'I Still Haven't Found What I'm Looking For.' I loved that song; it said to me, even if you are not sure what you're looking for, if you don't look, you won't find it. –Katie"

Beginning to Backslide

Even though I was thinner, stronger, and more energized than I had ever remembered being, there was still something off in my mind.

My anxiety had not abated at all, no matter how *in control* of my life I was starting to feel. A snippet from my journal that fall demonstrates the panicky and frenzied pace of my thoughts during a typical day:

"Today I wake with the same fear that grips me each morning. Am I doing this right? Did I choose to go to sleep at the right time last night? Have I slept long enough to repair my body without overdoing it? Did I wake early enough? Maybe I should've set an alarm...

No, I close tonight, I need my rest. Should I have stayed in bed longer then? No, nine hours is too long. You need to get up.

But I'm stiff. My muscles are sore. Maybe I should work out & stretch. No, what if that makes it worse? And anyway, I've got so much housework to attend to. Or should I run errands today? I really need to get some spiritual time in... I'm halfway through three books that I'd like to finish, but I'd also like to journal. But what about yoga?

Crap, I forgot the kids... I really should do something fun with them. Create memories. But there's so much laundry to do. Maybe they could help me? No, then we'll fight. No fights today.

I know, we'll have a playdate. They can see some kids, and I'll visit with my friend. But which friend do I text? Who haven't I seen recently? I need to be fair; I've been avoiding so many texts lately.

Ugh... No, the house wins. It's a nightmare. I've got to clean it so that I'll want to be here.

First, breakfast. Then a smoke. And coffee. Oh my God! It's almost 11! Okay, it's 10:30. But still –I'm losing time. God, why didn't I get up earlier?

I always do this! Always make the wrong choice, and now the day is ruined and it's not even noon.

Time for lunch. Great, now we're definitely not going anywhere. Paulo will be home soon, then we'll sit around and hash out dinner. Then we'll add to the already huge mess that we're now too worn out from the day's stress to clean.

We'll decide to watch a TV show with the girls— finally, that "quality time." Except that when they want a second episode, we'll fight. Then I'll scream at them to get ready for bed. Then we'll make up and snuggle. They'll sleep, we'll stay up and watch more TV and scroll through social media, and we'll do it all again tomorrow.

I hate these days. No; I dread them. I always make the wrong choices with my time, and I always end up disappointed."

Waking up to those daily panic attacks was taking its toll on me. The stress was redirecting me to my old, familiar ways of coping. As my disordered eating habits returned, my eczema worsened, my face started breaking out, my digestive system and sleep were whacked out, and my energy was gone. Work and home life felt chaotic, and my depression started coming back. I had pretty much abandoned my yoga practice, and I eventually stopped exercising altogether.

Despite what felt like lead weights pulling me toward the depths, I clung to the edge of the cliff with my fingertips, desperately refusing to let go of all the progress I had made. I did not want to give up! So, I trudged through another Whole30, using it as a vehicle to further inspect my inner world and what was tripping me up.

It was during that time that I finally opened myself to the truth that: 1) for most of my life, I've battled with alcoholism and escapism and 2) I'm choosing a different path now. I shared this realization with several close friends in an effort toward accountability. But even as I was making these strides in understanding my habit patterns, a new and unfamiliar pattern was establishing itself. I was approaching the first anniversary of my gramma's death as well as the impending holiday season along with all of its trauma triggers. The cold, dark winter months were doing all they could to bring me down.

> "It doesn't always come easy. In fact, it rarely does. Try again. And be okay with it."
>
> —Jeni Juarez

Starting to Accept a Longer View

As I fought hard against my propensity toward atrophy, a seed began to crack open and take root; that seed was the beginning of self-compassion. My writing began to change, and I began to offer myself forgiveness and understanding for my steep climb toward self-acceptance. I began to recognize the longing to love myself more. And in that moment, that love looked like proper nutrition, yoga, adequate sleep, nurturing relationships, appropriate boundaries, and quiet time for reflection.

I was starting to make peace with the journey, even joking in my journal:

> "Hey! I know you've spent a lifetime perfecting the art of justification and manipulation, but seriously, you know better. You know that you feel best when you honor yourself, so fucking do it."

I was calling myself out and speaking out loud the truth that I was still many lessons away from truly embodying self-love and self-acceptance; from actually believing that my worth was intrinsic to my aliveness and not based on my appearance or what other people thought of me.

I understood that from now on, I would be walking the razor's edge of being thankful for who I already was while simultaneously striving to become a better version of myself. A lot of shifts were occurring: the girls were growing in their independence and self-concept; I was no longer satisfied with my career track; and Paulo and my marriage deepened in intimacy and trust with each vulnerable conversation. The challenges were changing along with my perception of what life was supposed to look like.

4

Braving the Unknown

I was dragging myself toward the first anniversary of my gramma's death with one foot in and one foot out of life. It felt like these conceptual models of who I thought I was were beginning to crack, letting in some space for possibility. On December 7, 2015, I wrote:

"It has been December for a full week, and yet my mind is frozen. Trapped in November, not ready for what December has to offer.

Traditions (obligations)
Celebrations (mourning)
Gifts (debt)
Treats (discomfort)
Generosity (selfishness)

Like a fish out of water, I flip then I flop. Indecisive, unsure of whether to forge ahead toward positivity or to let go and drown in fear.

This morning as I got ready, I was listening to my music on a Bluetooth speaker with my phone left on the kitchen counter. Suddenly, the song not only turned off (paused) but my volume was mysteriously muted. Surely, that can't occur by itself... I panic, assuming the worst: that someone is here to kill me.

I check the first floor—clear. I peer timidly toward the basement stairs, fully aware that there is no way in hell I'm going down to look for an intruder. I decide to fake bravery, turn my music back on, and consider grabbing a steak knife. Instead, I reach for my mug of hot tea. I take a sip, knowing that it's far more likely that I'd scald someone rather than stab them.

Out of nowhere, a thought pops into my head: It was my gramma. She doesn't approve of my music, so she turned it off. "It's too early for vulgarity," I hear inwardly.

Wait, what? No, it's a freak accident. I've dropped this phone a lot. I decide I'm being ridiculous, so I decline to check upstairs for burglars, and I continue my morning routine.

Later, when it's time to get clothes, I realize I'm still unnerved. Grabbing my weapon of choice (hot tea), I go upstairs, first checking the girls' room, then the bathroom, then my room. All clear.

"Prove it's you," I say to no one, feeling as though I am not alone.

As I finish getting dressed, something draws me to my top drawer, where I spot an old, shabbily sewn gem pouch with bells on the ends of the pull-ties. My first thought is, "Oh yes! I forgot that I wanted to make my mom a set of runes." My second thought is, "I have not touched these in years." (Runes are an ancient divination tool. They are a series of symbols inscribed upon small stones, each with a particular theme or message, that can be interpreted in different ways depending on the inquirer and the spread being used. My mom's mother used to practice with them, so I made myself a set back in high school. Finding the rune set in my drawer after more than a decade of forgetting about them felt like a message sent across dimensions from her.)

I unwrapped the inner cloth to expose the twenty-four smooth black stones, each hand-painted with a white symbol. I closed my eyes and considered the question, "What is going on right now?"

I pulled Naudhiz: Need; Unfulfilled Desire. But what does that mean? What is this unfulfilled desire? Something tells me the answer will be revealed soon.

Starting to Break (up with) the Rules

My whole upbringing, everything about life was described in a linear way:

- Graduate from high school
- Go to college
- Choose a lifelong career
- Get married
- Buy a house
- Have kids
- Retire from the same job you got right out of college
- Die

So much focus was placed on the outward appearance of a successful life: completing each checkbox on the list, *in order,* while simultaneously accumulating as much money and material wealth as possible. I honestly cannot remember my parents ever telling me what to do in between checking the boxes. Life mostly felt like a relay race in that, every time I successfully achieved a level, there was no time to rest or appreciate it aside from maybe a wild weekend of celebrating with food and booze. Then, it was off to the next level.

Coming across those runes and the message of "unfulfilled desire" began to pique my curiosity about what I was doing and what I really wanted out of my life. I was beginning to sense that maybe my life wasn't so set in stone after all—that instead of feeling like a failure for not earning a high salary in a high-status job straight out of college, maybe I could create an entirely different benchmark for success: the satisfaction of a life well-lived.

The Third Option

> "From a tiny seed to a great Redwood, all great endeavors require a deliberate first step. And courage. Lots and lots of courage."
>
> —Jeni Juarez

Until my early thirties, I believed there were only two options when obstacles came across my path:

- Give up
- Try harder

During my life, I have tried both methods with earnestness. I tried forcing weight loss with strict diets and abusive workout regimens, only to give up and binge eat while obsessively watching my weight increase on the scale. When I was discouraged by my stagnation in my position at the bookstore, I tried forcing change through assertive self-promotion and accepting the most awful, random job interviews. Then, after a few months of disappointment, I would give up and accept that I might never leave my job. Never did I consider a third option: Say "Yes" to what feels like the next right thing to do and trust the unfolding process.

This kind of open-minded curiosity began to blossom within me as I began imagining new and different possibilities for my personal—and my family's collective—well-being. After finishing my ten-class pass at the yoga studio, I once again felt emboldened to look up the yoga teacher training programs in my area. Looking back, I'm in awe of myself and how much courage that decision took to make. It was a brazen act of defiance against a lifetime of living according to the rules of living that I had been taught.

I approached my yoga teacher training (YTT) research with the same kind of neurotic perfectionism that I approach any big decision. I looked up a handful of local studios, read their mission statements and program descriptions, and ultimately signed up for a beginner's class at two different studios.

One of them described their YTT program with academic precision, outlining expectations of book reports, community service, and other studious tasks that made my inner back-to-school nerd squeal with excitement. But when I went to the class, everything about the studio felt sterilized and strict. We were set up on either side of the room, facing each other. The instructor taught from the middle aisle, pacing up and down the row. I was feeling so many sets of eyes on me during the hour-long practice, and the energy felt judging. I left the class feeling like I needed another yoga class to recover from it.

I was disappointed by the experience because, from the outside, it seemed like the perfect fit for my Type A personality. But as I would continue to learn, when things don't go how you want them to go, it's often because you are being redirected to the right path.

"When the student is ready, a teacher appears."

—unknown

Finding My Teacher

Judging from the website for the other studio I was planning to check out, it didn't seem like the next one was going to be a good fit, either. The *About* web page talked about something called *bhakti yoga*—the yogic path of devotion or service to God. My first thought upon reading that was, "Gross. I don't want God in my yoga."

So, imagine my surprise when I walked into From the Heart Yoga & Tai Chi Center to see paintings of goddesses and hand mudras, statues of Ganesha (the Hindu deity with an elephant head), orchids, and peacock feathers. But the unique and beautiful adornment of the space wasn't what hit me the most. It was the energy of the room where Behnje and Rick taught. It contained within its walls the combined years of Behnje's and Rick's dedicated practice as both students and teachers, as well as the collective practice of the loyal community of yogis that they had built in the space.

I walked through the door and across the golden-hued wood floors to look out of the glass French doors leading to the garden behind the building. A Buddha statue, some older trees, a table, and some chairs punctuated the serene wintry scene. I immediately felt in my heart that I was home. I experienced this deep sense of belonging, like a long, settling exhale.

After only a few classes with Behnje, I decided that this was who I wanted to deepen my understanding of yoga with. Behnje shared with her students that her teacher taught her to take a decades-long view of their students; that she envisioned each of us in a pinnacle pose like handstand as soon as we walked in the door, but then she panned back to this moment, and the next movement that would lead us down the winding road.

Behnje taught in a way that I would describe as fiercely compassionate, with an attitude of, "You've got this, and I've got you." She did not coddle or placate, which is good. Because even though I *thought* I wanted to be babied, what I *actually* wanted was to be empowered, encouraged, and believed in. And that's what Behnje did. She showed me a strength and courage that lived in me that I didn't even know existed.

Going for It—The First Trust Fall

Now determined to participate in the 200-hour Yoga Teacher Training Program at From the Heart, I needed to reckon with the reality of our family's financial situation. I could not afford this training on our family's income alone. It was time to get creative and roll up my sleeves.

The first step I took was to reevaluate all our family's expenses and cut whatever we could. We switched cell phone carriers, canceled cable, changed our car insurance policy, and even refinanced our home. I applied the skipped mortgage payment, our tax return, and the reduction in monthly bills to my goal, but it still wasn't enough. We had a giant yard sale and brought tubs of children's items to a resale store, but it *still* wasn't enough. I realized I was going to have to do something that I hadn't done in a very long time: ask for help.

I started by grabbing my journal and describing what I had been experiencing before and since my grandmother's death, including physical therapy, discovering Whole30, self-care, and the profound impact that yoga had had on me. What I ended up with was a very vulnerable and heartfelt explanation of why this training mattered to me and what I had experienced leading up to this point. I was ready to do one of the scariest things of my life: start a crowd-funding campaign.

My friend Meg was a huge supporter of my new courageous undertaking. Ever an inspiration to me, Meg had been pursuing her passions as careers since college. So, she was no stranger to the exhilaration, uncertainty, and challenges involved with going after one's dreams. Because I was asking for community support, I felt like I owed my campaign contributors proof of my determination to make their belief in me mean something. So, I put my project manager's hat on and started to create a brand for myself.

Unrelenting Optimism was what came through for me: an unyielding determination to extract wisdom from everything, including and especially adversity. Meg offered to make buttons for me with "Unrelenting Optimism" written in pink script on a black background. The buttons, along with a handwritten thank-you card, would be sent to anyone who donated at least five dollars to my campaign. I also offered personal yoga classes and monthly email updates about my yoga journey to anyone who contributed fifty dollars or more.

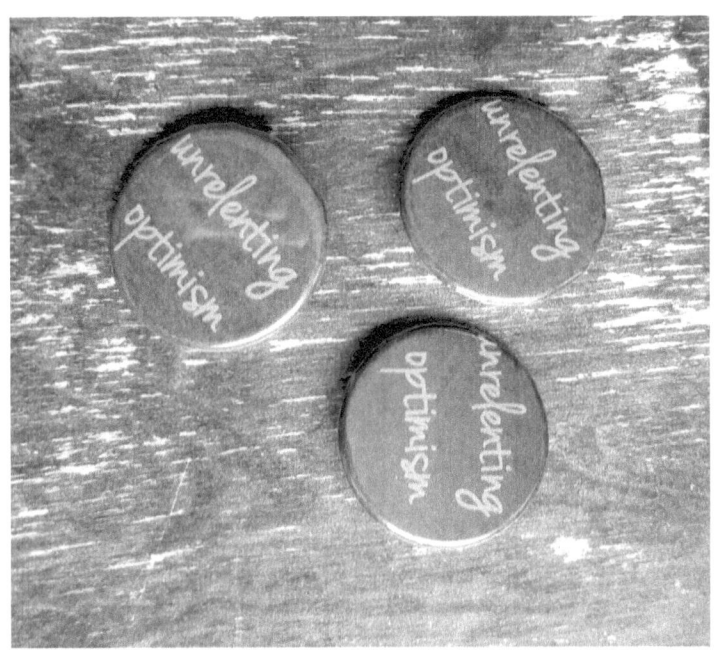

Unrelenting Optimism

To help me promote myself, Meg also created a brief video of me doing a yoga flow in the late winter snow behind her mom's house. She helped me overlay some narration onto the video, and I shared it on social media to amplify my cause. Here's what I said: "It [yoga] feels so peaceful yet powerful to me. It teaches me to honor where I presently am and what it took to get me here, but it reminds me to play the edge; to know that I am limitless."

Around the same time, I was working through my fifth round of Whole30. Only this time, I was also leading a group of six of my neighbors who were doing it with me, along with two curious spectators and eight more sparked with interest. I was once again tapping into my skills as a teacher and encourager, and I was beginning to acknowledge my abilities and my influence.

Seeing everyone persevere and succeed in a hundred different ways through that thirty-day challenge was so uplifting and empowering. I knew in my heart that this was who I was: a student, a teacher, and a leader. I loved all of the people I was working with, and I had a deep longing to saturate the world with that same love and support.

While I had no idea what the future would bring, I knew three things:

- It will happen at the right time
- It will be exactly what I need
- It will be beautiful

I knew this because I was witnessing the unfolding process, and it was already true. The synchronicities were guiding and affirming that I was headed in the right direction. My role was to value the process and to keep showing up for the work. In the end, my crowd-funding campaign was shared 122 times, and more than twenty friends, family members, and strangers contributed nearly $1,000 to my $3,000 tuition fee. Through Grace, community, and laser-focused determination, my dreams were coming true.

There was no way of knowing at that time how radically my life would change over the next five years. But one thing was certain: Things were never going to be the same again.

PART II

The Initiation

Atha Yogānuśāsanam

What is it that I desire?
      Freedom.
Freedom from anger, from fear,
From pride, from self-hatred.
      Freedom from expectations.
      Love.
Love for myself, for my family,
For my community, my world.
Love for God, for life.
      Joy.
Joy of connection, of fulfillment,
Of dreams, of miracles.
Joy of witnessing the joy of others.
      Spaciousness.
In my mind, between thoughts,
In my body, open and strong.
In my heart, wide enough to hold it all.
      Compassion.
Compassion for all beings and the
Suffering they endure.
Compassion for myself, and the
Sacred work to be done.

5

Obstacles and Allies

Growing up, my dad tended to repeat certain phrases as a judgmental, passive-aggressive way of correcting behaviors of mine that he deemed inappropriate or unpleasant. Hearing him say, "Oh, that's Christlike behavior…," or "That's not very lady-like…" no doubt encouraged my rebellious self to abhor any association with Christian conservatism or the damsel-in-distress trope later in life. But there was another frequently uttered phrase of his that has taken on new layers of meaning for me: "That's so unbecoming of you."

This *unbecoming of you* phrase, meant as a shame-based learning tool at the time, was actually a signpost guiding me toward my *sadhana*—my daily spiritual practice: the work of un-becoming everything that I thought I was supposed to be to instead be who I already was. I wouldn't appreciate that subtle but profound distinction until much later, but embarking upon my yoga teacher training was one of the most important steps in this new direction of authentic and whole-hearted living.

Yoga Teacher Training Begins

What a surprise I was in for with the addition to my already jam-packed life of an extra forty-five-plus hours per month of notetaking and asana (the physical practice, or *hatha yoga*), in addition to many more hours of reading, meditating, and trying to "take my practice off the mat" and into my daily life. Our classes met every other weekend for three hours on Friday night and seven hours both Saturday and Sunday. We were also expected to attend at least one hour-long class per week in addition to our reading and practice assignments. My hunger for learning far outweighed any concerns about the increased workload. I was so excited!

For the two months leading up to the training, I had committed to a daily practice that included *asana* (postures), *yamas* (behavioral restraints), *niyamas* (inner observances), meditation, contemplation, and *pranayama* (breathing techniques). The fruits of committing so fully to these various practices slowly began to emerge in the form of a deep sense of peace, curiosity, and focus.

And yet, as I walked into my first Friday night YTT session, barely on time, I was vibrating with nervous energy. My status as a novice was immediately clear. We were invited to find a "comfortable seat" on a stack of blankets on the floor. But no matter how I placed my body or what props I used, I could not get comfortable. I fidgeted like a child. I was out of practice in note-taking, so my arm was cramping as I fervently attempted to write down everything verbatim, as though it would be my one and only chance to ever hear or comprehend this information.

Learning about the history of yoga and yogic philosophy, as well as a broad overview of this particular method, Heart-Centered Yoga (see Box), was enough to tell me that I was exactly where I needed to be. The asana practice left me feeling stretched and grounded. I came home expecting to continue to read and practice, but as soon as I walked through the door, I was overcome with exhaustion and fell asleep.

We spent the rest of our first weekend discussing the first Universal Principle of Alignment—Opening to Grace—which was described to me as setting the foundation of the poses mindfully and with devotion. It's the willingness to receive love and support from a bigger energy and from others. My experience with Opening to Grace that weekend was a painful acknowledgment that, since those dark days of my early childhood, I had felt betrayed, cast out, and unsupported by God. I had spent so much of my life convincing myself that I was in control and that I could muscle my way through anything alone. I felt disconnected from life and the world around me, lost in my own sense of isolation and separateness.

But everything about this training experience challenged those beliefs. There were nine of us in the class. Danielle was the last to arrive that first evening. She sat in the back corner with me, and we hit it off right away. We had lunch together on the second day and discovered that we had quite a bit in common. Danielle had this free-spirited, grounding energy that I found both alluring and enigmatic. In addition to her new focus on becoming a certified yoga teacher, she was also a doula and a Reiki practitioner. Reiki is an energetic healing modality that recognizes and attunes the body's life force energy, the energy that animates all life. I couldn't help but imagine what it would've been like to have a friend like her when I was twenty-something, lost in my materialistic achiever role. But I was grateful to have her influence in my life now.

There was something so magical about the class setting. Here I was, barefoot in this beautiful, open space filled with intentionality and sacredness, completely removed from the outside world. In that space, I felt safe to be myself with no filters and no judgment. There was an element of trust and vulnerability among us all that enabled us to speak from the heart and let our tears fall if necessary. It felt glorious and so foreign from any recent experience I could recall, and it was the perfect environment for curiosity and self-exploration. By the end of the weekend, my hips ached along with every single muscle in my body; I was beyond exhausted. And yet, it was all I could do not to wish the next eleven days to hurry by so I could be back in that room on my mat.

Heart-Centered Yoga

There are many styles and philosophies of yoga. It is a 5,000+ year old practice, and despite the differences among styles, the goal is always the same— liberation—although it can be defined differently. The type of yoga that I trained in is called Heart-Centered Hatha Yoga, which finds its roots in Anusara. Founded in 1997 by John Friend, Anusara is based on the philosophy that life is a gift that we're invited to remember and celebrate within our yoga practice. Anusara means "flowing with grace," "going with the flow," "following your heart."

The two main purposes for practicing Heart-Centered Yoga are:

1) Self-Knowledge (Chit): Awakening, recognition, remembrance, self-realization, enlightenment, discovering the bliss of being (Shiva)

2) Delight of Creative Expression (Ananda): To enjoy the freedom of being. To make beauty, to love, to exult in the goodness of life, to celebrate the Supreme through art/music, to serve by adding more joy and laughter to life (Shakti)

There are 5 precise steps in Anusara Yoga's teaching methodology, called the "Universal Principles of Alignment™" (UPAs), which deepen awareness in the present moment and offer the potential for radical transformation. The first one is Open to Grace and Set the Foundation. (see, https://www.anusarayoga.com/methodology)

Cultivating Discernment

Behnje's teachings, no matter how literal or specific, always held a simultaneous universal application. During our third weekend of training, she taught us that an important aspect of our yoga practice was cultivating discriminative awareness. In a practical sense, this could be related to discerning how your body feels in a particular asana and engaging your muscles or modifying the pose in a particular way to make it feel the best in your body. In other words, pay attention to what feels freeing or supportive and what feels binding or harmful, and adjust accordingly.

My teacher simplified this teaching by repeatedly encouraging us to move toward that which is life-enhancing and away from that which is life-diminishing and to establish the appropriate boundaries. Of course, on the surface, that seemed obvious enough. But how often do we engage in habitual behaviors of mind and body that are not contributing to the overall enhancement of our lives? Contemplating this teaching on my mat sparked a similar curiosity about other areas of my life. Were my daily routines life-enhancing or life-diminishing? What about my diet? My relationships? My career?

Another theme of the weekend stemmed from our discussions around *swadharma* (our own capacity, value, and gifts that we bring to the table) and the Bhagavad Gita. According to my translation by Juan Mascaro, the Bhagavad Gita is "an intensely spiritual work that forms the cornerstone of the Hindu faith and is also one of the masterpieces of Sanskrit [the ancient language of South Asia] poetry. It describes how, at the beginning of a mighty battle between the Pandava and Kaurava armies, the god Krishna gives spiritual enlightenment to the warrior Arjuna, who realizes that the true battle is for his own soul." In the Bhagavad Gita, Krishna is both God incarnate as well as the warrior Arjuna's charioteer in the battle between the armies. Krishna exhorts Arjuna to honor his swadharma: his unique role in the world.

All this heightened awareness and curiosity around what in my life was freeing me and what was binding me meant that I could no longer pretend not to see what was now so obvious. Although I had radically changed nearly every other aspect of my life, including my values, my diet, my friendships, and my hobbies, there was one facet of my life that my intuition was screaming at me to change: my job.

It was time to stop thinking about it and talking about it and instead, really *do something about it.* I couldn't stand the daily beatdown from upper management at the bookstore over our financial metrics and whether we were hitting them. I felt sick thinking about how my team members were trapped in entry-level positions that didn't provide basic insurance or paid time off while I occupied a protected, full-time position. And I was *completely* fed the fuck up with having zero time or energy for my husband, my kids, my friends, and most importantly, *myself!* I dreamt of time for reading the books that I sold; of lunch dates with my girlfriends; of quiet mornings to myself.

I felt called to find a new job that would better both myself and the community, regardless of what I would lose in annual income. Feeling drenched in the toxicity of corporate greed and selfishness, I wanted to find a small, local business or a non-profit to work for. I wanted a change that would help me reclaim my soul and my peace.

I started sharing my feelings about looking for a new job. I updated my resume online, and I applied to work on three organic farms, at a natural health magazine, for a natural living blog, and at a yoga studio (as a receptionist). I wrote in my journal that it was time to open myself to new opportunities and to pay attention to the messages that might be coming my way.

One of the people I was regularly sharing my dreams with was my sister-in-law, Tammy. She and I had gotten close over the past year while doing Whole30 together and going on gym dates and nature walks. While walking in the woods one day with Tammy and our other sister-in-law (and my high school best friend), Anna, I shared that I was looking for a new job.

Tammy and Anna were both working at a locally owned butcher shop and were really enjoying it. Tammy joked that maybe she could get me a job there. Margie, the owner, was a super friendly and matronly person who loved to help everyone, but especially other mothers. I stopped and said, "Really? Would you?" She agreed to mention it to Margie on her next shift, and we all imagined how fun it would be to work together.

Game Changer

It was late July now, and only a few weeks after that walk. I was sitting stiff-necked at my desk, working on the staff schedule, when I received an "I love you" text from my dad. He followed up by asking me about my work schedule.

"I'm on forty-eight hours this week; fifty-six including the commute. I think I'm going to quit in September," I declared to him and the air around me.

He glazed over the comment, but I meant it. I meant it with my whole being. My job was no longer serving me, and I believed I could be contributing to my family and my community in a much better way.

Less than three hours later, as I sat for lunch at my desk, my phone rang. I didn't recognize the number, so I let my finger hover over the decline button. For reasons unknown, my finger traveled back to answer as I scrambled to pick up the phone to say hello. The foreign number belonged to Margie from the butcher shop. She was calling to ask if I was still looking for a job, and if so, when I could stop by to talk about it.

And just like that, only twenty-five hours after I told my dad that I was quitting the bookstore in September, I was sitting in Margie's office signing a letter of intent for employment starting September 4th! I asked Margie to give me four weeks to help my store prepare for my departure. Based on our agreement, I would be starting my new job right as the girls were returning to school.

I was going to be taking a fourteen-dollar-per-hour pay cut, but for the first time in my adult life, I was going to work part-time shifts. After eight years, I was finally going to be able to pick my girls up from school every single day, be home with them for bedtime, and enjoy the majority of my weekends with my family. This was going to be a HUGE shift!

Meeting Ram Dass and Maharajji

Slowly and sweetly, I was beginning to hear the inner call to come back home to myself. I began seeking for what I thought I had lost, but what was always hidden within me, waiting for my eyes to be ready to see and for my ears to be ready to hear. It seemed that whatever I was seeking was waiting for my heart to be ready to gently, patiently, remove the layers of armor I had imprisoned myself within for the sake of an imagined security from a scary existence.

Fully immersed in my yoga practice, I spent each day recommitting to the path of truth and love. I spent time reading sacred texts, practicing meditation and contemplation, moving my body through hatha yoga, and having beautiful conversations with Paulo, Meg, my coworkers, and my YTT cohort. I began to design my days in a way that kept my awareness aimed toward a greater level of consciousness and intentionality.

With all of this reorienting, it was becoming easier to notice what was supporting my path and what wasn't. I couldn't get into the same movies and music anymore. It was frustrating at first because I had built up a big part of my personality as someone who had a secret obsession with vulgar, angry, aggressive music. Until one day when Paulo asked me directly, "Why do you listen to music that degrades women?" I couldn't come up with an answer that made sense; it was time to let it go.

At teacher training, I told Rick and Behnje about how my musical tastes were shifting and that I really enjoyed some of the music they were using in their class playlists. They recommended I check out MC Yogi. I listened to a few songs of his on a streaming site, and my eyes were opened to a whole new genre of music that was uplifting, beautiful, and light-hearted. Letting the random playlist run its course, I eventually came upon another artist that was regularly featured on Behnje's playlist: Krishna Das.

Krishna Das is a kirtan wallah, which, in India, is someone who chants prayers and the divine names of God. Having always loved singing, including the singing of devotional songs and Gregorian chants, I had an immediate affinity for Krishna Das's music. Mostly call-and-response chants in Sanskrit, they quickly became a favorite form of meditation for me. That is, until I realized he also had *dharma* talks available to stream online as well. My Sanskrit teacher, Professor Douglas Brooks, once explained dharma as an implicit social contract that functions as a net that holds everyone together. "Dharma talks" refer to a conversation among spiritual seekers about how wisdom teachings relate to everyday life.

Krishna Das's dharma talks were an amalgam of stories about his life, his guru, the westerners whom he met while in India, and questions and responses between him and the audience to whom he was speaking. I *loved* listening to them. He was funny, direct, a little vulgar, and very authentic. He described ways that we could create a little space around the "Movie of Me" that we each create in our heads all day, every day, all life long. It was both refreshing and inspiring to listen to them, which I happily did while I was cooking, driving, and even while working.

In his talks, Krishna Das would often talk about his dear friend and guru brother, Ram Dass. Before he became Ram Dass, Richard Alpert was a prominent professor of Psychology at Harvard University in the 1960s. Noticing how even the most well-respected doctors and psychological theories still couldn't fully explain consciousness or "cure" neuroses, he began to research the use of psychedelic chemicals in expanding human consciousness with fellow researchers Timothy Leary, Ralph Metzner, Aldous Huxley, and Allen Ginsberg.

Their work became controversial as more of the American youth began experimenting with mind-expanding drugs during a time of great civil unrest due to the Vietnam War and the Civil Rights Movement. Both Richard Alpert and Timothy Leary were fired from Harvard, which set them each on different paths forward as they continued their research in different ways.

Richard decided to bring LSD to India, a country well-known for beings familiar with alternate planes of consciousness. He wanted to find someone who could explain how this drug worked and what it meant in terms of our understanding of reality. Through a series of seeming coincidences, Richard eventually met an Indian saint named Neem Karoli Baba, affectionately known as *Maharajji*, which means "great king." The experiences he had with Maharajji forever altered Richard's understanding of the nature of life. He was renamed *Ram Dass*, or Servant of God, and came back to the United States, where he could not help but talk about Maharajji, even though Maharajji had explicitly told him not to. Ram Dass then went on to write the book *Be Here Now*, which became a highly influential guide for spiritual seekers hungry for deeper connection and joy in their lives.

When I first began listening to podcasts of Ram Dass's old lectures, what struck me immediately was both his brilliance and his profound devotion to this bigger energy that he interchangeably referred to as God, Maharajji, Spirit, the Divine Mother, the

Universe, and other names. He had such a deep reverence of all faith traditions and their sacred texts, rites, mystics, poetry, music, and art. And even as he respected and revered them, he understood through his experiences with Maharajji that they were but many paths up the same mountain to the one Source.

My heart yearned to have this same relationship with God. The first time I heard Ram Dass playfully refer to himself as a spiritual dilettante (a dabbler), I smiled as spontaneous joy spread like warmth across my cheeks and chest. Yes! This resonated so much. It felt like someone was giving me permission to do what I always wanted—to freely explore my relationship with the Divine without demanding that I claim allegiance to a particular religious dogma.

I looked Ram Dass up one day while working at the bookstore, and I found a book title that jumped out at me, called *Polishing the Mirror*. The title struck me because we had recently been discussing in teacher training how spiritual practice polishes the mirrors of our hearts so we can remove the impurities and more clearly perceive the reflection of supreme reality, whatever *that* meant. I ordered the book for myself, noting with humor that it would arrive on my final day of work.

Hindsight Wisdom

My letting go of certain forms of entertainment, including senselessly violent or derogatory movies, music, books, and magazines, was part of a broader, subtle recalibration of mind that was occurring. Recognizing my life as a series of lessons guiding a blossoming of consciousness, I perceived each day as an opportunity to learn through direct observation of the present moment and self-reflection.

The term *abhyasa* in Sanskrit translates as steadiness and fortitude on the path of awakening. This consistent and wholehearted effort of Sadhana naturally leads to *vairagya*, or the letting go of attachments. As our longing deepens, we begin to release anything that isn't supportive of our desire for reunion with the Self.

I Cannot Force Faith

Despite the exciting news of a long-awaited job change as well as the profound experiences I was having during my YTT weekends, there was an aching heaviness that was taking hold in my heart. It didn't quite register the same in my body as depression or anxiety had in the past. No, this was different; I was in great despair.

My teacher explained that to feel despair is to feel longing. She said that we despair because we realize that we cannot do everything on our own; that to experience peace and freedom from suffering, we must surrender to our faith by turning toward the ever-present flow of Divine Grace.

I grappled for weeks with this idea of surrender. Up to that point, I believed that to surrender to God was to give up and to avoid personal responsibility for my life. I often saw examples of people intentionally choosing not to show up to life; those who simply prayed to God for abundance and then passively waited for good fortune to arrive. In my resistance to that, I had swung the pendulum to the other extreme in my own life by insisting that I was solely responsible for my success or failure at the expense of my own peace and contentment.

Logically, I recognized that this obsession with control was driven by my apparent lack of control as well as the presence of fear. And yet I struggled to accept the truth that life is ever-changing and that perhaps it was time to move *with* the current of life instead of against it. It was on the first evening of our fourth teacher training weekend that I wrote the words, "I cannot force faith" in my journal.

Contemplating what I understood as faith conjured a memory of my youngest daughter, Nolani. As a toddler, she'd come up to me, wrap her legs around my belly, and collapse her head onto my chest. Sometimes it was because she was emotionally churned, with tears flowing, breathing rapidly, seeking comfort. Other times, she simply wanted to feel that loving energy pulsing through me and into her. With her breath calm and eyes closed, she'd drift into meditation or even sleep as she took rest on me.

Nolani resting on me

That trust and confidence that she has in me—that I love her fiercely and unconditionally—would draw her magnetically to me as a source of stability. She has so much faith that I will be there for her whenever and however she needs me to be, no matter what she's feeling and how she shows up. And I honestly cannot think of a sweeter description for how I could imagine my relationship to "God" or the "Divine" to be.

The discussions we had in class helped shape a different understanding of surrender that draws to the middle of these two paths.

Yoga is about balance and connection, after all. While it's true that Divine Spirit is always with us, guiding us and setting before us assignments that bring us closer to our true nature, we also have a personal responsibility to show up for those assignments. Self-effort and surrender to Grace are equally necessary for a fulfilling life.

I was trying to force something that cannot be forced. Faith is something that simply happens. It emerges as a deep sense of trust in the unfolding storyline of the universe. But regardless, the challenge of discernment would remain: to have faith in God is not to relinquish responsibilities and let go completely, but a concerted effort with an open heart.

An Aversion to Heartache and the Seed of Universal Compassion

As we were wrapping up the first half of yoga teacher training, news broke that a twenty-nine-year-old man had killed forty-nine people and wounded fifty-three more in a mass shooting inside Pulse, a gay nightclub in Orlando, Florida. I struggled at first to engage with the media coverage of the shooting; the pain in my heart seemed intolerable, and I wanted to hide from it. Here I was, trying to devote myself to peace and harmony and love, and as soon as something tragic and horrifying happened, I became incapacitated by my fear.

My teacher Behnje took a much firmer stance. She held space at the beginning of each class that she taught that week in honor and remembrance of those murdered and mourning, and she called her students to action. She reminded us that even choosing to do nothing, to disengage, is a deliberate action. A choice. She let us know that she is not here to tell us what to think or what to do, but that we must do something. That "something" could be simply informing ourselves of what transpired, becoming familiar with the lives lost, signing a petition or sending an email to our representatives, or sending a donation to the families whose loved ones had perished.

This was the first time anyone had ever directly challenged me to act instead of feeling helpless in response to a crisis or tragedy. That evening, I pulled myself to my computer and found a memorial page that showed pictures along with the names and ages of all forty-nine victims. I read each name one at a time, taking a moment to acknowledge that they were people with lives, families, friends, dreams, and futures, and because of one person's hate, they were now gone.

When I could finally bring myself to read coverage of the tragedy, what stuck out most from the reading was a quote from the mayor of Orlando, Buddy Dyer: "We will not be defined by the act of a cowardly hater. We will be defined by how we respond and how we treat each other." This felt like an echoing of Behnje's call to action. And because of that experience, I vowed to learn how to turn toward, instead of away from, the suffering in the world.

Hindsight Wisdom

There are unspeakable acts of violence that occur every single day, all over the world. Yet most of these events do not receive media coverage, and if they do, only a fraction of the population even takes notice. I believe that my responsibility to act is threefold. I have a responsibility to be aware—eyes and heart open—even when it is agonizing. I have a responsibility to lead by example; to embody love and mercy in everything that I do and with everyone I encounter, no matter how challenging it becomes. And I have a responsibility to engage, to go out and interact with the world, to be a global citizen, and to see the family of humanity as an extension of me.

Living On God's Time

That summer, Paulo and I decided to take our family on our first camping trip. After considering all the beautiful areas of Michigan's lakeshore, we settled on Wilderness State Park near Mackinaw City. Because I tend to obsess over outcomes and prefer to do things "perfectly" over making mistakes, trying new things can be intimidating. I wanted to challenge these limiting habits in myself, so I purposely avoided my typical over-strategizing. I decided that for this new thing, Paulo and I would gather odds and ends for a few weeks and then make a list and fill in any holes the day before leaving.

The morning we were set to leave, we brought everything on the list into the front yard. It didn't take long to realize that it wasn't all going to fit into our 2007 Impala along with our two kids. We started pulling things to leave behind from the yard. We crammed our pillows in the rear window, tucked sleeping bags underneath the girls' feet, and the fishing poles (no hooks!) took up the air space between Paulo and me in the front seat as the poles curled from the front passenger floor to between the girls' heads in the backseat. We had no idea what we were doing, but we didn't care. Ever since our anniversary trip up north, we have been longing to bring our girls up there, too.

In the days leading up to our trip, Nolani kept telling us that she did not want to go camping. She had no context for what it would be like, and the uncertainty was stressing her out. Thankfully, she shook that anxiety quickly once we got up there. One of the most thrilling parts of our trip was observing the blossoming confidence and independence in our girls. After a few laps around the campground and some quizzes as to how to locate our "home," they were gleefully hopping on and off their bikes, cruising around together, and taking in the scenery.

While the girls basked in their newfound freedom, Paulo and I set up camp and started a fire. We heated our dinner over the fire before taking a swim in the crystal-clear waters of Lake Michigan. Paulo and I placed our chairs right on the water line with beers in hand and blues music pouring through the mini speaker. I sat there for a while, watching and listening to the waves crash over my feet. Another campfire, s'mores, and a late-night walk through the International Dark Sky Park (IDSP) made our first night complete. There is no light pollution at this kind of park, so you can witness the night sky as if you are sitting in a planetarium. (see, https://www. darksky.org/our-work/conservation/idsp/parks/)

The next morning, I took the girls for a short bike ride to Wilderness General Store for fresh, homemade donuts. Paulo worked his percolator coffee magic over the fire, and we feasted before heading back to the beach. We were never bored, and yet we never felt rushed. Instead of eating on a timed schedule, we simply ate when we were hungry, letting our bodies lead the way.

This was my first conscious experience of living on "God's time," as I called it, and it was by far the greatest gift I received on our camping trip. I woke up early, naturally, and allowed the day to unfold without concerns of time constraints or expectations. I simply floated on the fresh air and sunshine, letting my heart guide how to spend my day. No one was telling me what to do, and whatever I did (or didn't do) was completely okay. Camping nourished us in a way that other activities never had.

This same experience was evident in Paulo as he cheerfully attended to the duties of camping with a childlike spirit. This setting was exactly what our family had been needing, although we didn't even know it. At lunch on the second day, the girls told us that they wanted to move up north. More than anything, I wanted to say yes to them. Nature was speaking to us all, beckoning us away from the heaviness and obsession with imposed deadlines that wrap like vines around us in our day-to-day lives. I wished then and there to give this to them someday, although only time would tell how our lives were meant to be lived.

The second evening, we let the girls ride their bikes to the small beach area to play with the other kids. Paulo and I began breaking camp down in anticipation of rain the following day. Twilight was setting in, and the girls hadn't come back yet. We rode to the water to check on them only to discover them swimming near a momma and her two babies, blissfully indulging in the calm serenity of night-time swimming. My heart filled at the sight of them experiencing this unique calm. The sky and water took on the same milky-gray color, and the beachfront was completely empty of visitors. They were quietly floating in the undisturbed water.

After they were tucked into bed, Paulo and I stayed up playing cribbage by lantern light. As we reflected on the experiences of the weekend, we both committed ourselves to bringing a greater sense of wonder and delight in the natural world into our children's lives. It had been a long time since we had dreamed about the future together. The atmosphere we were imagining held so much hope and possibility—and it was only the beginning!

Hindsight Wisdom

It is a tragic reality that so many cash-poor people and people of color lack access to green space. For how much joy free play in nature can bring to a human being, let alone how that fertile opportunity for unstructured creative flow can impact their development, it is abhorrent how so many of us are relegated to concrete parking lots, train tracks, backyards, and alleys for playing as children. Oftentimes, existing urban green spaces and creeks or rivers are full of pollutants due to waste from neighboring manufacturing companies.

Of course, a child can thrive in some of the most oppressive environments, but that doesn't mean they should have to. If your family lacked the resources, safety, or awareness to adventure with you in your younger years, it's never too late to try! Check with your local Department of Natural Resources (go to your state's website and search DNR) or try an app like AllTrails to explore nearby hiking trails, bike paths, and more.

A Crash Course in Ambidexterity

I wasn't even three weeks into my summer break from yoga teacher training when I began noticing some hardly perceptible discomfort in my left shoulder. On a mission to achieve *adho mukha vrksasana,* or handstand, I had been intensely practicing my inversions. After a while, it became so aggravated and inflamed that I was experiencing numbing and tingling sensations down my left arm and into my fingers. I couldn't comfortably hold my coffee cup, and I kept unconsciously massaging and tugging at my shoulder, coaxing it to stop throbbing.

When I finally reached my self-abuse threshold and could no longer tolerate the pain and physical limitation, I texted my massage therapist at my chiropractor's office. At first, Anna could not see me the same week, but at the last minute, she had a cancellation right before the start of the holiday weekend. The thirty-minute session gave her just enough time to evaluate and scold me for lack of better self-care. She knows me too well—overly scheduled and incredibly stubborn. Anna empathized with me but reminded me that ignoring pain and discomfort is an irresponsible behavior that can take something relatively simple to treat and turn it into a very debilitating, sometimes irreversible injury.

She informed me that I was experiencing an Overuse Acromioclavicular (AC) Joint Injury. While it's highly correctable, healing it required a level of patience and diligence that I struggled to invest in myself when it comes to self-care. Paulo observed me moping around the house feeling sorry for myself as I conscientiously kept my left (dominant) arm against my trunk, imagining that it was tied to my waist at my elbow. I was instructed not to lift it perpendicularly to my body or above my head and to not make any circular motions with my hand (like wiping a table or waxing a car) for the weekend. Additionally, I was told to ice my entire shoulder front, side, and back at least twice a day for ten minutes and to perform small but specific stretching/strengthening exercises as much as possible. That paired with four to six weeks of treatment with her, I was told, would hopefully be enough to rehabilitate the injury before the second half of YTT started.

As I took in the sight of the eight loads of dirty laundry along with the six loads of dirty dishes, I realized that not only would I be unable to perform most of the housework that I had intended to complete on Friday, the beginning of my five-day weekend off from work, but that I would also be unable to use this free time to work on my yoga practice, go for bike rides, play on the playground, or even carry a cooler. I was *drowning* in self-pity over the thought of being still and asking for help.

Paulo told me, "Jeni, you've been feeling but ignoring the pain for a few weeks now, avoiding the reality of the situation. Now that you know, you're letting yourself get depressed about your limitations. You need to remind yourself that you are fine and that you just need to slow down and follow directions for a while. You'll be back to your everyday routine soon. You've injured this shoulder before when you fell off a ladder as a teenager. (How he remembers these stories, I have no clue!) Now it's time to acknowledge it and heal once and for all." God bless that man and his gentle wisdom.

I told him that I hated feeling limited, incapable, and in need of help. I tend to become protective and discouraged, overcome with a desire to lie in bed and mentally check out (dissociate). He called me to a different action—one that takes responsibility for the situation without placing judgment on it. So, I did what any reasonable yogi would do: I meditated on it.

While sitting, I remembered a pose that Behnje had taught us once or twice: the Armless Warrior. It is a variation of *virabhadrasana,* warrior pose, in which you grasp your arms across your chest instead of extending them outward. It's a call to remembrance; it reminds us that even when we lack certain abilities, we are still strong. We work within our present limitations and gently explore and play the edge.

I was overcome with the humble realization that although I temporarily lacked the full function of my left arm, I was still so incredibly capable in many other ways. This was not the time to feel sorry for myself. It was an opportunity for reflection, gratitude, awareness, and patience. And a time to ask for help.

No matter what precautions we take, no matter how informed and measured we are, life will continually shake things up. Many wise people have reminded us throughout the history of time that what defines us is not what happens to us, but how we respond to it. During my rehabilitation, I committed to being a good patient, following directions, and acknowledging that even when my body doesn't perform how I expect it to, I am still strong, still loved, and still a precious gift.

I'm learning not to feel sorry for myself when life presents unexpected challenges and instead choose to honor the challenges and what they are asking of me. I am so much more than my perceived skills and strengths. I am a manifestation of God's love and creative energy. And you are, too.

"Banat, banat, ban jai." (Making, making, some day made.)
—Lahiri Mahasaya

Sacred Summer

There are many ways to convey the meaning of Yoga, but each definition seems to stem from its root *yuj*, or to yoke. Yoga is about
union: union of the body/mind and heart, union with a bigger
energy, with divine consciousness, with community, with your
true Self. Essentially, these are all ways of stating the same thing.
Yoga is about how you relate to the universe. That summer was a
beautiful training ground for taking my yoga practice off my mat
and into my life.

Paulo and I took some time in August to celebrate our tenth
wedding anniversary (which was actually on September 17th) and
to reflect on how we've grown and changed over the years. We spent
a great deal of time in deep conversation about life, our purposes,
and how we envisioned our future together.

We also renovated the extra bedroom to create a sacred
space—our little yoga room—in which our family could seek
solace from the noise of the world outside. Meg's mom sewed
curtains that had flecks of shiny gold thread in the fabric, and we
left the space bare except for my rocking chair, some wall art that
reminded me of my gramma, a baby Buddha statue that Paulo and I
found at an antique shop, and a *puja table*—a space to place sacred
objects such as a bell, incense, gemstones, photos or *murtis* (statues) of saints or deities, and anything else the worshiper would like
to incorporate into their ritual.

The girls would often come to sit on the floor with me after
school to talk about hard stuff, and I used the space every day for
meditation, reading and contemplation, and my asana practice.
Paulo and I began a Sunday morning ritual of sitting on the floor
with our coffee while we talked about life.

Truly, the most pivotal moment of the summer took place on
September 3rd, when I punched out at the bookstore for the last

time. After fifteen years of dedication to my company and to all the wonderful people with whom I'd had the pleasure of working, I knew it was time to let go. The significant sacrifice of time paired with the ever-increasing stress was creating a dis-ease in my life. I was craving more of that precious "God's Time" that I had a taste of up north, and my intuition was no longer whispering but shouting that it was time to be brave.

As I prepared to leave my office for the final time, I remembered the Ram Dass book I had ordered for myself. I brought home my new book along with gifts and letters of encouragement from my coworkers as well as the remaining trinkets and photos from my desk. When I got home, I retreated to my rocking chair in the yoga room, contemplating the words of my youngest daughter: "We're really living life right now." I snuggled up with a cup of tea and began reading about bhakti and karma yoga in the words of this new teacher of mine, Ram Dass. I learned there are four primary types of yoga: karma yoga is the yoga of selfless action or *seva* (service); bhakti yoga is the yoga of devotion to God; jnana yoga is the yoga of knowledge; and raja yoga is the path of Ashtanga or the Eightfold Path.

> "There is a wisdom which knows when to go and when to return, what is to be done and what is not to be done, what is fear and what is courage, what is bondage and what is liberation—that is pure wisdom."
>
> —Bhagavad Gita 18.30

Grace and Redefining My Image of God

Something that Behnje had passed forward from her own teacher in our teacher training still stands out to me: "When we take one step toward Grace, Grace takes ten steps toward us." The weightiness of her words conveyed a depth of confidence that was hard to overlook.

She spoke of an underlying pulsation of loving energy, of *spanda*, that creates, sustains, and dissolves all things in the universe, and of how this primordial Love is yearning for us, patiently waiting for our longing for reconnection to emerge.

I've long been a believer in the concept of synchronicity, or "meaningful coincidences" as defined by psychiatrist Carl Jung. To me, they feel like whispers from a deeper dimension, checking to see if I am paying attention. This felt understanding relies on my ability to be sensitive, curious, and non-judgmental toward my inner and outer experiences. It seems that as soon as I allow myself the space to have greater awareness of my inner and outer landscapes, I begin to observe that circumstances tend to align for me in the most perfect of ways.

For example, I've noticed throughout my life that books seem to come into my awareness at exactly the right time to offer guidance on what I'm "working through" at that moment. And they always come in exactly the right order because each seed of wisdom seems to contain the blueprint for the next level of growth to be borne from. Perhaps you're experiencing some of that synchronistic timeliness with this book.

I've also experienced this with music, friendships, careers... nearly every aspect of my life, if reflected on through a lens of curiosity, could be viewed as the foundation for the next layer of experience. In other words, synchronicities can make it feel as if there is directionality to the seemingly random, unrelated people, objects, and experiences in our lives.

And so, through this lens, I found it particularly delightful to contemplate how Grace —my word for Divine Love/Truth/Intelligence/Energy/God/Creator/Formlessness—revealed her/it/himself to me. I began to see synchronicities not as lovely, random accidents, but instead as breadcrumbs and signposts guiding me from a dimension beyond the 3D world I was living in.

During my mom's visit that summer, we reengaged in the conversation about God we had tentatively started when I was "coming out of the broom closet" as a teen. I told her that although as a child I had felt so connected to Jesus, God, Mother Mary, and the saints, because of so many experiences of fake holiness and even violence within the church, I had developed a bad taste in my mouth anytime someone started talking about Jesus or religion in general. And now that we were talking about things like "Grace," "The Big Energy," "Universal Consciousness," among other translations for this idea of "God" in my yoga teacher training, I was brushing up against this inner conflict of believer and non-believer again.

After hearing me out, my mom mused, "Well, the word God is pretty loaded for most people. It pulls up a different image for everyone. Maybe it's because of this heavily pushed image of an old, white-bearded, vengeful, judging Father God that you are turned off to the word "God?" What if you imagine God as a woman? Call her Goddess or Mother?"

That innocent inquiry flipped a switch for me. Cherished memories flooded back from elementary school. I recalled images of the May Crowning during which we'd coronate and sing to a statue of Mother Mary in front of my Catholic school, and the Charismatic masses my grandparents took me to. Remembrances of praying the rosary, repeating the Hail Mary, and of course, my own persistent longing arose for a sense of motherly love, acceptance, and affection. Yes; the image of a patient, unconditionally loving *Divine Mother* or one of a genderless, interconnected, benevolent, and divinely intelligent *Universe*, was precisely the imagery my religious dogma- and patriarchy-traumatized mind needed to be willing to engage with mental concepts of "God" again.

Later that same week, while in teacher training, we were given time to contemplate our teachers. We were asked to remember and have gratitude for all the teachers who have inspired us throughout our lives. As soon as the bell rang, I scribbled the names of two dozen individuals without difficulty before the bell rang again, and we were asked to bring our attention back to the group. Ranging from my husband to my parents and grandparents, to my children, siblings, schoolteachers, friends, neighbors, coworkers, and even some total strangers, I've had no shortage of influential and inspirational beings who've helped me along my way in life. I recognized that Grace had been with me all along, even when I thought I was abandoned.

During that same practice, we were asked to contemplate the greatest gifts that we have to offer as a teacher. What surfaced in my heart was my authenticity, my own vulnerable humanity. I heard the words, "Live out loud, Jeni. Let the world see you." But the problem was, I still couldn't accept myself; I was afraid to be seen. I kept thinking, "I need to be purer first, I need to be more strict."

During the group check-in, I broke into sobs as tears streamed down my face. I'd been so emotionally churned that month, face-to-face with my perfectionism and my not-good-enoughness. When I shared with the group that what I needed was to exercise greater self-discipline to find my peace, my teacher interjected. "No, I don't think you need more self-discipline," she said in a quiet but fierce tone, "Perhaps what you're in greater need of is self-compassion."

I faltered while trying to hear her words clearly. I struggled to imagine what it might feel like to love myself without conditions or expectations, but I believed it would feel like freedom.

Hindsight Wisdom

When I finally freed myself from the constraints of religious dogma, I gave myself permission to explore a vast, unfathomable vision of God that exists beyond all organized religions and their often problematic, violent, money- and power-seeking human leadership. I could appreciate the core messages of the prophets, saints, and mystics without getting lost in the hypocrisy of the church. The outcome for me has been a more intimate, sweeter relationship with the Divine.

"Once we get a taste of the freedom that comes with letting go of our stuff—anger, righteousness, jealousy, our need to be in control, the judging mind, to name just a few—we start to look at those things in new ways. That is the teaching of being in the moment. For someone who understands that this precious birth is an opportunity to awaken, is an opportunity to know God, all of life becomes an instrument for getting there—marriage, family, job, play, travel, all of it. You just spiritualize your life."

—Ram Dass, Polishing the Mirror

#MeToo

As I've been practicing yoga, certain things have surfaced in my awareness, demanding that I face my fear of the past and release myself from the toxic hold my memories had on me. And, like many women across the United States, I was shaken to my very core when predatory sexual comments made by then-presidential candidate Donald Trump were released in the media. Each time I saw a meme or an article about it, it hit me in the chest like a pellet gun of remembrance.

"You know, I'm automatically attracted to beautiful I just start kissing them. It's like a magnet. Just kiss. I don't even wait. And when you're a star, they let you do it. You can do anything...Grab 'em by the pussy. You can do anything."

— Donald Trump[2]

---

2 https://www.nytimes.com/2016/10/08/us/donald-trump-tape-transcript.html

Paulo and I had been together for thirteen years at that point, yet I had only recently begun to open up to him about the near-daily sexual harassment that I received from other men. From being touched on the hip or rubbed up against from behind to being told things like, "watch out before I come over there and spank you," "you should smile," or "resistance makes me crazy." And my least favorite: the spine-chilling feeling you get when you notice that you're being thoroughly "taken in" visually by a man with violent hunger in his eyes.

Throughout my life, I have known what it feels like to be treated as prey, to be disrespected and made to feel like an object meant for enjoyment but unworthy of love. I have been taught to believe that I am not safe by myself in certain places (like the mall, bike paths, downtown) and at certain times (literally whenever). As a fat teenage girl, it seems that I was either regarded as an easy target (needy, low self-esteem) or too unattractive to pursue and therefore "one of the guys"—the physically safer option.

Such a great cruelty is the unwritten rule of society, which dictates that women avoid speaking on any topic that makes other people uncomfortable. And let me tell you, sexual harassment and abuse have made us so uncomfortable that even as women, we silently teach one another to keep these offensive and demeaning experiences to ourselves or to simply accept them as normal or inevitable. "Oh, he's just like that." "He's an old pervert; he didn't mean any harm." "You shouldn't have been drinking so much." "That was a long time ago, you should let it go."

But in truth, these things that happen to us and around us do not define us. And with so many strong and outspoken women, such as former first lady Michelle Obama and Glennon Doyle (author of many wonderful books, including *Love Warrior*) among countless other celebrities and "everyday women" standing up, refusing to be silent any longer, I decided that I would no longer let shame keep me silent, either.

My yoga practice was literally squeezing the painful memories out of me, releasing me from their chokehold. I no longer felt compelled to hide the fact that I am also a survivor of abuse. And I vowed to myself never again to stand idly by as I observe any individual, woman or man, be harassed or dehumanized in front of me.

This critical breakthrough led to a public sharing of my private pain and suffering due to previous sexual trauma. I summoned my courage and spoke my truth to my husband first. He held me with a firm, encompassing embrace as I shattered into a panic attack in his arms. Feeling the rapid pulsation of my heart as my breath quickened, I cried and cried as he rocked me and held me close.

I confessed that I had been scared to tell him because I didn't want him to look at me like a wounded, broken, helpless victim. I didn't want him to see me as fragile or damaged goods. His compassionate eyes and steadiness let me know that these fears were illusory, keeping me trapped in a prison of memories.

Later, I decided to post about my experience on my blog, sharing the link as a #MeToo status update on Facebook. In doing so, my eyes were opened to the fact that I was not alone; that I had so many soul sisters who've been through the same fire as me and even worse. And we all had buried our pain deep down into the fibers of our beings, suffering in silent loneliness. I didn't learn until recently that the "me too" movement began way before the hashtag, ten years earlier in 2006, actually. It was created by Tarana Burke in response to her experience with a young girl sharing a tragic story of sexual violence, which galvanized her commitment to bring resources, support, and pathways for healing to survivors, and to queer, trans, disabled Black women and children and people of color in particular. (See, metoomvmt.org)

The truth is, we never fully escape these shadows of shame until we drag them into the daylight and strip them of their toxic power over us. They manifest as depression, disordered anxiety, drinking problems, disordered eating, substance abuse, disordered codependency, self-mutilation, abusive relationships, and so on.

I reflected in my journal later that, "It's fascinating how fear swells up into my throat like a knot, begging me to hold my truth in and stay silent. And yet, as soon as I speak it, my heart loses ten pounds of grief, and my smile cannot be contained."

> "When you bear what you think you cannot bear, who you think you are dies."
>
> —Ram Dass, *Polishing the Mirror*

We are not looking for pity when we speak our truth. We are not looking for retribution. We are not looking for attention. We are reclaiming our narratives as a form of medicine. We are love warriors, and we are healing, together.

Noticing the Fear

Now approaching the culmination of the 200-hour Yoga Teacher Training, it was time for us to learn how to create class sequences that focused on Heart Themes and Alignment Principles. In this method of yoga, each class includes a theme that aims to connect us to the essential divine goodness of our true nature. The theme is generally connected to one or more virtues, such as compassion, fortitude, and integrity, which are expressed through the asanas of the class sequence. It was thrilling to suture together all the pieces of knowledge I'd accumulated over the past several months and to fully immerse myself in the mindset of a teacher.

I had been giving more focus to the contemplative side of my practice, and I could see how it was altering my perspective in grand and peace-inducing ways. Slowly clearing away my old stories of not-good-enoughness and perfectionism, fear surfaced as the next layer of attachment to face and work through.

For my class sequencing homework, I chose the theme *Courageous Expression*. There was a strong focus in my language for the meditation/centering on how Grace's protection provides us the freedom to express ourselves creatively. Interestingly, my peers pointed out that there was so much emphasis on the security aspect that my actual theme of expression didn't even come through. While it still created an overall positive energetic feeling of safety for them as my students, my internal fears had distorted my intention of focusing on freedom. I ultimately re-wrote that sequence four times before I was finally able to convey my intent in a clear, impactful way.

After our weekend of teacher drills and peer evaluation, I spent some time with the feelings of fear that always seemed to be right near the surface of my consciousness. There are life-diminishing tendencies within me to feel disempowered and incapable of protecting myself. It's as if a fearful, anxious, childlike part of me has never been fully acknowledged, so she lingers in the shadows of my mind, occasionally tainting not only my perceptions but also my behaviors and belief systems. I had a growing awareness that much if not all the dis-ease that I've experienced in my life has stemmed from unchecked fear.

I awoke the morning after that weekend of teacher training to a persistent urge to go hiking in the woods behind my grandparents' old house. I went up to the secret place where I used to spend hours daydreaming and writing as a child, the same space in which I had spoken to my grandmother during my meditative trance months earlier. This hike, which proved to be an incredibly healing journey, seemed to represent on a more recognizable scale how I had transitioned from being a curious, playful, exuberant child to a panicky, calculating, untrusting adult.

Armed with a journal and my copy of the Bhagavad Gita, I began my nervous journey up the hill. Immediately, all my senses were ignited. With each step I took, I frantically scanned for poison ivy. Every falling leaf that crinkled on its way down alerted my ears and eyes as my breath caught in my throat at the thought of another human being in my vicinity. I noticed that I was rushing forward as if in a hurry, looking at the ground in front of me with tunnel vision. I couldn't even begin to appreciate the beauty and fullness of nature that surrounded me until I was three-quarters of the way to the top.

Once I came to the clearing before the peak, my breath began to calm. My panoramic vision slowly returned, and I felt my muscles soften as I realized the significance of overcoming this irrational fear of being in the woods alone. Then, I could feel *everything*. The energy around me was soothing and peaceful. Everything about that time in the woods felt magical and nourishing, and I knew it was only the beginning. Each day since then has offered fresh opportunities to be curious about my fears, to draw them nearer, and to observe them instead of repressing or avoiding them.

In the woods behind my grandparents' house

New Traditions Heal Unobserved Grief

Grief is a long and winding path. It takes you to the darkest valleys within yourself and then springboards you to the tallest peaks, sometimes within a single day. There are days, weeks even, that I feel strong and steady until a bittersweet memory or thought surfaces in my mind. Within a fraction of a second, I'm tumbling down to the floor.

One such tumble happened while I was chatting with my boss at the butcher shop. The conversation came around to buying Christmas gifts for the impending holiday season. My witness self watched as my mind began to whirl, my mouth rambling off soundbites of opinions and anecdotes about how I'm not a big fan of materialism; I can't afford to buy gifts for everyone that I love, that's not what's really important anyway, blah, blah, blah…

That was all true, but I was dancing around the deeper wound. My whole perspective of the holidays had been tainted with a shadow of grief. The regret for missing so many experiences due to my old work schedule and the grief of losing three of my four grandparents during the holidays and within four years of each other made it feel impossible to muster joy and wonder from Halloween to New Year's Day.

Reading between the lines of my self-righteous statements to my boss, I realized that the truth was that my heart was broken. I finally gave up my armor, looked her dead in the eye, and said, "I want to figure out how to make my heart beat again." She gazed at me with knowing eyes and said, "I have a song for you." She played Danny Gokey's, *Tell Your Heart to Beat Again*, loudly as we both silently took in the words and the music and continued our work, dropping the conversation.

I wanted to feel a different kind of way this holiday season. Although I knew that I'd never return to who I was before I began losing the physical forms of those I love, I knew that I wanted to rise above the consuming darkness of grief unobserved. Upon this realization, the still, small voice within encouraged me to take a new perspective: This year would be unlike any other year. I am learning;

I am waking up. I am delighted to notice that I have worked the entire month of October without setting up a single holiday merchandising display or needing to dig deep to get excited about company-wide sales contests or required promotional events.

As I breathed in the gratitude of this awareness, my curiosity was piqued by what other stale perceptions I could re-frame. Recalling my recent hike behind my grandparents' house, I decided that instead of focusing on Halloween so much this year, I would see if Paulo and the girls might like to learn about and celebrate a tradition from their cultural heritage, the Mexican Día de Muertos, or the Day of the Dead.

Día de Muertos is a very old, very sacred tradition in pre-Spaniard Indigenous Mexican culture. As someone born outside of this heritage, I acknowledge the importance of learning about, honoring, and respecting this important tradition that is the religious and cultural legacy of the Native peoples (Mexica, Maya, Tlaxcaltec, Chichimec, and others) of what is today known as Mexico. Due to colonization, it became illegal for hundreds of years for the Indigenous Peoples of the Americas to practice their cultural and spiritual traditions or even to speak their native language or wear their traditional regalia. The truth of this pervasive trauma and attempted cultural genocide must be acknowledged and reckoned with for us to move forward in collective healing.

I had read in an article online[3] that, "Assured that the dead would be insulted by mourning or sadness, Día de los Muertos celebrates the lives of the deceased with food, drink, parties, and activities the dead enjoyed in life... Día de los Muertos recognizes death as a natural part of the human experience, a continuum with

---

3 https://creativeartsguild.org/events/annual-events/dia-de-los-muertos/
   about-the-holiday

birth, childhood, and growing up to become a contributing member of the community. On Día de los Muertos, the dead are also a part of the community, awakened from their eternal sleep to share celebrations with their loved ones."

I picked up some *cempasúchil* (Mexican marigolds) and a couple of new candles for the *ofrenda* (home altar). When my family came home, I shared my ideas with them. They were very excited to learn more about their culture and the significance of this holiday and to honor their ancestors. On Día de Muertos, we went to the supermercado down the street from our house to pick up *pan dulce* (sweet bread) for ourselves and our offering. Once home, we all set about the house, looking for pictures and mementos of deceased loved ones as we began to assemble our ofrenda.

Once we had it set to our liking, we turned off the lights, sat in a semi-circle on the floor in front of it, and breathed it all in. As my eyes flickered over each photo and trinket, my heart felt juicy, full, and calm. The girls said in near-unison, "They're here with us, I can feel them." Paulo and I could, too. As we listened to Spanish music and ate our pan dulce, we felt the embrace of wisdom and love from our ancestors all around us.

We each took a moment to share a prayer of gratitude and remembrance, thanking our family and friends for their impact on our lives, for sharing their light with us, and for carrying us through when times have gotten hard.

It was a very warm and comforting feeling to intentionally honor and remember those who have passed on. I asked for guidance and support through the coming weeks as I learn a new way of being during the winter—a softer, gentler, more self-compassionate version of myself—that self-honors and allows space for all the feelings while remaining playful and engaged. We all agreed at bedtime that this would be a new family tradition, and I instinctively knew that this was a snippet of the freedom that I'd been looking for.

Last Day of YTT

The last day of our 200-hr Yoga Teacher Training also happened to be the sixth anniversary of my grandfather's death. I wrote a letter to my mom in my journal that morning, part of which read:

> "His memory sparks a lot of emotions in me. On the one hand, I felt completely and unconditionally loved by him. He would've given me the world if he could've. He indulged all of my curiosities and dedicated his days to making me happy. On the other hand, he would, at times, deeply upset me, offend me with his fearful, judgmental opinions, and make me feel physically unsafe.

> It is auspicious that I would end YTT on a day that already holds so much significance, especially because of the way that my spiritual practices have enabled me to open, reexamine, and heal some deeply rooted wounds such as these. I also know that this is not a finish line. It is simply an affirmation that henceforth I dedicate my life to the awakening of my own inner being and to the service of humanity, even as a householder, and perhaps because of it. This is the embarking on a lifetime of curiosity and learning and engagement. And I am so grateful and excited."

I share this personal sentiment with you because it sutures the many lessons I learned during the seven months of teacher training. While I spent the better part of two decades missing out on the joys of life for fear of the suffering, I'm learning to feel my heart beat again. I'm learning to unbecome who I thought I was supposed to be, and instead, I'm discovering the beauty of who I truly am, of who we *all* truly are, which is simultaneously a unique expression of the Divine and a microcosm of the bigger energy of life.

Second Anniversary: A Letter to my Gramma

"I am gentle with myself today. I think that you would want that, but that's not why I'm doing it. I desire an openness, an aliveness that will only come with unrestrained breath and a calm mind. Many tears have flowed freely this week as I deepen my focus on you, but today my eyes feel soft and supple and bright, and for now, tear-free.

In the brief moments where I can feel my chest tighten and my shoulders hunch and round, I breathe patience and compassion into that tightness, and I feel the release. This morning, I slept late, awakened by kisses and coffee and my Beloved. The snow-covered earth, delicate and shimmering, encouraged quiet and peacefulness.

Paulo and I made a feast for breakfast: chocolate chip pancakes, bacon, eggs, hash browns, and decadent coffee. We worked together, no bickering or whining – I <u>know</u> that was you. Thank you for that."

6

Taking My Seat

Atha Yogānuśāsanam: Now, the Practice of Yoga Begins. This is the first of Patañjali's Yoga Sutras (a collection of aphorisms, short statements that express a general truth). Patañjali is regarded as an early CE Indian sage who was the first to organize and record the theory and practice of yoga as derived from much older traditions. Each time I've read Patañjali's sutras, I feel exhilarated because it reminds me that each moment is new. No matter how many times I've stepped onto my mat or read a classic spiritual text, it's as though it's the first time because I'm experiencing it with a different quality of awareness. My practice changes from the morning to the evening, from yesterday to today, and it will most certainly change again tomorrow. It's an ever-evolving path inward that is entirely unpredictable, just like life.

Letting go of the old storylines of who I *thought* I was, I felt fully immersed in the play of life for the first time in a very long time. It was a welcome change to have more time with my family and friends as well as a dedicated yoga space. Working at the butcher shop was teaching me about my own physical strength and learning agility, and my new schedule gave me plenty of opportunities to immerse myself in my practices.

And yet, my journal entry from January 7, 2017, was all over the map. I was fresh out of teacher training, money was tight, and we had some family members temporarily living with us. I was in a tough spot mentally.

"Although several people have asked me when I will begin
to teach classes, I've been scared to take the next step.

Afraid to fail? Or am I afraid to succeed? I'm noticing the pattern of self-sabotage. When I'm near a breakthrough, I have two consistent tendencies:

1. I distract myself with a million different things until I "run out of time" for productivity or/and
2. I devise this over-the-top, highly oppressive, strictly sequential To-Do List as though it were an intricate list of things I need to finish <u>before</u> I do what I want to do.

Here's an example of my self-sabotage. Before I can teach a yoga class, I must:

- Finish my website, including a comprehensive recipe/meal-planning page, which I haven't started
- Sign paperwork and file to become an LLC; acquire a business credit card for tax purposes
- Order business cards (why??)
- Buy new, professional-looking yoga clothing
- Finish decorating the yoga room
- Have several classes' worth of themes & sequences prepared and practice them all extensively for memorization
- Re-read all of my notes and handouts from YTT
- Finish reading my 500-page book on sequencing (I'm on page 55)
- Have all common poses memorized by their Sanskrit terms
- Be in top physical/emotional condition (...what?)

If I need to check off this entire list before ever teaching a formal class, by my calculations, I may never do it. This is what self-sabotage looks like for me. This is what unchecked fear looks like for me."

The next day, Grace showed up in the form of an email from my very first yoga teacher, Katie. With her simple email, everything changed:

> "Jeni,
> Happy New Year! I have followed your progress through TT via your blog. Now that the holidays are over, and hopefully we are settling in for the winter, I was wondering if you have given any thought to teaching. Give me or Jennephyr a shout or email.
>
> Katie"

To which, hours later (after obsessive contemplation and four drafts), I responded:

> "Hi Katie!
> Thank you for reaching out. I am absolutely interested in teaching. I've been practicing a little on family, but I know that the best way to find fluidity and confidence is to just start. How would you recommend I proceed?
>
> Jeni"

> "I am not afraid; I was born to do this."
>
> —Joan of Arc

I then sent an email to Jennephyr, the studio owner, requesting a teaching audition. After teaching my first hour-long class to them both, Jenn hired me on the spot and gave me a Wednesday evening slot to teach my class, which I named Heart-Centered Hatha Yoga in honor of my teachers and their method. Within four months, I was teaching twice per week.

Darkness Falling

Between all the classes I was teaching and the classes of Behnje's I was attending, I felt in a very high state. My whole being felt lighter and more joyful. I experienced a deeper sense of connection to nature and to the people I encountered, whether a loved one or a total stranger.

While meditating with my teachers, my consciousness would expand, and profound insights would arise. Once the meditation was over, I would hurriedly record my experiences in my journal as if they were treasures to collect. I also began to unconsciously attract people who would tell me how amazing I was, feeding my ego in exchange for a hit of the energy radiating from me.

I must admit, I was starting to feel a bit special, as though I had succeeded in attaining something through my efforts. And through this impure, egoic exchange, I was depleting myself quite rapidly. It was as if a weighted blanket had been cast over my mind and body, making everything feel more grueling.

I didn't have the awareness yet to see that I was falling into a common pitfall on the spiritual path, which Tibetan Master Chögyam Trungpa Rinpoche refers to as "spiritual materialism" in his book *Cutting through Spiritual Materialism*. He explained this as a fundamental distortion in which we "deceive ourselves into thinking we are developing spiritually when instead we are strengthening our egocentricity through spiritual techniques."

I was overlaying my achievement-based mentality onto my spiritual practices. Because I saw the teachings as existing outside of me, they became something for me to accomplish as an individual. Underlying this striving was the subtle belief that I was somehow inherently flawed or lacking, and that only through persistence would I obtain spiritual "success"—in other words, I'd finally be "good" or "worthy."

This perspective reinforced the sense of separation between me and the world, making me the ultimate subject and everything else object. The power of my mind's habit energy continued the ongoing storyline of my small self as a main character—a fundamental ignorance or confusion that forms the very basis of my suffering.

By Grace, I recognized this forcing energy as a subtle form of self-judgment, of unworthiness. I began to operationalize what I had learned in my practices by taking a discerning look at my self-aggrandizement and its shadow, self-doubt. I played with different perspectives, appreciating that it's always much easier to see flaws and faults in others than it is to see them in myself. I began to inquire how these shadow traits lived in me. I did *not* enjoy what I unearthed in the process.

After feeling so high, so connected, and so full of love during the yoga teacher training, the inevitable low was crushing. It seemed as if I was falling off the path, doomed to a life consumed by anxiety, depression, and unsupportive coping strategies.

Reckoning with the Highs and Lows

This marked the beginning of a rather unsettling time during my spiritual journey. I didn't yet understand the notion of egoic, or psychological, death: the death of who we *think* we are. But here I was, standing at the edge of the cliff of Jeni-ness—my limited, small self constructed by society, my parents, and my mind—wondering whether I could survive the unfathomable leap across the ocean to the mysterious other shore.

Whereas before, and especially as a teen and young adult, I wished my life away by staying insatiably busy and in a self-induced fog, I was now, sometimes painfully, very present in my life. To bear witness to my own self-destruction filled me with anguish. It didn't matter what I "knew" was good for me or how much I said the words "should," "must," or "ought to," my body/mind would faithfully run the same old programs whenever my emotions signaled to it that my self-concept was not safe. It was as if a battle between my will-power and my habit-power were taking place within my mind.

Now that I had seen how I was constantly hiding from, ignoring, and band-aiding the scars of my youth out of fear, I had no choice but to face them. At times, I felt as though I had been stripped bare in a cold room with nothing but mirrors surrounding me. It was a burning away of all the identifications, all the beliefs, all the armor that I had accumulated throughout my life. This "unbecoming" felt eerily like annihilation. Every moment of every day was a learning experience, showing me all the stories that I had been taught to tell me about myself.

Endless thought streams of identification flowed through the background of my mind: I'm a perfectionist; I'm anxious; I'm an empath; I'm a trauma survivor. During my meditation practices, I would ask myself, "But am I?" Over time, I noticed that as easily as I could identify myself in both positive and negative terms, I could dispute those labels and change them. All that was required was curiosity, attention, and kindness.

This marked a pivotal shift in the way I related to myself. I was developing an additional perspective beyond my entrenched ego view. It was as if I were simultaneously looking out from my eyeballs as well as from slightly above, slightly behind my own head, including myself in a bigger story. Instead of the main character, I saw myself as one of infinite characters who are simultaneously diverse expressions of a united whole. I watched this being named Jeni as she went about her days. And in seeing her plight, how she had endured so much heartache and suffering, my judgments about her began to soften.

I noticed how she craved belonging, how she desperately wanted to do and be good so she could feel safe in her relationships. I saw how she clung to the expansive, light experiences she had while on her mat, and how she pushed away the contracting, heavy experiences she had everywhere else. And one day, miraculously, a new, more compassionate inner voice spoke within her, coming through in her journal entry:

And here I am once again, on the other side of Christmas, quickly approaching a new year. I'm beginning to see the cosmic humor— the cyclical nature, the recursiveness of it all. If ever I was on a wagon, not only have I fallen off, but my foot got stuck and I'm now being dragged behind it. However, I am relating to it differently this time.

As my belly swells with bloat and discomfort after binge eating, I rub it lovingly and find bigger clothes. When my mind is foggy and my body is exhausted, I drink some extra coffee or take a nap. As my hands rip apart, consumed with eczema, I scald the itch away, and then I apply treatment. When the mood strikes for a drink or a smoke, I partake and then observe my energy slowly drain away from me as a headache creeps in. I eat and eat and eat until I feel sickly full, and then I sit in my agony until I am empty enough to take another bite.

All of these behaviors cause my mind to shut down. I lose interest in doing anything besides watching the days slip away. I await bedtime so that I can be done with this day, with all its chores and responsibilities.

I've been here countless times before, always accompanied by feelings of fear, panic, disgust, anger, and hopelessness. But now I'm witnessing it, investigating it with curiosity and non-judgment. I was struck by the realization that if I want off this merry-go-round, it will require a new program, a new way of relating that includes new responses. I long for something different, to see what exists beyond the boundaries of my comfort zone and my fear.

7

Turning Toward the Cave of the Heart

In one of his dharma talks, Ram Dass invites the listener to imagine they are making their way down a wide staircase to the subway station in New York City, right before the rush hour. Upon reaching the bottom of the stairs, you discover a locked gate with a sign on it that reads: No Exit.

You begin your climb back up when suddenly, a sea of people begins flooding down the stairs. You try to explain to them that there's no way through and to turn around, but everyone's too distracted and rushed or busy on their phones. Meanwhile, you're finding it harder and harder to move against the mass of people moving frantically to nowhere. You now know that the path you had planned to take won't get you to where you want to go, yet it takes all of your effort to maintain your balance as you walk against the flow of traffic. You accept that everyone else will eventually figure it out too, so you focus on getting yourself back to the fresh air instead.

This is a beautiful metaphor for what some experience when they begin to wake up to the ways they've been trapped in a futile cycle of craving and aversion, their happiness and contentment always out of reach. We may feel compelled to inform everyone we meet that "things won't make you happy," or that "you're looking outside of yourself for something that you can only find within," but honestly, no one can even hear that message until their hearts and minds are ready to. It's the greatest secret that is actually not a secret at all.

So, you do what you can to keep working on yourself, releasing the limiting storylines of who you think you are. You learn, little by little, to let things go more easily and not to get so attached to people, objects, experiences, or outcomes. You accept that you can't change people's minds, but you can keep deepening your ability to be present. You can keep working to open your heart and calm your mind so you can hear what the highest action is to take at any given moment.

> "The time is always now. Nothing else exists besides this moment. Be bold, have faith, and do what must be done."
> —Jeni Juarez

Recognizing the Expansion

The first half of Trump's first presidency was nearing an end, and there was so much upheaval happening. People were waking up, and things were being shaken up. The #MeToo movement brought forth a tidal wave of sexual harassment and assault survivor stories. Powerful men were being fired and held accountable, and women across the world were marching for intersectional rights. New horrific instances of police brutality against Black people were in the news constantly. Stories of families being separated left and right due to mass deportations kept coming through the media. And our tax and healthcare systems were radically benefiting the rich while the lower and middle classes struggled.

In our microcosm, our family was shifting as well. People were questioning the status quo, overcoming addictions, and finding the courage to pursue their interests. Things were changing indeed. More and more, I was beginning to hear and heed my inner voice. I felt that my next step was to embrace what I was afraid to do but that I knew I must: reach out beyond my tight, limited social circle and help build community.

Behnje was continually affirming this appreciation for the collective at the end of each yoga class. She would first offer each of us gratitude for showing up and gathering together, and then she'd offer gratitude for the wise, compassionate beings from whom this wisdom has been passed, like an ever-burning torch of illumination from teacher to student since time immemorial.

My intuition was telling me that it was important to find the courage to make new friends and join ever-widening circles of inspiring people who are dedicated to evolving our culture in a way that is rooted in universal compassion, truth, and wisdom. I was sensing an inner pull to attend community events and to become a more active contributor to my community.

In the stillness, I also heard a call to strengthen my will so that I could have the courage and fortitude to immerse myself in my passions and discover my purpose. Playing small and barely getting by wasn't going to work anymore; it was time to open myself to my highest potential.

The Wisdom of "I Can't Deal with This"

I was going on my second year at the butcher shop and while it was still a far cry from the heavy stress I remembered from the bookstore, I was feeling that antsy, frenetic energy again that was telling me something was out of alignment.

Even though I was originally hired to work only during the weekday mornings, my limited availability eventually became a fairness issue once we got to the summer. Since all the other employees were required to work some closing and weekend shifts, I agreed to work a few closes and a weekend shift each week in exchange for fewer total days worked. With the shorter hours of operation, it would still allow for family dinner and bedtime routines every day. However, my body was not appreciating the schedule change; the ten-hour days on my feet, along with the repetitive heavy lifting and cutting motions, were wearing on my muscles and joints. Not only that, I was beginning to be relied upon for managerial responsibilities like ordering, training, and discipline, but my pay wasn't increasing.

I was struggling to enact boundaries because I felt like I owed Margie for taking me on and accommodating my scheduling requests. It was a small business with an even smaller profit margin, and she was doing everything she could to make up for the low wages. And yet, there was a crankiness among the other employees, too. I soon began noticing myself mumbling or internally saying, "I can't deal with this."

It startled me at first, hearing myself utter "I can't deal with this" so often. Why couldn't I? What was the problem? I sat with this curiosity for several days until the realization hit me: It doesn't matter where I work or what kind of work I do; if I'm not being real with myself and speaking my truth, there will be dis-ease. And the truth was, I was slowly creeping back toward the familiar pattern of working full-time hours, including nights and weekends, only now for much less money and without any insurance benefits or paid time off.

This season of transition was now ending; I was never meant to stay at the butcher shop forever. I needed to get real about what my dream was so I could take real steps toward it.

Learning a New Way to Pray

My brain was like a knotted-up ball of yarn that I was trying to untangle. Inside I was screaming, *"I don't know what the fuck I'm doing!"* All I knew was that my body and mind were unsettled at work and unsettled at home. Once again, I was dragging myself through the days and feeling cornered.

Paulo and I were making about $200 less per month than what we needed to cover the basics, so our debt was piling up. Our clothes were slowly wearing out, and we didn't have the money to buy new ones. I asked my neighbor and friend, Becca, to give the girls haircuts in her driveway, and she even gifted the girls some new school clothes that fall.

I remember a particularly humbling day when our little neighborhood family wanted to celebrate the end of summer with a potluck dinner. With my head down, I thanked them for the invitation but said that we couldn't afford to contribute to the community meal, so we were going to stay inside. They *immediately* countered, without a hint of pity, that there was more than enough to go around, and to please come and let them love on us. I wanted to cry. It felt like I had a softball in my throat as I agreed to let go and allow them to care for us.

Years of prideful independence (read: fear of vulnerability) had built up this resistance toward being the receiver instead of the bestower of generosity. Paulo and I both had a strong self-identification as people who do things for others, not as people whom others do things for. But there was no avoiding the sacredness of reciprocity during this time. I saw how accepting love from our friends was nourishing them as much as it nourished us. And by allowing this generosity to flow through us, I got the sense that it was Grace in disguise; all these beings were like embodied angels, rooting for us and wanting to see us thrive.

Understanding this, my angry, defeated thought of, *"I don't know what the fuck I'm doing!"* slowly turned into a jovial, shoulder-shrugging, *"I don't know what the fuck I'm doing!"* I began to wonder whether it even really mattered that I knew what I was doing, or if it was more important that I did what I thought was *the next right thing to do.*

I decided that instead of trying to manifest a very specific, clear result through laser-focused determination, I would try a different approach. Letting go of outcomes, I dreamed about the aspects of my ideal job. Would I work alone or in a team? Would it be a consistent schedule or flexible? Would I work inside or outside? Would I create or sell a product or a service?

What came through for me was a scaffolding of values and needs:

- I want to work during the day, during the week, so I can be with my family after school and on weekends
- I want to work no more than 30 hours per week so that I have time and energy for myself, for others, and for the things that matter most to me
- I want to work in an industry that aligns with my integrity; I will not participate in the exploitation of resources, employees, or customers for the sake of profit
- I want to work by myself or with a small, intimate team in a setting that honors my autonomy and my talents
- I want to sell a product or service that I believe in and to do it in a way that respects the earth and people
- I want to work in an environment that enables me to continue learning and growing in ways that can become an offering to others

After clarifying the parameters of my ideal profession, I shortened it to "I want to work part-time, during the day, during the week, in an industry that reflects my integrity and values, in an environment that allows me to continually learn and grow in ways that benefit others." Once I had that memorized, I began telling anyone who would listen. I told my husband, my friends, my family, and my co-workers; I even began telling my customers at the butcher shop.

Except for my closest support system, every single one of them told me that what I was looking for didn't exist. And yet, amazingly, their naysaying didn't deter me. I wasn't seeking outside approval or validation on this. I deeply believed that if I imagined the framework but relinquished the details, I could trust that whatever unfolded next would be the next right step toward my future becoming.

Hindsight Wisdom

People-pleasing and a refusal to ask for help are results of personal, intergenerational, and cultural trauma. In the personal realm, these behaviors can reflect a history of our own needs not being sufficiently met by caregivers, friends, or partners. It can also reflect a distorted belief that our perceived value stems from how much we self-sacrifice in service of "the other." When they become lifelong coping strategies, these behaviors are passed down generationally. They become a family trait of coping with personal difficulties on one's own. Many of us have habitual tendencies to struggle and suffer silently, pretending to the outside world that everything is fine when you know damn well that things are not fine. It's what our parents did, what their parents did, and so on.

In the cultural realm, these behaviors can be traced to the enduring impacts of patriarchy, settler colonialism, chattel slavery, the bootstrap mentality of capitalism, and the Protestant work ethic. All these ideologies suggest that life is meant to be inherently more difficult for certain subsets of humanity and that for everyone else, if you're struggling, it's all your fault and somehow also your responsibility to correct by yourself.

An Angel Named Karen

I first met Karen as a customer at the butcher shop. She was already a friend of Tammy's and Margie's. She was a Pampered Chef consultant and had hosted PC parties with them in the past. Suspicious of all multilevel marketing companies as so many of them tend to prey on the young, the poor, and mothers, I initially declined the offer to host a party.

After some persuasion by Tammy and Margie, however, I not only hosted a virtual Pampered Chef party with Karen, but I also attended a PC team meeting at her home. Knowing that I needed an income injection and wanted more flexibility in my schedule, she generously offered to pay for my "starter kit" and to mentor me as a direct sales consultant. There were no strings attached—I wasn't putting any of my own money into it, and I could end the agreement at any time.

Karen withheld nothing; she shared her ideas, her party materials, and her guidance as I tried out this new experience of self-employment. We became fast friends, and she even began attending my yoga classes.

I started spending a lot of time with Karen. We would get together and talk about life, purpose, and spirituality. I shared with her how eating more whole foods had changed my health on all levels, and that I wanted to empower other people to take charge of their well-being, too.

She helped me imagine the possibility of using my "parties" to teach people to cook in a more body- and soul-nourishing way. I marketed myself as someone who'd come to your home with my kitchen gear and teach you and your friends how to prepare easy, nutrient-dense meals that contained no processed foods or sugar. Selling the PC products was incidental instead of my focus, and the result was that I sold a lot more without even trying.

Karen and I were learning and growing together, enjoying this symbiotic friendship that was rooted in mutual respect and concern for each other. There wasn't a power dynamic between us, even though there was both an age and socio-economic gap between us. Our hearts were connected, and we had much more in common than we did differences. We wanted to see each other succeed and feel fulfilled, and we were openly vulnerable and honest with each other to that end.

After a private yoga session at my house one day, Karen and I were having coffee together at my dining table. She said, "I've been reading this book that feels very timely, and I want to help you manifest a blessing in your life. Tell me what it is that you're looking for professionally."

I shared with her my recently crafted mantra: "I want to work part-time, during the day, during the week, in an industry that reflects my integrity and values, in an environment that allows me to continually learn and grow in ways that benefit others." Karen gave me a list of local organizations and affinity groups to look up later, and we let the conversation drift to a new topic.

A few weeks had passed, and I was sitting in the corner of the butcher shop, eating lunch during the midway point of my ten-hour shift. I was gazing up at the schedule tacked to the wall, feeling edgy about my upcoming shifts, when I got a call from Karen.

"You will not believe this. I just got a newsletter from the Grand Rapids Center for Mindfulness in my email, and they have a job opening for a part-time office assistant. You would be perfect for this job. I know, because I worked that job for Carol until five years ago. Send her your resume and let me know when you do. I'll call Carol and personally recommend you for the job," she said.

I felt electrified. I couldn't believe it; *this was really happening!* I got to work on updating my resume and cover letter as soon as I got home from the butcher shop. I sent it to Karen, my mom, and a few of my most trusted writer-friends, hoping for some encouragement or suggested edits. When no one responded within the first few hours, I decided to trust my intuition. I polished it up and sent it to Carol.

I didn't hear back right away, so my enthusiasm began to wane. I was about to start job-searching again when I received a call from Carol for an interview. I met her at a coffee shop because the Center didn't have a brick-and-mortar location. Everyone worked from home, and they rented space to teach their mindfulness classes.

"Everyone" makes it sound like a large team; it wasn't. The Center had been without an office assistant for a few months at that point, so Carol was responsible for creating the newsletters, answering the calls and emails, and running the financial and administrative pieces while teaching two eight-week sessions at a time. There were three other core instructors along with two additional specialized instructors who were dear friends of Carol's and were always willing to collaborate on an offering. The office assistant was the only person on the payroll, and it was a vacant seat that needed to be filled as soon as possible.

Immediately, Carol expressed her concern that I was overqualified for the job and that she couldn't pay me enough. I countered that, contrary to "normal," what was most important to me in this season of life was not money, but time. I was longing for more open space and fluidity in my schedule, and I was willing to sacrifice the opportunity to work up a professional ladder to get it.

I waited three weeks and went through a second interview with Carol as well as a phone interview with the Center's other co-founder, April, before I received and accepted the job offer. *This was huge!* Not only would I be working around fifteen to twenty hours per week, but I was also going to be able to write my own schedule, have nights and weekends off, and *work from home!*

Mindfulness-Based Stress Reduction and a New Kind of Boss

When I reflect on my first few months working for Carol, I cannot help but smile. Since everyone worked remotely, my training took place at her private home. Her house was beautiful and large, set sweetly among old-growth trees, rolling hills, and a creek. Often, we would see deer relaxing in her backyard, which looked more like a nature preserve than a yard.

As I arrived each morning, Carol would greet me with a hug. She'd invite me to make myself a cup of coffee and to help myself to anything else I might like. Once we finished our initial check-in, we'd head up to her office, where she'd sometimes put me to work on a project like cutting flyers or creating newsletters, or she'd walk me through an office procedure like responding to emails or updating the website. We would take an hour-long lunch break together on her screened-in porch, and she would prepare us a salad and quiche, followed by more coffee or a cup of tea.

I was so used to listening to music and chatting while working that the silence was a little jarring at first. Carol agreed to let me listen to music on my headphones, but I very quickly gave up when I realized how challenging it was to listen to music and type at the same time. Instead, we'd sit together quietly, with only the sound of Carol taking a long, steady, deep breath every so often. Hearing her audibly breathe was a helpful trigger to notice that I was holding mine, so I soon began mimicking her mindful breathing, too.

Carol loved talking to me about yoga. As it turned out, not only was she a 500-hour Registered Yoga Teacher, but she also had taught at Behnje's yoga center many years ago before opening her own studio. Yoga had been Carol's primary practice until she happened upon meditation and decided to dedicate her training and life's work to learning and teaching Mindfulness Meditation.

We would occasionally break from work to try a few asanas or partner stretches, and she permitted me to go through all her saved class sequences and books from her yoga teaching days. There was no hesitation; she was simply delighted for me and my path, and she wanted to support me in any way that she could. The depth of love and appreciation I felt from her meant more than any bonus or perk from any job I had ever had. Even so, she gave me a dollar raise a month after I started because she immediately realized how much I was going to help the Center.

I felt like I had hit the lottery. Not only was I doing meaningful work for a wonderful human being who believed in me and validated my talents, but I was also receiving my wish to work somewhere that allowed me to continue learning. Part of my job responsibilities included taking the classes that we offer so I would better understand what we did and what I was selling.

I signed up for the eight-week Mindfulness-Based Stress Reduction (MBSR) course that was initially pioneered by renowned meditation teacher, author, and professor of medicine emeritus at the University of Massachusetts Medical School, Jon Kabat-Zinn. I must confess that I was feeling a little arrogant about the whole thing since I had been teaching yoga and practicing meditation with my teachers as well as independently studying how stress affects the body. I didn't think I was going to learn much more than I already knew, but I was looking forward to it, nonetheless.

The MBSR classes reminded me of yoga teacher training. They lasted two and a half hours and were a combination of learning, practice, and contemplation/reflection. I was struck by how empowering it is to deepen my understanding of the inner workings of the stress cycle and how it affects my mood and mental/physical health. As it turns out, I still have *a lot* to learn.

Through this intensive practice, I was building an inner resiliency and honing my capacity to create space between my direct experiences and my interpretations of them. Mindfulness empowered me to have a choice in how I responded to stressful situations instead of being pushed around by them. As my attention and focus strengthened, so did my ability to notice nuance and hear my intuitive wisdom more clearly.

Reflecting upon my mere thirty-four years of living up to this point, my heart was humbled by the awareness of Grace permeating each step on my journey. Even in the periods of greatest darkness and despair, I was being held, taught, and guided to what was the highest for me. I could not recognize this before, but I could see it now, and I was grateful.

Since completing my 200-hour YTT and abandoning my previous career track, three major lessons have emerged:

- Nothing is permanent. We are constantly changing and growing, and our lives are incredibly brief. And although we have tendencies to think/behave/feel in certain pathways, we can choose to change those pathways and create new tendencies. We can change our lives for the better.

- We are not meant to live in isolation physically, emotionally, or spiritually. We are interconnected in so many ways, both known and unknown. When we deny ourselves a sense of community, we deprive ourselves of the natural experience of belonging. To live as though we do everything for and by ourselves is as difficult and ineffective as remaining stagnant and expecting that someone else will rescue us with no effort from ourselves.

- As I deepen my practices of self-care, I cultivate a greater sense of love, compassion, and acceptance for myself. This tender kindness then naturally extends to all other human beings. I have experienced expansive joy and peacefulness through offering love and compassion to those whom I encounter. From my children and husband to family, friends, and co-workers, to neighbors, acquaintances, and strangers, my love and desire to serve grow more and more each time I do my practices and reconnect to the divine presence within me and all of God's creation.

And so, on the Spring Equinox, on the heels of my birthday and a new moon two days prior, I made a vow and wrote it in my journal. Feeling the increased vibratory energy all around and within me, I chose to co-participate with it:

- I commit to my heart, to my community, to the page, and to the Universe that I choose to make 2018 a year of self-study and discipline with the intention of growth, abundance, expansion, and freedom.

Falling into Love with Maharajji

Wandering around the library with the girls one day, I came across a book that caught my attention. It was called *Love Everyone: The Transcendent Wisdom of Neem Karoli Baba Told Through the Stories of the Westerners Whose Lives He Transformed* by Parvati Markus. Recognizing Neem Karoli Baba's name from the Krishna Das and Ram Dass podcasts, I checked it out and dove into it before bed that night.

Several of the stories told in the anthology were familiar to me from the podcasts I had listened to. I honestly cannot recall any story that stood out among others, but I do remember that near the center of the book, there were some color photographs of Neem Karoli Baba. At first, that didn't matter much to me. I briefly looked them over and continued reading. But after a day or two, I noticed myself stealing glances at one particular photo of Maharajji throughout the day. I'd flip open the book for a glance while bringing up the laundry and before going to sleep. It was as if there were a magnetic force bringing me to view his picture again and again. In Hinduism, this is known as *darshan*, the beholding of a deity, revered person, or sacred object.

Maharajji wasn't a teacher per se. He did not require austerities or service from his devotees, nor did he initiate them into a particular lineage. He didn't write books or conduct lectures. Maharajji's primary offering was that of loving presence and unconditional compassion for the suffering of humanity. Whenever a devotee would ask Baba to tell them how to raise kundalini or become enlightened, he would simply tell them to love everyone, serve (feed) everyone, and remember God. He would often say, *Sub Ek*—All One.

The photo of Neem Karoli Baba (Maharajji) in Love Everyone

I felt a tugging as if I were being pulled by a string connected to my heart. I discovered Ram Dass's website, LoveServeRemember. org. It had a beautifully curated collection of articles, videos, and podcasts of Maharajji's teachings as expressed through Ram Dass and the other Westerners who'd traveled to India in search of something they couldn't explain but had found in their experience of this man in a plaid blanket.

While perusing the site, I clicked on the events page and discovered an announcement for an upcoming retreat called Open

Your Heart in Paradise (OYHIP). It was set to run the first week of December. My jaw hit the floor when I saw who was hosting the retreat: Ram Dass, Krishna Das, Jack Kornfield, Sharon Salzberg, Joseph Goldstein, Mirabai Bush… these were meditation teachers, wisdom teachers, and authors who had significantly impacted my life these past few years, and they were all going to be at the same retreat! And if that wasn't enough (it was), it was happening in Maui!

Now, you must understand, without significant logical explanation, my heart has always been drawn to Hawaii. For reasons beyond my comprehension, I've always felt an affinity to Hawaiian culture, even naming my daughter Nolani from the combination of two Hawaiian names: Noelani and Nalani. I had always dreamed of visiting, but knowing how expensive and far away it is, I never believed that trip was meant for me.

Seeing this retreat announcement changed all that; I felt in my bones that I was supposed to go. I knew that Ram Dass had suffered a severe stroke in 1997 and that he was continuing to participate in these retreats (this being the twelfth year of the biannual retreat) despite the strain on his health. I kept hearing this urgent voice inside telling me that if I was going to meet him, it needed to be this year.

The spark of possibility led to an idea, which led to a self-declaration. My next step was to share it with someone else. I met up with my sister-in-law Anna, to whom I had recently passed my copy of Ram Dass's book. We were at an event for my nephew when I pulled her aside and conspiratorially whispered, "Are you willing to dream with me?"

I told her about the retreat in Maui and that I thought we should go. She had traveled to Maui with another classmate when we were in high school, and she told me once that she wanted to go back someday and bring me with her. I knew it was a long shot because we both were in financially precarious situations, but I also trusted our capacity for magic when we were united in a common goal.

Although Anna expressed cautious enthusiasm for the idea, there seemed to be too many obstacles for her to commit to joining me. I could relate; there were going to be plenty of challenges to overcome. But I believed to the core of my being that this was meant to happen. I decided to pitch my idea to my other magical-thinking best friend from way back, Meg.

I met up with her and repeated my question: "Are you willing to dream with me?" As soon as I laid out my idea, I was met with an enthusiastic, "HELL, YES!!"

"Okay, but the only way this is going to work is if we fully believe that it's possible, no half-hearted maybes or mights. We have to believe with our whole hearts that if it's meant to happen, it will. We need to be willing to show up and do the work, but the details will be resolved as if by magic."

She agreed, and we adopted my statement of "the details will be resolved as if by magic" as our mantra.

Can I Do Both?

It had been a matter of days since I shared my dream of the OYHIP retreat on Maui with Paulo that another big announcement came through: Rick and Behnje were going to offer their first-ever 300-hour Yoga Teacher Training program starting that summer. My head was spinning. I had been asking them since the last day of my 200-hour training if they'd ever consider doing a continuing/deepening/graduate program, and now they were going to do it *the same year as the Maui retreat!*

Reflecting on my Spring Equinox intention for a year of self-study and discipline, I asked myself, "Can I do both?"

I was so afraid to talk to Paulo about it. Here I was, asking my husband to help me aggressively save a quarter of our family's annual income for these trainings in the spirit of my own continued growth. I was dumbfounded when he immediately agreed to it.

"When you do this work, Jeni, you do it for all of us. We all heal when you heal. So, if you believe that this is what's next, then do it."

I was shocked. I could not fathom the depth of this man's love and faith in me. At that moment, I affirmed my heart's longing that these opportunities were meant for me and that if I put in the effort and opened to Grace, it would indeed manifest.

It was time to get to work. I continued to teach two to four yoga classes per week, work part-time at the Butcher Shop and the GR Center for Mindfulness, and sell Pampered Chef. I also began donating plasma, carpooling kids from school, babysitting, and teaching private yoga classes. I even rolled seventy dollars' worth of pennies, nickels, and dimes, and hijacked all of the bottle returns in our house for my cause. I felt like a teenager raising money for spring break. I was intensely focused and dedicated because this was the depth of my longing.

And yet I knew I wasn't going to get there without Grace. I needed to ask for help because even with all my efforts, my family could not fully sustain this financial undertaking alone. I humbled myself and once again set up a crowdfunding campaign. While I didn't receive as many donations as I did for my first campaign, the love offerings I received from a few key individuals were enough for me to make the down payment on the 300-hour YTT program. I was going to do both.

Dreams Coming True

Only three months had passed since setting my Spring Equinox intention. Meg and I had already booked our plane tickets and lodging a few weeks prior, not wanting to risk a price hike or lack of availability. There was no going back; whether we got into the limited-capacity retreat or not, we were going to Maui!

When the day to register for the Ram Dass OYHIP Retreat came, I made a little ritual out of it. I went to a yoga class that morning, enjoyed a lovely post-yoga conversation with a friend, and went home to create a sacred space as I waited for registration to open at noon. I prayed and meditated until my alarm went off. Then I grabbed my phone, clicked the link, entered my information, and submitted it. It was official: I was going to the retreat! Later, I learned that the retreat sold out in only twelve minutes with a record-breaking 400 participants. Baba's Grace was covering every step.

I tried reaching out to Meg, but she was in California filming a reality TV show, and part of her agreement was that she had very limited contact with the outside world. We were both disheartened to discover that she had missed the registration for the retreat, but it didn't matter; we were taking this trip together, and it was going to be amazing.

Two days later, my girls finished second and fourth grade, I moved my office home from Carol's house, and I put in my notice to the butcher shop. For the first time, I was going to be working from home and spending summer vacation with my daughters. Not only that, but in another week, I would begin my 300-hour YTT adventure. Life felt like a fantasy. My heart was bursting with gratitude for the lightness, clarity, and peace of this season. My fervent prayer was that I drink it in slowly, enjoying and appreciating the unfolding. The best was still to come.

8

Nothing Worth Having Comes Easy

There is a Zen story of a Chinese farmer whose horse ran away one day. The farmer's neighbor saw what happened and said, "Oh, farmer, what bad luck you have!"

"Good luck, bad luck... who knows?" replied the farmer.

The next day, the farmer's horse returned with two wild horses. The farmer's neighbor saw the horses and said, "Oh, farmer, what good luck you have!"

"Good luck, bad luck... who knows?" replied the farmer.

Later that day, as the farmer's son was out trying to break the wild horses, one of the horses threw the son from him, breaking the son's leg. Seeing what had happened, the farmer's neighbor said, "Oh, farmer, what bad luck you have!"

"Good luck, bad luck... who knows?" replied the farmer.

The following week, the king's officers traveled to the village to conscript the eldest sons for war. Because the farmer's son had a broken leg, he was not taken off to war. Seeing the men leave, the farmer's neighbor said, "Oh, farmer, what good luck you have!"

"Good luck, bad luck... who knows?" replied the farmer.

Things Aren't Always as They Appear

From an outer perspective, the blessings were raining down. I was settling in nicely to my new work-from-home job, eagerly anticipating the start of yoga teacher training, and delighting in the slow countdown to Maui and the Ram Dass retreat. And yet, from an inner perspective, it was a really difficult time for our little family.

I'm challenged to describe the complexity of issues Paulo and I were individually and collectively up against. There was some financial strain both from the adjustments in income and my now intense savings plan for my upcoming training. Our car needed some significant repairs, and we were beginning to run into some home repairs that could no longer be put off, either. The girls were starting to experience bouts of depression and anxiety as they approached puberty and contended with ever-increasing expectations at school on top of the spillover of my and Paulo's emotional reactivity.

I started gaining weight as soon as I began posturing myself as a health coach for Pampered Chef, and I slowly crept back up the scale to my highest weight in four years. I sensed once again that I was trying to force something that was out of alignment with where I was going. I loved teaching and cooking for people, but the parties almost always took place on nights and weekends, and the people I most wanted to support in the kitchen were not the people who wanted and could afford PC products. I hated that I was selling unnecessary, single-utility items to mostly affluent white women. So, when school ended for the girls, I thanked Karen for all of her love, guidance, and support, and I told her I was parting ways with PC.

But something else—something much more painful—was triggering my alarm system as well. While I was spreading my time and energy outside of our home, Paulo was left with the girls and feeling very much in the background of my life. And as I was developing a routine of going to yoga every Thursday night and Saturday morning, he and a friend from work were establishing a Thirsty Thursday routine. What started as a shared six-pack on Thursday nights slowly devolved into an eighteen-pack or more on Thursdays, Fridays, and Saturdays. I was not thrilled.

At first, I protested, shamed, and judged Paulo. I started slipping into old manipulation strategies that I had learned from my childhood, trying to get him to be how I wanted him to be. Of course, this didn't work out as I had planned. Not only was I stoking painful emotions and depression in Paulo, but I was fomenting strong feelings of resentment and depression in myself.

I was so overwhelmed with worry over his health and safety, not to mention the future of our family. Having been together for so many years, we had both walked each other through periods of depression, grief, and addiction at various times. Both of us have so many trauma wounds from our childhoods that it has been a literal fight for our lives on occasion. I tried nagging, withholding affection, and even the silent treatment to get him to change. And by Grace, I began to recognize what I was doing and how I was hurting him. I also saw that the traits I was condemning in him lived in me, too. And in doing so, my perspective began to broaden and shift.

I realized that I was trying to control him out of my own fear. He had his reasons for wanting to escape on the weekends. And instead of loving him through his pain and supporting him the way he had always supported me, I was falling back on familiar habits of blaming and shaming him to manipulate his behavior until I got what I wanted. Worse yet, I was spending so much time focused on his unhealthy habits that I was totally overlooking my own. I was immersed in self-righteousness and using it as an excuse to disengage from myself and my marriage.

Since I knew that codependency wasn't going to fix things, I instead focused on spending time with the girls while Paulo socialized and slept his weekends away. I took them to the park and the bookstore, and we'd have girls' nights in my bedroom on the weekends. Paulo and I effectively began living two separate lives, and I started to wonder how long I was willing to live like this.

Hindsight Wisdom

To be in a long-term relationship, it is both sacred and necessary work to bring our shadows into the light of awareness so they can be dispelled once and for all. The potential richness of a relationship rooted in open honesty, trust, and intimacy far outweighs any momentary shame of bearing witness to one's own inner experience. And a relationship lacking that steadfast commitment to intimacy is already a house built on sand.

300-hour YTT Begins with a Test

The day had come when my yoga teacher training was to begin. It was a sunny Friday in June, and we had plans to go to my aunt's house to swim in her pool beforehand. I had us all packed up and ready to go when Paulo got home from work. He came inside, and something seemed off. He asked me to take a walk with him.

As we walked down our street, Paulo told me that he had been fired. There was no cause; he hadn't violated any policies or made any errors. The supervisor simply said that the company was headed in a direction that did not include him. Paulo had given them six years of exceptional work, during which he taught himself how to use, maintain, and repair every single machine on the shop floor. He was one of the highest-paid employees, and he handled almost all the new hire training for the company even though it wasn't a part of his job responsibilities.

The job loss hurt him a lot. He felt betrayed and rejected on top of the immense weight of knowing that he was our family's primary earner. We both shed a few silent tears, but we agreed to trust that we were going to figure something out. That's when it hit me: I was about to start paying almost $400 a month for my teacher training. I told Paulo, "I think I need to quit. This isn't the right time. We might need this money to pay our bills."

He adamantly disagreed. "No, you need to go. We will find a way to make this work."

I felt sick to my stomach, but I agreed not to make any hasty decisions. So, we packed up the girls and headed off to my aunt's house. We laughed and swam, never letting on that our family had just taken a huge blow of shocking news. We even took some silly pictures that still make me smile when I look at them. On our way to From the Heart for my training, we told Elaina and Nolani what had happened. We reassured them that we are a strong, resilient family and that we were not afraid. They seemed to take it in stride, trusting that we had things under control.

That night after the training, I stayed to talk to Rick and Behnje about Paulo's job loss and to say that I might be dropping out of the training. They expressed tender concern and offered to give me a couple of months to make the first payment to give us time to sort things out. They wanted me to stay, and they were willing to work with me to make it happen. I thanked them for their flexibility and decided I would continue for the time being.

Paulo grieved for the next nine days. He was so consumed with sorrow and shame that he could barely get off the couch. But on the second Monday of no work, he decided to contact the unemployment office and get his paperwork rolling. As part of the stipulations for unemployment benefits, he had to prove that he was actively looking for work.

So, on his way home from the grocery store later that afternoon, Paulo pulled up to a building that sits on the opposite side of the road at the end of our block. Not only did he get an on-the-spot tour and interview, but by the end of the following day, he was offered a job. It was going to be a four-dollar-per-hour pay cut and without benefits, but the owner seemed to be an honest and fair man. He promised that if Paulo worked as hard as he claimed to, his paycheck and opportunities would reflect that. And it was a major perk to work less than 1,000 feet from home!

The next day, Paulo walked down the street as I walked upstairs on our way to work. He came home for his morning break and visited with the girls and me, and he was home again to eat lunch with us at noon. This was going to be our new normal. Good luck, bad luck… who knows!

The Sandpaper of Life

Whatever preconceived notions I had about how wonderful and enlightening this time during teacher training would be were thrown out the window by the second weekend. The harder I tried to be peaceful, the more frenetic I became. The more intensely I practiced, the less freedom I felt in my asanas.

Emotionally, I felt like I was being tossed around by thirty-foot waves. I kept panicking about whether I would be able to save enough money for Maui. I vacillated between projecting an image of body acceptance and secretly obsessing about losing weight. I was drowning in self-doubt and impostor syndrome.

Meanwhile, our nagging home repairs reached a point of no return: our bathtub got a crack in it, so every time someone showered, the water would rain down into the basement right next to our washer and dryer. We were going to have to do a full bathroom remodel to fix it. As soon as we began construction on it, our upstairs drainpipe became so clogged that we could no longer use the sink or toilet. With no functional bathroom, we relied on the graciousness of our neighbor for over a week.

Miraculously, the week after Paulo had been fired, he received a letter offering the option to transfer his 401K to a new portfolio manager or cash it out. We decided to accept the tax liability and cash it out to help us repair both bathrooms and attend to the much-needed car repairs, too. It wasn't quite enough to cover all the expenses, but thanks to a small loan offered by a friend's mother, we had enough money to give our home some much-needed attention. Finally, we were starting to breathe a little easier.

All that anxiety stew mixing around in my mind would've been enough, but then my little Nolani went ahead and threw something else into the mix. As I tucked her into bed one night, she confessed to me that she had always wished for a little brother or sister. I fell silent; this was a touchy subject for me.

The year after Nolani was born had imprinted traumatic memories on me. I was so chronically stressed and exhausted during that time. I was working forty-plus hours a week, binge drinking on the weekends, and casually drinking most other nights, and constantly running around trying to keep up with the girls and the housework. I told Paulo then that I couldn't imagine having any more kids; my mental and physical health couldn't take it. He was heartbroken because he had always imagined having a bigger family. But I stayed firm, and eventually, he let go of the hopes of more children.

And as he did, I slowly began to question whether our family was complete. I must've mentioned it subconsciously so many times, because a little more than a year before Nolani's confession, Tammy had challenged me in the butcher shop.

"I don't think you're done having babies," she said, matter-of-factly.

"Um, that's crazy. Why do you say that?" I asked.

"Because you won't stop talking about it," she said.

So, when Nolani shared her wish with me in bed that night, all I could say was, "Well, Nolani, there's a lot of magic in our words. So now that you've put it out into the universe, we'll have to see what happens."

I also told her that I wasn't the one whom she needed to convince; her dad would need to be on board, too. She laughed and said there was *no way* she was going to bring it up to Paulo.

"He'll smack me on the mouth if I say that!" she declared.

"No, he won't, give him a chance," I replied with a chuckle.

It took her a few more days to work up the courage to tell Paulo her wish. And when she did, he was completely taken by surprise. I can't imagine the whirlwind of thoughts and emotions her statement may have sparked in him, but I knew what it was doing to me.

The thought of having another child followed me like a shadow through each day after that. As I'd entertain the thought, so many questions and fears would bubble up with it. What about Paulo's drinking? What if he dies or goes to jail, and I become a single mother to two teens and an infant? I'm thirty-five now; that's considered geriatric in the world of pregnancy and childbirth! What if there's a complication? And oh, the weight gain... I don't know if I can handle the mental battle of gaining weight again and experiencing my postpartum body. And what about the girls? They're eight and ten now. That's a huge age gap! We'd be starting over, signing up for another eighteen years (at least) of caring and providing for another being. And does that mean we need to have *two* more children? Or would this baby be like an only child? *Can we even afford another baby?!*

Speaking My Truth

Ruminating over all of this in my head wasn't working. I was riding a mental merry-go-round of theoretical pessimism. The more future catastrophes I imagined, the more anxious, fearful, and uncomfortable I became. There was no point in opening to the possibility of another child until we both addressed the very dark shadow looming over our marriage.

I saw clearly that if things stayed exactly how they were, our lives together would be relegated to a monotonous repetition of survival and short-lived highs. Drifting further apart, most of our time together would be spent arguing. I feared we might both languish in this kind of environment. I was longing for the authentic intimacy I had experienced with Paulo before, the kind that was borne out of vulnerability, respect, and passion.

But I was terrified. I knew that if I drew a line, I needed to *mean it*. I was afraid that being 100% truthful and up-front with Paulo could lead to a separation. But the obvious irony was that by not being 100% truthful, a separation was already subtly occurring. I began to seriously consider what it would be like to leave Paulo, and my heart ached at the thought. I realized that it didn't matter whether I stayed or not. Either way, I was going to be challenged, I was going to learn, and I was going to grow.

In my journal, I wrote:

Where do I go from here? How do I make you see that you are a treasure and that your life is worth fighting for? How do I continue to fight for both of us, and is there a point at which I should stop?

I'm so unhappy in our marriage at this moment. And I have been for months and months. How could I support myself and the girls without you, without undoing all that we have worked so hard to create? How could I go on alone, not sharing in the miracle of life with you?

If you don't find your way out of the darkness soon, I fear that I'll have to learn anyway, because you might destroy yourself.

Please God, help me remember how much I love this man. Help him realize that life could be so much more fulfilling if he could find the strength to do the work. Heal our broken hearts so our daughters won't know the pain of a broken home.

I won't give up until you tell me that it's the only way to save us all.

The situation reached an apex on our anniversary in 2018. It was a Sunday, and I was wrapping up a teacher training weekend. I needed to go to the grocery store straight after class to pick up some food for dinner and the rest of the week. But as soon as I got to the parking lot, I started to bawl. I was so unhappy, and I couldn't imagine a way forward for us that included addiction.

Knowing that there was no way the tears were going to stop, I walked straight into the store, red-faced with silent tears streaming down my cheeks. A few steps in, I ducked down a home goods aisle for some privacy as I wept. I pulled my phone out and texted Paulo: "I am deeply unhappy." I continued with my shopping as I cried, my vulnerability laid bare for the world to see. I surrendered to the emotions and let them fall like purifying raindrops from my cheeks.

The conversations that ensued were very difficult and uncomfortable. They stretched on for hours at a time, spread out over days, then weeks, then months. We were digging deep into the whys and hows and what's next. I told him that I did not want to divorce him; that I knew we were not done with what we were meant to do together. But I could not continue in this relationship while he avoided his pain in such a destructive way. He was slowly killing himself and missing out on so much. We deserved better. He deserved better.

It was a difficult boundary to draw because it didn't include an ultimatum, but I think that's why it worked the way that it did. It wasn't conditional; it was a clear and firm statement of, "This is not okay with me. This crosses the line." By Grace, Paulo saw the raw truth of the situation and chose himself and his family as he began to walk the very difficult road of sobriety.

It's been seven years, and Paulo has since said that he never knew more deeply that I meant what I said than he did that day. My words were in harmony with my deeper truth, and the energy they carried was a powerful force to reckon with. In saying that which was hard to say, a space was created. And this space held the possibility of outcomes vastly more complex and interesting than the bleak, passionless experience of giving up.

PART III

The Return

Great Mother

The ocean is Mother,
     the waves, her children.
She holds us in her embrace,
     softly, soothingly,
          clearing away our sorrows.
She gives us Life,
     giving, giving, giving,
     with no want in return except gratitude.
Her children, wild and playful,
     beg to be noticed.
They dance and play,
     tugging at my pant leg.
They hop over rocks,
     making a big scene,
     racing to be first to
          reach the shore.
Try as they may to become independent,
like a magnet,
          Mother draws them back home.
Again and again,
     they return to Source,
          to Mother.

9

Budding Trees

"The world is always richer than the ideas we have about it. The filters we put on our perceptions determine what sort of world we live in. If you go through the world looking for _____, you will find _____."
— Joseph O'Connor & John Seymour, *Introducing NLP*

Joseph and John get it almost right with this. Our mental filters do, in fact, distort how we interpret the world. But I would argue that *we* do not place the filters on our perceptions. At least, not initially.

When we are born, we are immersed at once within a complex web of pre-existing beliefs. Our understanding of the world around us becomes shaped and colored by the beliefs and behaviors of our primary caregivers, our location in space and time, our access to resources, and much more. Everything we experience, from the most mundane to the most delightful or traumatic, imprints a memory onto us that informs how we relate to and interact with our slice of the universe.

And all of this is done without our permission or understanding until we realize that this is so. Once we become aware of how biased, limited, and unclear our perspectives are, we are empowered to clean our lenses, or at least to remove a bit of the residue. Through Grace, we glimpse the limitlessness of the mind.

Perspective Change

Right around the beginning of the 300-hour yoga teacher training, I had a beautiful conversation with an old high school friend. We were each sharing about how our life plans had changed over the years and how we were now aspiring to different goals. I came right out and asked her, "What is it that you want?"

"I just want to be happy," she said.

I paused for a moment, took a breath, looked at her, and asked, "What does that even mean? Suppose you get the perfect job, find the perfect partner, buy the perfect home, and find yourself in perfect health; then what? Do you hold your breath and sit on your hands until you die?" We both laughed, but it opened a great conversation.

This was a big moment of clarity for me. Seeing my own striving in her eyes, I experienced a felt understanding that by pushing and pulling so hard in my life, I was creating profound stress and suffering for myself. I noticed this subtle but ever-present mental and physical straining as a tell-tale sign of fear and an absence of faith and confidence. I began to understand viscerally what the Buddha had explained through the Four Noble Truths.

The Four Noble Truths are the first teaching Shakyamuni Buddha gave after he experienced enlightenment under the Bodhi tree.

1. All life is suffering. Birth is suffering, aging is suffering, illness is suffering, and death is suffering. Not getting what we want is suffering. Getting what we don't want is suffering.
2. All suffering is caused by the clinging of the mind.
3. The end of suffering is caused by the end of clinging of the mind.
4. The path to this end of clinging is the Eightfold Path (the Buddhist practices).

The only lasting solution to all of this uncomfortable not-getting-what-I-want or getting-what-I-don't-want stuff was to *let go of all the wanting*. It was my attachment, my craving or desire for things to be different than they were, that was making me so damn miserable. I knew this was true because when I was grounded and attentive, I could feel the tug of these clingings, breathe some space between my thoughts, and mentally/emotionally/physically let go. And in this letting go, my experiences became much more easeful and calmer. There wasn't a sensation of gripping tightly to or bracing against outcomes, and that felt very spacious and equanimous.

This understanding led to a paradigm shift. It wasn't my job to muscle my way through life, strategizing or manipulating situations to my benefit. I didn't have to be afraid of the circumstances of my day-to-day life or what imagined catastrophes might lie in the future. This shift in perspective was an invitation to learn how to stop frantically swimming against the natural river flow of life and instead float tenderly upon its current. It was an invitation to *relax* a little and stop taking everything so seriously all the time.

The reality is that there is nowhere to stand. Change is the only constant. Any sense of certainty or security is a mental delusion born out of fear of the mystery of life. And the only freedom from this is a radical acceptance of *what is* in this moment, without an accompanying storyline. I was being asked to let go of expectations, opinions, and detailed goals and instead commit again and again to cultivating the inner spaciousness from which my own inner guidance arises. So, instead of relentlessly pursuing happiness, I would work toward a general feeling of equanimity or okayness toward whatever was in my awareness at that moment.

I accepted that life was not going to stop throwing curveballs. My looks would continue to change, and I would inevitably get ill or injured and lose a job or a friend. Every person I've ever known would eventually die, including me. But that didn't mean amazing things wouldn't happen along the way. And even the tragedies contained a poignant richness to them that, at times, inspired awe.

Through my spiritual practices, I have learned how to pay better attention to my life while I'm living it. Even simple things give me immense joy when I'm paying attention. Stargazing, watching a butterfly land on a flower, hearing a baby giggle, watching dust motes float in the sunlight, listening to an exquisite musical composition; life continually presents a buffet of sweetness and wonderment if I have the sensitivity to notice.

I'm not saying it's easy work. I'll probably spend the rest of my lifetime (at least) watching myself react to situations that I once labeled as "bad" or craving things I once labeled as "good." But I do believe that over time, I can develop this profound, grounded steadiness that will allow me to meet the challenges of life instead of resisting them. I believe it because I've already tasted it; I know it exists.

What I've realized is that every single terrible, awful, no-good, very bad day (or week or month or year) that I've had has taught me something. They've made me stronger, wiser, and more compassionate. I can't declare with full integrity that I wish any of those "bad" experiences had never happened. In my heart, I know that every experience of my life continues to prepare me for what's next. And anyway, while it might *seem* like perfection to have everything I want all at once with no struggle, that honestly sounds rather ephemeral if not boring. I'm learning that life is meant to be messy and wild and uncertain. Instead of bracing myself against the winds of change, I wish to dance with them.

Hindsight Wisdom

I first read the word "equanimity" in Sharon Salzberg's book, *Real Happiness at Work*. In it, she says that

"Equanimity is the voice of wisdom that helps us accept what cannot be changed in the moment and learn to say, 'Right now, this is it.'" Sharon explains that being equanimous is not passive acceptance or a feeling of helplessness; it's defined as mental calmness, composure, and evenness of temper, especially in a difficult situation. The Buddha explained that equanimity is the realization that nothing is permanent and that cultivating it becomes a basis for wisdom, compassion, love, and freedom to naturally arise.

"Set the intention to pay attention to your experience when you're struggling, because struggling means there is something you're resisting to accept."

—Joseph Goldstein

Marriage as a Practice

In his teachings, Ram Dass would often discuss the yoga of relationship, of how our interactions with other beings are grist for each other's mill of awakening. Over time, we realize that all we see are projections of our own minds. This teaching became more evident as I reframed my marriage to Paulo as a spiritual practice.

As I learned to be more direct and vulnerable in my speech, Paulo felt safer being more vulnerable, too. That mutuality of felt safety and respect opened the doors for a greater depth of spiritual intimacy than we had ever experienced. It was as if we were embarking upon self-guided marriage counseling. We both began to view our marriage as a sacred practice. We committed to using the content of our experiences as individuals and as husband and wife to break free of our false beliefs and settle more and more into the present moment with kindness, compassion, wisdom, and equanimity.

For this to happen, I had to come to terms with the fact that I've not only been wounded in my life, but that I have also wounded others. Whether consciously or not, I have caused suffering in the lives of the people I love the most, including and perhaps especially Paulo. Sitting with that revelation made my heart break. I don't want joy or peace at the expense of someone else's; I want a joy and peace that is inclusive of all beings, including and especially Paulo.

I also had to reckon with the truth that I am not an island. A significant reason why I'd been able to learn, grow, and heal over these past several years was because of the unflinching love and support of this precious man. He has never, not once, called me a bitch, annoying, or bossy, although it could've been a fair assessment. Even when I was at the peak of my binge drinking and eating, he never told me I was getting too fat or drinking too much alcohol. He gave me the space and the support to simply be me, so the decision to change was mine and not due to some ultimatum or manipulation tactic.

When you are well-loved despite your shadows and shortcomings, magic happens. Radical transformation happens. And if I wanted the best for Paulo, then the only logical thing to do was love him exactly as he was and is. All I could truly do was work on my own stuff and do my best to become a safe environment for Paulo to open his heart, should he choose to. I had to let go of my desires and instead give him the space to *be*.

> "The curious paradox is that when I accept myself just as I am, then I can change."
>
> —Carl Rogers

Ram Dass was known to say, "If you think you're enlightened, go spend a week with your family." It's funny, but it's true. How could I ever hope to foster any kind of community outside the walls of my home if I couldn't manage to live harmoniously with the people who lived inside? How could I possibly be satisfied with any achievement "out there" if I wasn't first showing up for my responsibilities to my Beloved and to my precious children? I was beginning to appreciate that there was nowhere to run; everywhere I went, there I was with all my stories and my neuroses. Getting my own house in order needed to be my first priority.

This renewed perception of love and relationships became even clearer through a bedtime conversation with Elaina. One night, desperately searching for ways to trap me for longer snuggles, my oldest daughter caught me off guard with her question: "Mom, what does love feel like?"

My mind whirred, scanning my thoughts for a response about this emotion that has been sung, written, spoken, and cried about more than any other in human history. To me, it's utterly indescribable, but for the benefit of my then 12-year-old, I gave it my best shot.

"Well, darling, there are many ways to describe what love is and how it feels. All I can give you is my perspective. To me, what a lot of people think is love is really a chemical response in their brains. An attraction to someone else triggers a bunch of hormones that make you feel euphoric, and that person becomes all you can think about."

I continued, "This is what most people mean when they say they have 'fallen in love.' It creates a longing, a dependency. You feel so good when you're around them that you don't want to be around anyone else. When you're alone, you wish you were with them. It feels like they've given something to you that wasn't there before and, without them, you would no longer have it. This head-over-heels, disorienting love is how I felt toward your dad when we first met.

"Then, once that initial endorphin rush begins to wear off, a type of transactional, possessive love begins to settle in. It's a love that says, 'I'll love you if you are like this, but not if you are like that.'

It's possessive because it's a kind of love that you want all to yourself; it feels like it's in a limited quantity, and because you found it, it's yours and only yours. People can become jealous or paranoid if they think they might lose that transactional love," I said.

I gave a side glance to check if she was still with me. Surprised that the conversation was holding her attention, I pressed on.

"It seems to me that most of us live the rest of our lives in this transactional, possessive love. It feels good when it feels good, and when it doesn't, we become bitter and resentful. When that happens often enough, we're tempted to drop it and run to something better. In the long run, a new relationship wouldn't necessarily be better. We eventually butt up against the same unresolved issues that came up in the previous relationship. Really, we're longing for that initial wave of disorienting, endorphin-filled love," I said through a sigh.

I continued, "What I've come to understand through my life experiences is that there is a higher, purer form of love than this. It's the energy that creates and permeates everything. It is what we're made of, and it's also what holds everything together. Now, that might sound confusing, so let me break it down through my and your dad's story.

"Through my spiritual practices," I said, "I began to realize that I had forgotten how to love myself early on in my life. Growing up, I learned that 'I'm a good girl if . . .,' and 'a bad girl if . . .' and love was used as a punishment or reward depending on my behavior. This taught me that love and affection, as I understood them, were transactional and could be taken away. It robbed me of my understanding of my intrinsic worth, the value that I had simply for being alive, a value that could not be added to or taken away. That was a tough realization, but it was important.

"Through understanding this transactional love that I had with myself, I was able to recognize how I was reflecting it onto all the other relationships in my life. I loved my best friend when she was a 'good best friend,' and I hated or ignored her when I thought she wasn't meeting my needs or treating me how I thought she should. I loved my parents when they behaved how I wanted them to, and I hated them when they made mistakes. All of this 'if, then' did nothing but add paranoia, depression, and self-righteousness in my life, and none of that feels like true love."

I continued, "What began to help me flip the switch on my understanding of love was a Buddhist meditation practice called Metta, or Lovingkindness. It's a practice where you decide on certain phrases expressing well-wishes, and then you repeat them, sending them first to a benefactor (someone who has never let you down), then to a neutral person, then to yourself, then to an enemy, then to all beings, everywhere. The phrases that I use are, 'May you be safe. May you be happy. May you be healthy. May you live with ease.' These are what work for me, but they can be changed to whatever feels right to you," I said.

"Practicing Lovingkindness meditation slowly began to change how I viewed myself. Before then, I couldn't remember ever wishing myself well, even though I complained when things were not going right. It's as though I believed I didn't deserve happiness, good health, or a calm heart. Doing this practice helped me realize that I wanted to be happy and pain-free, and so did everyone else, even my greatest enemy. It showed me that we're more alike than we are different and that we're each vulnerable to self-hatred and heartache. Metta invited me to bring in more self-compassion, which slowly turned into compassion for other beings. This changed my understanding of what love feels like."

Elaina was drifting off to sleep, so I went to the yoga room and grabbed my journal to complete my thoughts on her question.

"To me, love feels like a warm embrace that holds the world together. It is the understanding that there is no 'other,' only more reflections of my inner consciousness. When I look at my husband from my heart, I can see his beauty and his innate worth; I can recognize his suffering and his longing for happiness, and I am overcome with a desire for his well-being," I wrote.

Tears began welling up in my eyes as I continued. "This love is not possessive. If his highest good did not include me in the storyline, I would accept that. It would be painful, but only on a certain level. It's not transactional. Even on his worst days, when he's definitely not 'behaving how I'd prefer,' I still love him, perhaps even more strongly because I understand that underneath those behaviors and beliefs, he is struggling to remember how much he deserves to have a happy, easeful life. The love I feel for him is not dependency. It's a love that wants what's best for him while not losing sight of what's best for me. I hold both views simultaneously, and recognize the exquisite dance we are in.

"This kind of love holds a longer, higher view. It comes from an understanding of the many levels of consciousness on which we exist. On the material level, we're in bodies, in a marriage, in a family, playing roles. Being able to hear the 'right' way through an incarnation is difficult, and it requires a quiet, focused mind. All this to say, I do not take my relationship with my husband for granted; I know that physically, it will one day come to an end, whether that is because ending it is the 'right' thing to do, or because one of us has died. It won't benefit me to hold on too tightly to him (possessiveness), because everything will ultimately change.

"On a soul level, I feel that we've been together for many incarnations, many lifetimes. We're using each other to wake up; to deepen our understanding of what life is really about. Perhaps in past lives, I was the husband, child, father; perhaps he was the wife, child, mother… But it's clear that the connection between the two of us is beyond this world. We teach each other.

"There is no hierarchy; we are simply a reflection of each other. When I see something unbalanced or shadowed in him, I intuitively know that it's something that lives in me and that to heal it, I must go to the source of it within me. He plays the same game when he's looking at me; this is the foundation that Lovingkindness practice laid for us. We are learning and growing together in this tenuous, ephemeral dance of life, and I cannot fathom nor describe the full depth of a love like this. It just is."

The Power of Satsang

In Hinduism, there is a word for a spiritual community of like-minded seekers of Truth: Satsang. In Buddhism, it's called the Sangha. And it is considered in both to be a sacred jewel because, especially in these times, it is truly a blessing to find conscious, sincere people to walk through life with.

Hindsight Wisdom

Back in the seventies, Ram Dass would encourage folks to "hang out" with holy books like the Bible, the Tao Te Ching, or the Bhagavad Gita or to read the words of or contemplate the great beings of the world such as Jesus, Buddha, Anandamayi Ma, Ramana Maharshi, and others. He explained that keeping our minds oriented toward the wisdom and deep compassion that emanate from such sources can be a wonderful support in the absence of Satsang or Sangha.

Now we have YouTube videos of wisdom teachers at our fingertips, along with audio recordings of meditations and podcasts. Yoga and meditation centers have proliferated across the United States, and you can join virtual group meditations online. It's much easier to find Satsang these days; *all you need to do is look.*

In my own life, I reflected on how I had many friends and acquaintances, but it was the people who were willing to engage in these deeper, more vulnerable conversations with me that I was deriving the most nourishment and joy from. It was through my conversations with them that I was able to more honestly examine my own motivations and beliefs. These shared experiences of awakenings truly *were* sacred jewels; the progress we made together was far more than I could have ever achieved on my own.

Discovering spiritual sisterhood with Meg was especially life-giving. In the months before we went to Maui, we did some serious soul work together. We would connect once or twice a month for coffee or tea to unpack life experiences and to dream together. We believed in each other and cheered each other on. There was no competition or comparison; we sincerely wanted the best for each other, and we didn't feel threatened one iota by the other's successes.

A sweet memory that I have of Meg was when, while we were talking, I shared how I felt a little stuck and unsettled in my life. She asked me, "In what practical way can I help you?"

After some thought, I said that food prepping for the week is a keystone habit for me, meaning it supports everything else. She came to my house that Sunday and let me "put her to work" for about three hours as we tag-teamed my meal prep for the week. She insisted that I not feed her as I normally would, and she graciously left when the work was done. To me, this is true friendship. It got me on a roll, and I made the same effort on my own the following weekend.

Hindsight Wisdom

How often do we see our friends suffering and we say, "**Let me know** if I can do anything to help you?" But how easy is it for you to articulate your needs, even to your spouse or your closest friends? I deeply valued Meg's intentional verbiage: "In what practical way can I help you?" There's an immediacy to it. The question requires the responder to consider what would benefit them, and it holds the friend accountable to follow through with the help they are (likely genuinely) wanting to offer. When we take the time to build each other up, we ALL rise.

Me and Meg

YTT Wisdom

The end of the summer brought a three-month series of Master Classes with the same annual guest teachers as before. Although they are each traveling teachers with hundreds of students around the world, these three particular weekend sessions somehow felt directly related to what was up for *me* at the time. I've learned, particularly from teaching yoga, that we tend to have collective experiences that only seem to be specific to us. When I write my theme, I go inward and observe what recurring insights have come up for me that week. Often, more than one student will later say that a class theme seemed like it was written "just for them."

In August, internationally renowned Yoga Instructor Desirée Rumbaugh taught us ten hours of asana over three days. Her focus was on breaking down movements into their smallest components. The intention was not only to strengthen each part of our bodies through muscular engagement but also to deepen our subtle awareness of what was going on *within* our bodies.

Des offered many helpful soundbites within her theme, such as, "Somehow, some way, everything is working out for me," and "The most important and intimate relationship you'll ever have is the one with yourself. Do you know yourself?" She taught us that we should be making the asanas work for *us* (using them to clear congestion and to open and strengthen the body), instead of working for the *asanas* (forcing our bodies into the shape so we can feel like we've "achieved" them).

One thing Des said that stuck out was about the impetus of us "reporting our pain," whether in a yoga class or a relationship or elsewhere. Importantly, she added that after we report it, *we* must do something about it. We are self-responsible. She warned us against blaming a teacher or authority figure because, at the end of the day, we must trust our own inner wisdom. I interpreted this as no one is going to rescue me. *I need to have my own back.*

Sonam Targee, an Ayurvedic and Chinese medicine practitioner, came in September to teach us aspects of *Ayurveda,* the "science of life." Ayurveda is a comprehensive, traditional healing system rooted in over 5,000 years of study and application in the culture of the Indian subcontinent. Similar to Chinese medicine and a sister science to yoga, ayurveda empowers us to learn about ourselves deeply and to work collaboratively with the natural world to continually bring ourselves back into balance.

We practiced many ways of moving energy in our bodies, balancing our *doshas* (our unique constitutions), and self-care based on our doshas. Sonam encouraged us to notice our tendencies and to honestly ask what is out of balance, which points to what is needed for us to come back *into* balance. He shared that Ayurveda is an invitation to recognize our inextricable connectedness to the universe, of which we are a microcosm, and to use that wisdom to bend the flow of life in our favor.

On the Saturday of Sonam's weekend, he hosted a Kirtan that Paulo and I attended. It was one of the most peaceful kirtan experiences that either of us has ever had. We left feeling drenched in love and utterly rearranged cellularly. The intensity of that experience gently passed, and the following day, Paulo and I had a powerful emotional release. I cried for what seemed like an eternity, and we recommitted to our marriage on the eve of our twelfth anniversary.

The following week was rife with emotional turbulence as we navigated deep conversations about longings and healings, followed by periods of noble silence and contemplation. Then, on Friday, a quantum shift occurred. Our night began rough; my energy was very frenetic, and Paulo could tell. He gently acknowledged it, but instead of trying to fix it, he calmed me with his compassionate presence. We dropped the girls off with my stepmom and left to go on a date.

On the way to our destination, Paulo began sharing some painful memories from his past that he had never shared before. This act of courageous vulnerability opened something in our relationship. Throughout the rest of the night, we slowly, compassionately, began processing some of our childhood wounds together. It was cathartic and intimate to see and be seen in that way. I was struck that even after fifteen years together, we were still learning about each other; there was always more to discover.

The final master class weekend brought Douglas Brooks, Professor of Religion at the University of Rochester, to teach Hindu mythology and philosophy. He shared stories that invited us to consider what it means to live wholeheartedly. The myths discussed over the four sessions gave us a framework to contemplate how we, like the *nagas* or sea serpents, possess toxicity within us that can be used to digest and integrate our life experiences (food) if we are cognizant of its existence. If we are unaware, however, our toxicity can become a cause of wounds in ourselves and others.

Douglas, in his profoundly educated, poetically loquacious manner, shared the calling to examine and integrate our shadow sides. He argued that *we* are our most underutilized resource and that our work is to bring together our broken and missing pieces to create our own unique artistry as a commitment to a greater depth of intimacy with the world. The teachings he offered were an invitation to accept the uncontrollable nature of life while simultaneously learning how to fully inhabit our lives.

Throughout the Master Classes, the theme was listening to and honoring our experience exactly how it is. Life is inherently unbalanced, and there is no one coming to rescue us. There is beauty and sacredness in all aspects of life, and no finish line exists. It is up to us to listen deeply, align deeply, trust deeply, and love deeply. That is what it means to truly live – *be all in.*

Maui

With the master classes now complete, it was time to prepare for my upcoming retreat. Even getting to Maui was a teaching! Of course, there was the yearlong effort that ensued after I first approached Anna and Meg, asking, "Are you willing to dream with me that this is possible?" to repeating to Meg, "All the details will be resolved as if by magic." I felt from the very beginning that I was being pulled by my heart to Maui and to Ram Dass.

I had to overcome so much false programming of my unworthiness of such a vacation and of my selfishness for wanting to go. It was an opportunity to believe in my divine right and ability to follow my dreams, as much as it was an opportunity to speak up and ask for help from my community. And with equal parts belief, sincere commitment, and support from my family and friends, my dreams were coming true.

Our flight was set to leave the Monday after Thanksgiving. I spent the weekend connecting with Paulo and the girls, shopping, cleaning, and preparing food in anticipation of my departure. The reality began to set in for us all that I was going to be away from home for ten full days, and we all started getting a bit jittery. I knew that Paulo would figure things out and that everything would be fine, but I also acknowledged, painfully so, that I had been carrying the lion's share of the household responsibilities for the past several years and that my absence was going to challenge *them* as much as it would challenge *me*.

As I lay in bed Sunday night, terror settled into my bones. What if I don't come back? What if the plane crashes into the ocean or there's some catastrophic weather on the island while I'm there? What if this is my final goodbye? A lump formed in my throat as I contemplated the gravity of those potentialities. As I nearly gave myself over entirely to that immense fear, the quiet, steady voice inside began to speak to me from within.

These potentialities are never *not* in play. Each day that I wake up is a miracle, as is each time I return home from a day spent driving, working, or otherwise. And one day, those miracles will run out, and it will be my last. I could choose to hold myself back and teach my children to live in constant fear of the unknown, or I could choose to be brave, walk directly into the uncertainty, and teach my children to delight in the miraculous adventure that is life with great appreciation and joy. So, I did my *japa* (repetition of my mantra), listed my gratitude, and drifted off to sleep.

I was up at 4:15 the next morning to get ready for a 6:30 a.m. flight to Chicago. Despite a winter storm advisory the night before, our flight was scheduled as "on time," and school wasn't canceled. We were confident that despite everyone's warnings, our trip would go precisely as planned. We couldn't have been more wrong! The entire day would prove to be a beautiful lesson in surrendering to *what is*.

As we arrived at the airport, I received a text that school was canceled. Shortly thereafter, another text came through that our flight would be delayed four hours. As we waited in line to check in and see about changing our itinerary (since the delay would mean missing our connection to Honolulu), we remained calm and confident. The woman at the ticket counter decided that the only way to get us to Maui that day would be to switch us to a different airline and reroute us to Minneapolis, then LAX to Maui. What a fortuitous decision, as we later discovered that our original flight to O'Hare was canceled entirely.

That could've been enough drama right there, but no, our resolve would continue to be tested. Our plane to Minneapolis sat on the tarmac for a full hour waiting to be de-iced, so our connection to LAX was already in flight before we landed. Every person we met was delightful, and we luckily found seats on the next plane to LAX so as not to miss our flight to Maui. We traveled for twenty-three hours, then drove another hour to our vacation rental. We stopped at the store for coffee, wine, beer, and snacks. When we arrived, we unpacked, made a toast, and settled in for bed. The waves were so loud that we could hear them all night as they crashed onto the shore. It was warm, but the breeze of the trade winds made for perfect sleeping conditions.

Meg and I were up early the next day as the birds sang us awake. After the sun rose, I made myself some coffee and headed down to the shoreline for my first glimpse of the Pacific Ocean. As I approached, I saw the mountains of Molokai in the distance and the waning moon still visible in the clear blue skies above me.

Experiencing the power and majesty of the incredible ocean swells, I began to weep.

I had done some reading about the history, traditions, and culture of Hawaii before traveling there, so I could develop a bit of cultural competence and respect before visiting. Prior to this, I had no understanding of or sensitivity toward what the native people of Hawaii, as with so many other countries and islands in the global south, had endured due to the greed and righteousness of European colonizers.

Captain James Cook was the first European to make contact with the Hawaiian Islands in the late 1770s. Over the following hundred-plus years, missionaries, businessmen, and eventually politicians would travel to the archipelago to establish Christian boarding schools and churches, sugar plantations, hotels, and military bases. A military coup in the late 1800s led to the signing of the Bayonet Constitution, effectively stripping the Hawaiian monarchy of its power and disenfranchising the Hawaiian people.

Hawaii was then annexed by the United States just before the turn of the century after a failed attempt to overthrow the occupation and restore the Hawaiian Kingdom's last sovereign, Queen Lili'uokalani, to the throne. Sixty years later, after enduring the suppression of their language, culture, and religious practices, including hula, as well as the brutal World War II attack on Pearl Harbor by the Japanese, a vote was held to establish Hawaii as the 50th state of the United States of America.

As I stood on the shoreline, I was struck by how the land and people had been so deeply wounded by the effects of colonialism and militarism. Observing the people and culture of Hawaii, I felt as if the island were an example of what could be possible if our collective country could endeavor to decolonize our minds and recognize our connection with the earth and her inhabitants. My understanding of colonization includes a delusional sense of hierarchical authority of one group (commonly wealthy, Christian, and of European descent) that leads to the invading, conquering, subjugation, and exploitation of another group (those indigenous to the land). In this sense, to decolonize our minds is to identify and then overwrite the attitudes, ideologies, institutions, and behaviors that stem from this false and harmful self-righteousness that excuses or supports such behaviors of violence and oppression.

Despite the brutal and despicable ways in which the ancestors of native Hawaiians were treated, the people's resilience and enduring love of life are evident. They are not victims, but warriors, wisdom keepers, scholars, scientists, and artists. There is a deep sense of sacred reciprocity that permeates the relationships among people and with nature. An ongoing movement to reclaim their culture, language, and sovereignty persists, and even the native music is filled with messages of friendship, respect for Mother Earth and humanity, and aloha. "Aloha" speaks to that which cannot be put into words; it is a resonance to the spirit of each other, a reciprocity of love, tenderness, and honoring of one another.

Everything about the island of Maui felt sacred; I could sense divine feminine energy all around us. I delighted at the plumeria trees outside our condo, how they offered their beautiful, fragrant blossoms to the earth as if propitiating the goddess herself. Overcome with a feeling of tenderness, I found myself speechless in the presence of such raw beauty and power in the symphony of life that surrounded me.

On the road to Hana, nature's bountiful grandeur continued to unfurl. We saw feral cats, mongoose, goats, and birds. Monarch butterflies were abundant all around the island, and orchids grew wild everywhere, even out of the rock face as we drove through carved-out mountainsides. Occasionally, we would see trickling water down the rocky walls, and vines hung over the roadway, clinging to trees and creating a tunnel-like passage. We saw countless small waterfalls in the distance as we crossed old, rocky bridges. As Meg expertly navigated the twists and turns of the narrow road, I gazed with awe at the dense forestry and cliffs.

The second evening marked the beginning of the Open Your Heart in Paradise (OYHIP) Retreat. Meg walked me to Nāpili Kai Beach Resort, where it was to be held, and then she was off to explore the island on her own. Attendees were free to come and go as they pleased, but there were scheduled dharma talks, guided meditations and contemplative practices, qigong, yoga, and kirtan daily from 6 a.m. to 9:30 p.m.

We were invited to swim in the ocean or connect with other retreat participants during the breaks, and we were fed delicious, whole, and local foods for breakfast, lunch, and dinner. The entire retreat experience was meant to be a banquet for the senses, the mind, and the soul. It was an exquisite environment to immerse ourselves in various *bhakti* (devotional) and meditation practices to quiet our minds and open our hearts.

Taken at the Ram Dass OYHIP retreat winter 2018

What struck me most throughout the days was the loving energy being exchanged by everyone. The way folks made eye contact with tender, caring eyes and loving attention was disarming at first. Many attendees were already dear friends, having come several times to the biannual retreat. I became fast friends with a few individuals as well as a group of women who had traveled together. We would save room at extra-large tables to share meals, sitting near each other during the talks and kirtans. The conversations were lovely, and I found myself recording in my journal some of the wise, sweet things both the teachers and the participants were saying.

On the third day, I noticed a flyer near the check-in table that said:

Explore your Heart with COMMUNITY.
Gather - Listen - Meditate - Chant - Feed
Sign up to be matched with Ram Dass Meetups near you.
Ramdass.org/fellowship

It had crossed my mind the day before, while sitting with this beautiful satsang of Neem Karoli Baba devotees, that all the teachers from those initial pilgrimages to India back in the 1960s and 1970s were now in their seventies and eighties. I started to have the sinking realization that these teachers were not going to live forever; that the younger generations, those who never even *saw* Maharajji in the body and yet were irrevocably affected by his love, would need to continue gathering lest this path of the heart be lost to time. I snapped a photo of the flyer for later.

I brought up this contemplation while sharing lunch and stories with the group of women whom I had befriended. We agreed about the value of having a physical spiritual community to learn and grow with, without having to travel halfway across the world to do so. The problem was that most attendees lived in places like

California, New Mexico, Colorado, and New York. I managed to meet one person that week who was also from Michigan, although on the other side of the state. I began to wonder what it would be like to lead a small community fellowship in my hometown. My new friends encouraged me to consider it for the sake of bringing Maharajji's satsang even more to the Midwest. But would anyone even come?

We wrapped up the retreat with a sunrise meditation followed by a traditional closing ceremony led by Lei'ohu Ryder & Maydeen Ku'uipo 'Iao, as well as group swimming and singing in the ocean. Ram Dass's caretakers guided his water-friendly wheelchair into the ocean so he could join us. Encircling him were floating flower petals and all of us attendees. As a matter of tradition, he gleefully declared, "Oh buoy, oh buoy, oh buoy!" before leading us in an echoing rendition of *Row, Row, Row Your Boat* before we all parted ways.

Everything about the retreat and the remainder of the trip truly was a dream. I remember vividly a moment when I was swimming in the ocean, watching the sunset. I said out loud, "This is perfection; this is enough."

A gentleman nearby heard me and smiled, arguing, "No, you can always have *more!*"

Shaking my head, I said, "No, I am full and satisfied. If I died right now, I would be at peace."

With this awareness came the realization that this contentment was exactly what I'd been yearning for all along; the antidote to the fear I had been consumed by the night before we'd left. And while it didn't hurt that I was having this experience while swimming in the Pacific Ocean and watching the sun dip beneath the water, in my heart I knew that this contentment was wholly accessible within each moment of my life. Everything was okay, even if it didn't always seem like it. This peacefulness felt both familiar and extraordinary; the miraculous was contained within the mundane.

With the retreat now complete, Meg and I fit what seemed like three vacations' worth of adventure into our final thirty-six hours together before heading home. We went parasailing, ate at a hidden local restaurant, watched the sunrise from above the clouds on the sacred Haleakalā volcano, visited the Ali'i Kula lavender farm (my favorite experience), and even attended a (very colonized version of) luau. Each moment I lived there is inscribed within my heart, and the memories and dreams are as juicy and wonderful as the days themselves.

10

Shadow Work

There is a wonderful Ram Dass and Maharajji story that shares an account of when Ram Dass, after being told by Maharajji that it was time to return to the United States, began to panic over the amount of neuroses and impurities of mind he still had.

"Maharajji, you can't send me back. I'm too impure," pleaded Ram Dass.

Standing up from his wooden platform, Maharajji moved close to Ram Dass, carefully looking him over from every angle. Returning to his seat, Maharajji said, "I don't see any impurities."

It was then that Ram Dass appreciated that, in the eyes of the One from which all is created, we are without mistakes. This is an invitation to radically love and embrace oneself regardless of one's neuroses, past actions, and shortcomings. A term for this in Sanskrit is *purno'ham*: I am complete; full; whole.

Having tasted this purno'ham experience while in Maui shifted something in me. The awareness arose that, by having a precious moment of *santosha*, a moment of pure contentment in which I did not feel deficient, defective, or in imminent danger, I had expanded the spaciousness in my mind and being, even if only a little. And although it was a subtle shift, the benefit of that extra space was my strengthened resilience and capacity to bear witness to suffering, both mine and others.

Over the next two years, I would return to many familiar pain points in my life's labyrinth, only now from a distinctively higher, broader perspective. I would be graced with the courage, capacity, and community needed to reexamine the many personal and transpersonal traumas that had so relentlessly tried to obscure my connection to myself and to the whole of which I am part.

Hindsight Wisdom

It's important to note that the uniqueness of the environment and conditions in Maui wasn't necessary. I had accessed this experience of santosha before, but only then was I finally able to put it into words.

At that moment, it was as if my entire life had flashed before my inner eye. And taking full measure of all the connections, moments, bliss, boredom, and tragedy, I felt to my bones that *it was enough*. I had been enough and done enough. I had given to the world in thought, word, and deed what I could, as best I could, and my contribution was *enough*. I immediately sensed that the steady ground of enoughness was fertile soil, cloaked with mystery and impregnated with the possibility of infinite futures.

It was time for me to begin engaging with what is known as shadow work. Our shadow includes all of the denied aspects of ourselves—the parts of us that we can't accept, so we push them out of our conscious awareness. We reject these parts because they make us feel guilty or shameful. Things like greed, jealousy, sexual desires, aggression, selfishness, or cruelty are more obvious examples of aspects we would want to hide or reject, but shadows are not necessarily overtly harmful. They can also include aspects such as people-pleasing, codependence, self-sabotage, and passivity.

The problem with voting our unsavory aspects off the island of "me" is that these shadow parts continue to heavily influence how we interact with the world around us. And they can have profoundly negative impacts on our relationships as well as our ability to live a fulfilling life. We become fragmented. We break ourselves apart and tuck these unsavory aspects of ourselves away so we can convince ourselves that they aren't a part of us. But the problem with that strategy is that what we resist, persists.

What's required for us to engage with our shadow is the ability to self-reflect without value judgments of good/bad, right/wrong. We need some space between our ego self and our higher self so we can view our lives through the lens of the witness. This space is naturally created over time through our spiritual practices, including meditation, yoga, contemplation, mantra repetition, chanting, and many others. And it is this inner spaciousness that enables us to anchor into a place within that doesn't take our thoughts, words, and actions personally.

The process of shadow work involves turning toward these rejected parts with the intention of accepting and integrating them back into our self-concept. It's about embracing our full selves, with all of our flaws and imperfections, and coming to understand that there are no bad parts of us. This reclamation of our wholeness is key to revealing our intrinsic loving, peaceful, compassionate nature. After all these years of whole-hearted, consistent practice, I was finally ready to begin this part of my journey.

Spiritual Bypassing

I have a beautifully poignant memory from my 200-hour yoga teacher training that I return to often. It was when Behnje made clear that "this is not 'hearts and flowers' yoga; this is about cultivating the inner strength to meet life as its equal."

I remember the feeling of my body bristling and tensing at that statement. Hearts and flowers yoga was *exactly* what I wanted! I wanted to throw away all my heartache, my body hatred, my traumas, and my neuroses. I wanted to have a permanent experience of blissfulness by transcending apparent reality and spending the rest of my existence on another plane of consciousness. Am I the only one who thought that's what "enlightenment" or "heaven" meant?!

Actually, I know I'm not. Certain schools of yogic philosophy, as well as some of the major world religions, promote this idea of liberation or redemption in which we as human beings no longer exist. It is rooted in a false belief that our bodies and nature are dirty and sinful—that they're something to be ashamed of and beaten into submission.

This ideology of transcendent liberation is exemplified in the person who thinks they can be terrible their entire lives, then receive a sacrament of forgiveness right before death like a get-into-heaven-free card. It's in the person who ignores the suffering of humanity across the globe and instead retreats to a personal oasis, trying to meditate away reality. It's in the person who thinks that nothing exists beyond this life and so believes it's best to be as gluttonous and self-serving as possible, since the repercussions of their behavior are not "their problem."

This is a tantalizing, escapist fantasy, no doubt, but countless beings who've walked this path before us warn that this is a mind trap. No matter where we go, there we are. And what happens somewhere else eventually will impact everyone, everywhere. Through Behnje's words, I was challenged to actually *live* as the embodied being that I am and not only as a bundle of thoughts in my mind, to experience life directly and co-participate in the story instead of rejecting, dissociating, or avoiding the messiness of it.

This reflects a teaching from Buddhist teacher and psychotherapist John Welwood. In his book *Toward a Psychology of Awakening,* he coins the term "spiritual bypassing," and defines it as using "spiritual ideas and practices to sidestep personal, emotional, unfinished business, to shore up a shaky sense of self, or to belittle basic needs, feelings, and developmental tasks." He calls it an attempt "to rise above the raw and messy side of our humanness before we have fully faced and made peace with it."

Some examples of spiritual bypassing include:

- repressing or denying difficult emotions
- overemphasizing the positive
- feeling a sense of spiritual superiority compared to another
- using spiritual practices like meditation or yoga to "feel good" and avoid painful emotions or unresolved trauma
- emphasizing detachment to the extent that we're not addressing interpersonal or real-world problems

So much of what we call the spiritual path is really just about cultivating mental and emotional maturity. It's about cleaning up our shit—our melodrama, as Ram Dass used to call it—so we can release the stickiness of our storylines and embrace the freedom and joy of fully living our lives in the present moment.

Ram Dass regularly spoke of Krishna's demand of the warrior Arjuna in the Bhagavad Gita: "Be one in self-harmony, in Yoga, and do your duty, but relinquish the fruits of your actions to Me."

Krishna calls us all to action without attachment or aversion, action that arises from awareness. It is an invitation to ask ourselves, Am I avoiding taking necessary action out of fear or aversion to possible outcomes?

Am I being in the world in a way that alleviates suffering as much as possible while remaining grounded and not getting lost in it?

Am I using my spiritual practices or devotion as a way to avoid my dharma, as Arjuna attempted to do in the Gita?

Am I coming from a space of awareness, and are my thoughts, words, and actions dedicated to truth and love? Or am I living in my contracted state of mortality and fear of death and pain?

As I contemplated these questions and got real with myself, no bullshitting or spiritual bypassing, the best "next step" for me was revealed. Just as the moon cycles and seasons each run their divinely intelligent courses, I became aware of how certain pain points and focuses of attention cyclically came into my awareness, inviting me to extract the wisdom available within them.

This felt like an extension of something I had learned from Behnje about creating class themes based on what was "up for her" at that moment. I have recalled this teaching often, using it as a searchlight upon my awareness. As I witness my daily experiences and thoughts, I scan for repetitive messages, symbols, or conversation topics. If something comes up more than once, I investigate a little deeper to see what consciousness is trying to show me.

An example of this is operationalizing what is understood by many as the Law of Reflection. The Law of Reflection is a metaphysical law that states that everything we perceive in the world around us is a reflection of our minds. You can consider whether this is true for you by noticing how, when you're in a bad mood, suddenly everyone is annoying, or how, when you fall in love, everything seems more beautiful, or how, when you're afraid, it seems like everyone and everything is a threat. In modern psychology, this could be described as projection.

This projection of self onto others is an adaptive defense strategy that we often use to avoid acknowledging our own unmet needs, uncomfortable emotions, or shadow aspects. What we don't want to acknowledge or accept about ourselves, we easily project onto those around us. We even do this for our more "positive" traits. We admire certain qualities and talents in others that we feel uncomfortable claiming in ourselves.

So, operationalizing the Law of Reflection in service to my spiritual development involves bringing awareness to the aspects of other people that I find worthy of negative judgment. As I notice myself pointing the proverbial finger at someone else for their selfish/greedy/harmful behavior, I turn my pointer finger back toward myself and ask, "Why is this so salient to me? Why am I noticing this? Where does this exist in me and my experience?"

This is a psychologically painful process of self-reflection. It's a stage of clear-seeing and truth-telling that I believe we all encounter eventually, especially when we're consciously committed to alleviating suffering for ourselves and others. We cannot arrive at a state of universal compassion, healing, and integration until each being's grief and pain is heard, validated, and held. That starts with ourselves, but it ultimately expands outward until it includes everyone.

Most people would prefer to skip the "feeling our feelings" part and hurry back to an artificial kind of peace. But that kind of peace isn't real—it's tenuous and hollow. The Cosmic Mother in us all understands to Her bones that to create something new and beautiful, we must accept the incubation period, the transition, and the painful birthing process.

So, if, for example, I'm sitting in my self-righteousness pointing out behaviors that exemplify white supremacy and homophobia, I had better be willing to examine (and have others examine) my own toxic ideologies and tendencies. I have to cultivate the strength to bear witness to it all; to take it all into myself, alchemize it, and bring it back out into the world as something new and beautiful. We are all both/and. We each possess a shadow side that, as the name implies, is not visible to us. We've been wounded, and we've caused wounding in others. And, facing that illuminating awareness, I recognize that there is much work to be done.

For me, that work looks like seeing reality through clear lenses and not through the viewpoint of my trauma wounds and neuroses. It looks like radical self-love, courage in the face of fear, and speaking my truth. The work is recognizing the suffering that exists in all beings and doing what I can to alleviate it without making things worse or making it all about me. It's operating from my highest integrity while being unattached to the fruits, whether pleasant or unpleasant, of my actions.

It can't be all hearts and flowers.

Committing to Step Two: The Reckoning

From my perspective, true liberation is not an escape. In fact, I see it as quite the opposite. Freedom is living our lives more deeply, on purpose, and in community with others while releasing attachment to expectations, possessions, relationships, and outcomes. It comes from honoring our authentic selves, keeping an open and tender heart, and being in direct relationship to reality. No more avoiding or glossing over what makes us feel uncomfortable.

After all the years of fearing and resisting my own broken heart, after the years of trying to feel safe and secure in an inherently uncertain world, I was finally feeling strong *enough*, safe *enough*, to begin integrating all the wisdom I had accumulated along my journey. I understood that I didn't have to fear my heart breaking. Because each time my heart breaks open, more space is created to hold the suffering of the world, and my heart eventually stitches back together, only stronger, more integrated, and more beautiful.

It was time to be brave and turn toward my pain. It was time to start digging deeper into my oldest stories and wounds—the ones that hijack my personal power and limit my freedom.

The first warden of my freedom was my lack of confidence in my own resourcefulness and capability. All my life, I felt subordinate, victimized, and helpless. I did not *fully* believe that I could have my own back. So, one of the things I had to do to reclaim my power was to let go of dependency and transactional love. And nowhere in my life was this more visible than in my financial reliance on my parents.

As my grandparents had done for my parents as adults, my mom and dad each enjoyed the opportunity to show their love by spending money on me and my family. They'd pick up the check for a family dinner at a restaurant, fund the occasional family vacation, and even help buy needed household items like food, furniture, and stuff for the kids.

Having both grown up in low-middle-income families and then endured the harsh realities associated with being a single parent in a post-Reagan America, they both seemed to take pride in their buying power. And because I was stuck in a pattern of learned helplessness, I gladly became the beneficiary of their conditional generosity. I say conditional because, after many cycles of arguments, hurt feelings, and misunderstandings between us, I realized that the unspoken agreement was that by accepting their "gifts," I was entering into a contract of silence by revoking my right to dissent.

It was not uncommon for these expenses to be thrown in my face later. My mom would complain that she was still paying off something or should never have bought it in the first place. My dad would use his purchases as opportunities to suggest that I find a new job or spend my money differently. I realized that by letting them spend money on me, I was expected to keep my mouth shut if my opinions differed from theirs and be as overtly grateful as possible.

It was as if we were acting out a play of extended childhood in which they were the gatekeepers of resources, and I was the child whose opinions and feelings were invalid and unimportant. And once that awareness came through, there was no ignoring how I was helping to keep us all trapped in our storylines. I was complicit in our lack of freedom because I was not acting with integrity and maturity. And if I were truly committed to the liberation of all beings, I needed to break that contract.

It was time for me to remember that:

- I am strong, wise, capable, and resourceful. I am unafraid of hard work, and I have never *not* succeeded in accomplishing what I set out to do.
- I am not alone; I am held by a beautiful community of like-minded family and friends who have never hesitated to offer me support when needed, and who have also learned to give freely and without condition.

- Telling the truth is more important than "feeling" safe.* If we equate "feeling safe" with not being harmed or killed, we are already living in delusion, because we will, all of us, someday die. The freedom to respectfully disagree is far more important than most of us appreciate.

---

*If you are in an imminently dangerous relationship, *being safe* is your number one priority. Please know that there are people out there who want to support and protect you as you rediscover your own strength and freedom. What I am referring to here is the opportunity for those of us in physically safe environments to feel safe, since in many respects, we already are, only we don't believe it.

For anonymous, confidential help:
- RAINN.org (Rape, Abuse & Incest National Network)
- National Domestic Violence Hotline 1-800-799-7233
- National Sexual Assault Hotline 1-800-656-4673

Breaking this unhealthy power dynamic was challenging and sometimes even paradoxical in practice. Paulo and I began to pay for ourselves and our children at restaurants, and occasionally we'd pay for our parents, too. Sometimes, we would decline offers of loans or gifts in favor of finding an alternative solution, while at other times, we'd accept a loan or gift while continuing to speak and live by our values, risking potential confrontations and uncomfortable conversations. And then there were times that we'd clearly say, "Please do not offer this if there are conditions tied to it. I will accept your generosity only if you are giving it freely."

If you can relate to this financial dependency with your parents or with any of your relationships, for that matter, I cannot understate the value of breaking the contract of silence. At the end of the day, we each long for authentic, loving relationships, including the ones with those who were previously our primary caregivers. And authentic, loving relationships are built upon a foundation of trust, honesty, humility, and compassion. If you're hiding parts of who you are to keep the peace, your foundation is cracked.

I'm Part of the Problem

An important insight arose with this new contract-breaking approach. I saw that I was playing a role in perpetuating my own suffering, including the pain of disconnection I felt when I armored my heart in response to tragedy. It was apparent to me that when I wasn't fully present to the *here* and *now* with an open heart, I tended to act in a way that minimized discomfort for myself, even if that meant turning away from the suffering of others.

I saw that if I wasn't consciously a part of the solution, I was unconsciously a part of the problem. And up to that point in my life, there had been no more painfully obvious example of this truth than in my personal confrontation of how, through both action and inaction, I uphold systems of white supremacy. Not unlike my aversion to bearing witness to the hate-motivated mass murder at the Pulse Nightclub years ago, I was woefully unprepared to bear witness to the immense suffering within Black communities, Indigenous communities, and communities of the global majority. But try as I did to avert my gaze, my heart kept imploring me to lean into the horror of it all.

Having been raised in and immersed within so many systems of oppression that were benefiting people who looked like me at the expense of people who didn't, it has been more than a little difficult to clearly see the reality of it all. Growing up, everyone in my family was white, everyone in my church was white, and, until college, everyone in my school was white. My whole adolescence was perhaps subconsciously but nevertheless orchestrated in such a way as to keep me entirely oblivious. The crack in the cement wall of my obliviousness was the fruit of my self-compassion practices. And the light of awareness that shined through that crack was from Paulo.

Hindsight Wisdom

It is cruel irony that experiencing trauma in our lives both opens us to the capacity for empathy (the ability to feel the pain of others) and impinges our capacity for compassion (the ability to feel the pain of others *and* be called to act skillfully in response). The untended wounds of abandonment and unworthiness make it extremely difficult to examine the ways we hurt other people, and they can undermine our confidence in our abilities to help.

Paradoxically, practicing mindful self-compassion allows us to work with these childhood wounds in an alchemical way. I have personally observed that as I learn how to be tender toward my own pain and offer acts of love to myself in response to that pain, I feel safer to be my authentic self. And as I become more settled in my own being, I grow my capacity to bear witness to the suffering of others and be likewise moved to some form of supportive action.

I have also observed that while practicing empathy alone tends to drain me energetically and has a subtle aspect of martyrdom to it, practicing compassion is energizing and imbues the whole environment with feelings of connection and belonging. And if feeling nourished by community isn't enough incentive to lean into the heavy lifting that is "inner child work," then let us be motivated by the awareness that lives and livelihoods are violently impacted every day that we shy away from it. Our collective children are counting on us to heal these wounds once and for all, so we can chart a new path forward for humanity.

As I grew my ability to bear witness to and hold space for my own suffering, so too did my strength and capacity grow to include those outside of myself. And again, faced with the truth that until we are all free, none of us are free, I saw that universal liberation was intimately tied to my individual willingness and capacity to see suffering in all forms and my individual willingness and capacity to do what is possible to alleviate that suffering. Grace, through Paulo, showed me the cement wall of ignorance blocking me from recognizing my complicity in race-based violence.

"Nobody's free until everybody's free."
—Fannie Lou Hamer

It was in large part due to the Black Lives Matter Movement, sparked by George Zimmerman's acquittal of his murder of seventeen-year-old Trayvon Martin and emboldened by the highly visible, fast succession of murdered unarmed Black Americans since Trayvon's death in 2012, that this paradigm shift occurred. When I was first confronted with the senseless murder of Trayvon, the ground of my being was rocked. He was a precious child with a kind and gentle appearance. He was just being a kid, grabbing snacks from a convenience store, when his murderer decided he looked suspicious enough to shoot.

My daughters were two and four at the time. I'll tell you, a mother has to have very protective armor around her heart or fiercely closed eyes to not shatter at the announcement of the death of a child. I was horrified and enraged. And then also embarrassed because so many other unarmed Black and brown children and adults have been murdered at the hands of adults, both by citizens and police.

Why was this the one that shook me? I truthfully have no rational answer to that. Regardless of the cause of my previous ignorance, I was awake to it now. I was overwhelmed by the pain of reading about and seeing the footage of all these senseless and inhumane killings. My heart ached with grief, but I felt helpless on how to change it.

Drenched in self-pity, I lamented to Paulo about my heartache. "I don't understand how to help change this. I don't know how to talk to Black people about it. I'm so sensitive to their pain and rage that I feel so disingenuous when I try to speak on it. I feel like they're looking at me like the perpetrator, and it makes me feel defensive."

Paulo looked at me, and with a serious gaze and calm voice said, "Do not ever talk to another Black person again. Just don't. You hear me? Don't ever talk to a Black person again… Only talk to human beings."

In that instant, my ego and my heart shattered. I became so highly aware of how I was placing bodies in separate categories of humanity. The pain and rage I was projecting was a creation of my own embodied white supremacy; my own sense of Us versus Them.

Although I had no concept of author and activist Ibram X. Kendi's work yet, my heart told me at that moment that there was no such thing as "not racist." I was either passively maintaining the oppressive, hierarchical status quo of the dominant culture or actively working to dismantle the status quo of the dominant culture as it exists both in my mind and in the world around me, while simultaneously doing my part to create a wiser, equitable dominant culture, including its systems, policies, and institutions. As Kendi wrote in *How to Be An Antiracist*: "One either believes problems are rooted in groups of people, as a racist, or locates the roots of problems in power and policies, as an antiracist. One either allows racial inequities to persevere, as a racist, or confronts racial inequities, as an antiracist. There is no in-between safe space of 'not racist.'"

But I struggled at first to engage with our country's darker history toward those considered the minority (ironically, because they actually represent the global majority). I viewed the study of history as an arrogant, hypermasculine song of devotion to dominance over life, so I was disinterested in learning about it. Over time, I confronted this resistance and found myself getting angrier with each new revelation, as well as how our country's history had been utterly whitewashed. I resented how fetishized conquering and invading were in my textbooks. Why didn't anyone ever take note of the unwieldy economic driver that is strategic war?

Why do we collectively accept the violent consequences of endless military conflict, such as the raping and murdering of women and children; the kidnapping and military indoctrination of young men; the desecration of sacred lands and temples; the pollution and ecological devastation; child labor exploitation; the physical/mental/emotional traumatization of military personnel? All because of the awkward question of what to replace that revenue stream with, as well as what to do with the massive human resources committed to the cause of "spreading democracy and Christian ideals" and "protecting national security?" While that may be true for those at the highest levels of power, for so many of us, it's a bit more straightforward: we've been trained to look away and keep quiet out of self-protection.

Since I was a young girl, there was something in me that raged against the insanity of it all, but I had no outlet to express it. My intelligence was continually disparaged by men older than me, politely reminding me that I didn't know what I was talking about by virtue of my age and gender. Afraid of retribution and discouraged by continual verbal suppression, my mind repressed this rage, and I traded my humanity for an illusory sense of security as my ancestors had done when they first came to this country.

As I've previously mentioned, I do not know much about my blood-and-bone lineage. My grandfather began a genealogy search near the end of his life, but none of this was shared with the family as a whole. I can't even tell you my great-grandmothers' maiden names, nor their stories of immigration. I honestly never even cared that I didn't know until I began reading Resmaa Menekem's book *My Grandmother's Hands: Racialized Trauma and the Pathway to Mending Our Hearts and Bodies.*

In his book, Resmaa speaks to something I never once in my life had heard or considered: That, aside from the collusion between European royal and priestly classes seeking to colonize the world, anyone who dared to risk it all to emigrate from their home country to the U.S.A. surely did so to escape poverty, oppression, and war. They were terrorized and traumatized human beings who came seeking safe harbor, land, and better opportunities. And they either consciously or unconsciously accepted the silent contract set before them; that, to move up the socially constructed socioeconomic hierarchy of the United States, they had to sever their heart connection to humanity.

My European ancestors slowly relinquished their memories of the old country along with their spiritual practices, medicines, traditions, and culture, and instead embraced a new identity as a "white" American. They collectively averted their gaze from the horrors of chattel slavery and the attempted genocide of the Indigenous Americans. They chose individual survival over collective liberation, and in doing so, they severed their connection to themselves, dooming their future generations to a loss of ancestral memory that ushered in a new form of "internalized oppression" for us all. Internalized oppression refers to the condition in which members of targeted groups, due to extended and deep exposure to stereotypes, myths, and misinformation, begin to turn their experience of oppression and discrimination inward. They unconsciously believe what is generally said about their identity subgroups. For example, women are so consistently taught that they are weaker, less intelligent, and less worthy of success than men, that many begin to believe the lies and behave as though they are true.

And so, in light of my commitment to the work at hand, I understood that it was time to engage with my young country's political and military history. I did so to extract the wisdom that could be gleaned from a reckoning of pitfalls, mistakes, exploitation, and injustices. I began seeking out lesser-known historical accounts of the birth of the United States of America and what atrocities against humanity we collectively accepted as necessary collateral damage for the colonization of North America. What I discovered by scratching the surface made me sick to my stomach.

Faced with how genocide, exploitation, and racism had been baked into our belief systems, our culture, and the institutions of our society *from the very start*, I felt nothing but shame and overwhelm. How could I have simply *not seen* this before? The cognitive dissonance was very disorienting. Part of my daily yoga practice became the contemplation of this reality and how it lives in me, as well as sitting with the very uncomfortable resulting sensations and emotions as they arose.

I became an observer of my awkward white girl smile when passing a Black person. I began noticing how I would use African American Vernacular English (AAVE), a dialect of English created by Black Americans, even changing the intonation of my voice, depending on who I was around. I relived memories of my own subtle and not-so-subtle acts of racial violence (mislabeled as "microaggressions"), remembering the ugly and unkind words spoken from my ignorance. I began noticing how nearly every space I entered was overwhelmingly filled with white bodies. I sat with the discomfort, the guilt, and the rage.

And I continue to do so because acknowledging the truth isn't the same as embodying the truth. Embodiment implies "unconscious competence," and that takes *practice.* Because what we resist persists, and the only way to get rid of shadows is to turn on the light.

According to the psychological theory of **Conscious Competence of Learning** (https://www.mccc.edu/~lyncha/documents/stagesofcompetence.pdf)

1. *Unconscious incompetence*: You have a particular deficiency in skill or understanding but don't realize the deficit
2. *Conscious incompetence*: You realize the particular deficiency but don't yet know how to resolve it
3. *Conscious competence*: You practice in earnest to overcome a particular deficiency in skill or understanding
4. *Unconscious competence*: Practice becomes so firmly established that competency becomes your natural state

Reading books by and following some social media accounts of Black and Indigenous female activists, I learned that we white women are extra late to this conversation. And equally embarrassing, historically, Black, Indigenous, women of color, and queer women have always gone to bat for ALL women's rights, but white women are often conspicuously absent when it comes to "intersectional" rights (Kimberlé Crenshaw's legal theory, defined as "the study of overlapping or intersecting social identities and related systems of oppression, domination, or discrimination). So as tempting as it was to jump in as a "fellow suppressed voice" in this white, hetero, patriarchal country, I saw that the wisest, most supportive thing I could do in that moment was to sit down, shut up, listen, and learn.

My first step in this particular journey was to reckon with the hard truth that Black and Indigenous women and men have been carrying on this fight for hundreds of years, demanding to be treated with the respect and dignity owed to a human being from people hell-bent on invalidating, dehumanizing, exploiting, and committing violent atrocities against them solely based on how melanated they are.

I see and honor in particular the Black, Indigenous, and women of color who are reclaiming their divine right to rest and to express themselves creatively. This is not so easy when systems are created expressly to prevent certain groups from having leisure time. My heart aches as I realize the energy it often takes to keep white folks comfortable as a means of self-preservation while demanding one's right to be heard, validated, and uplifted.

I have personally experienced how exhausting it is to argue with some white folks about the existence of white supremacy and the violence it perpetrated and continues to perpetrate. How easy it is to imagine that we became a post-racial society after the passage of the Civil Rights Act of 1964, when the reality is so far from that. There is so much unacknowledged shame and grief preventing us from accessing the resilience necessary to stay in difficult conversations with one another. And I realize that a big part of my privilege as a white woman is to have the choice to bow out of the conversation whenever it gets too uncomfortable because it's not *my* right to exist that I'm trying to prove (yet).

Antiracism in practice for me so far looks like identifying and unlearning white-centered education and cultural dogma. It looks like self-education of the accomplishments of BIPOC (Black, Indigenous, and People of Color), especially Black and Indigenous women, and personal reparations/resource reallocation to local mutual aid programs that benefit BIPOC communities, to bail funds for social justice activists, and to Black and Indigenous entrepreneurs, wisdom keepers, and energy workers. I strive to amplify the voices of Black, Indigenous, and women of color in leadership, education, and art, and to decolonize myself by lessening my materialistic and competitive drives, doing ancestor work, and healing my own generational trauma. I endeavor to call out racist, misogynist, and heteropatriarchal language, policy, and laws whenever I see them, and I take note of my cowardice when I do not.

Facing my countless unearned advantages that were given to me based on my skin tone, as well as my complicity in the continuation of existing systems of oppression, has been some of the most psychologically uncomfortable shadow work I have yet encountered. And I'm so grateful that I have taken this work up. It is not lost on me that I am married to, the mother of, the sister of, and the friend of people of color. Owning responsibility for my conscious and unconscious culpability in race-based bias and violence against people of the global majority is a critical first step in becoming complicit in their, my, and our liberation. If I think it's painful simply to acknowledge the existence of this systemic violence, that is but a minuscule fragment of pain versus that which is experienced by those actually living the repercussions of that reality.

But upholding and/or allowing the continuance of racist ideology is not the only way in which I am part of the problem of white supremacy. White supremacy also expresses itself through classism, ableism, misogyny, homophobia, transphobia, xenophobia, fatphobia, mass incarceration, and other forms of "body terrorism" in an attempt to justify the power held by a few at the expense of the many. In the book *The Body is Not an Apology,* author Sonya Renee Taylor defines body terrorism as the efforts of our media and political and economic systems to perpetuate a state of self-hatred and body shame so as to support body-based oppression.

And I have done my share of harming people whom I subconsciously judged as "less than" by weaponizing my education and grasp of the English language; by using ableist and homophobic slurs; by mom- and woman-bashing; by manipulating and exploiting people for my own selfish gain; by participating in environmental violence through unrestrained consumption of food and goods; and, generally speaking, a complete disregard of my impact on the world around me. Learning to notice and name the many ways white supremacy has been infused into my worldview, beliefs, and even personality traits sometimes feels like digging through Mary Poppins's magic bag.

I'd like to reiterate here why self-compassion is such a crucial piece to us exploring our shadows. Because if I am still stuck in the belief that I am not enough—not intrinsically worthy of love, acceptance, and safety—then when I see how I've hurt others, I will become overwhelmed and incapacitated by shame. I will lack the inner resourcefulness to tend to my heart when confronted with my flaws, even if they are merely a result of my programming.

But if I can be tender and forgiving toward myself, I can find the strength and courage to make small changes in the everyday experience of my life. I can use my voice to participate in local, state, and federal government; I can help build local community and volunteer my time and energy; I can be open to adapting my language in a way that respects all expressions of humanity; I can purchase a water filter instead of countless water bottles; I can source my food and goods locally and ethically when possible; I can purchase less single-use and individually-wrapped products and practice repurposing and recycling; I can let my clothes wear out, trade with a friend, or purchase items from a secondhand store instead of contributing to the massive use of water and chemicals in the commercial textile industry; I can pick up trash that I walk past outside; I can support local businesses and artists when purchasing gifts; I can purchase used toys or engage in bartering/gift economies for household items; I can occasionally walk, carpool, or use public transportation instead of drive my car everywhere.

Hindsight Wisdom

I will be forever grateful to have discovered the Buy Nothing Project through a friend. The Buy Nothing Project is a worldwide gift economy centered on the mission of creating community and reducing environmental impact.

In a gift economy, all exchanges are done freely, without payment, trade, or condition. The Buy Nothing Project creates hyperlocal community networks to encourage folks to get to know their neighbors. Instead of throwing away useful items or donating to resale stores, you can post items in your local Buy Nothing Network to see whether someone in your neighborhood could use them.

In addition to offering your items and services up to the community, the Buy Nothing Network invites members to ask for items they need or want and to offer gratitude and appreciation for what they have received either physically or emotionally from the group.

Check out the Buy Nothing Project app or look up your local Buy Nothing Network on social media to join in on the love!

This is a long-term commitment. Awareness does not guarantee action, and I have to be willing and prepared to accept that I cannot change all these behaviors overnight. The compassion I extend to myself during this process of transformation is crucial to my success. It is also crucial to my ability to relate to those around me. I cannot expect everyone else to see and do as I feel compelled to; we each must walk our own path and arrive at our own understanding, through Grace. Because, let there be no doubt: It is by Grace that I have the eyes to see the violence I have caused, and it is by Grace that I am empowered to learn and grow. Freedom does not come from following the status quo; in this arena, I must be willing to stand on my own.

> "Whenever you find yourself on the side of the majority,
> it is time to pause and reflect."
> —Mark Twain

The Toxicity of Perfectionism

In a seemingly endless procession, Grace was presenting opportunities to explore my long-avoided shadows, providing me with multiple views of what was preventing my liberation (and by proxy/ association, the liberation of us all). Next up on my journey was the investigation of an insidious destroyer of connection, expression, and relationship: perfectionism.

Hindsight Wisdom

I'd like to clarify what I mean by perfectionism. I understand this to be a personality trait categorized by unreasonably high expectations and the belief that it's possible to achieve perfection. For some of us, it's rooted in a deep longing for approval or praise (read: insecurity/ inadequacy); for others, it's because one or more of our caregivers displayed this kind of behavior in our formative years, so it just feels normal.

It's also a function of white supremacy culture. Perfectionism serves to maintain the status quo of the people and ideas that are in power. Ask yourself, what are the standards that are considered perfect? No mistakes, no messiness. Looking, sounding, and behaving in a certain way. The unrealistic ideals we set out to achieve are rooted in the false belief that one way of living and being is superior to all others.

From where I am now standing, the violence of perfectionism seems so apparent. It limits not only the individual, but also society at large because it hinders creativity, which is always messy and experimental at first. In the same way, it attempts to diminish the beauty and innovation potential of existing among diverse cultures and perspectives. And yet, for much of my life, this constant striving for perfection in my expression of Jeni-ness seemed entirely logical and achievable. My ego justified its mission through the fear of embarrassment, the fear of failure, and a longing to be loved and accepted.

By reckoning with my perfectionism, I've acknowledged how much it sucks to suck at something and how ego-boosting it is to be an expert. I had a direct experience with this when I started working at the butcher shop, when I started teaching yoga, and again when I was hired at the GR Center for Mindfulness. In each instance, I had no idea what I was doing until I trained with someone who knew more and then developed competence through practice. Despite that icky, uncomfortable feeling of being "bad" at something, the reality is that I can only grow in my skills, knowledge, and talents if I'm willing to try something new. Perfectionists tend to hate trying new things and actually tend to be risk-averse because pursuing new, risky opportunities requires a willingness to make mistakes.

When I'm working on a task, even if it's something I love, perfectionism will steal my joy. My mind gets so overly focused on the future (where anxiety lives) that it's almost impossible to experience the present moment (where joy lives). When I'm too caught up in the finished product, my awareness is not open to what is happening right now—it's focused on not messing up. I miss out on the joy of the process and the adventure.

I also began to notice how whenever life was feeling particularly unstable or uncertain, I would automatically begin hyper-controlling things that were within my capabilities, including obsessively cleaning my house, getting overly rigid with exercise or nutrition, or busting out the hour-by-hour schedules and to-do lists. I defended my controlling tendencies with inner proclamations of self-indignation: "Well, what's wrong with that? It feels great to be in control and have whatever I control be perfect!"

What I did not immediately realize was that by holding myself to these insurmountable standards, I wasn't only beating myself up. I was taking those in my innermost circles down with me, too. Since unachievable expectations were the norm for me, I also unconsciously projected them as the norm for everyone else. And every time they failed to achieve those impossible expectations, my ego would suck me into thoughts and feelings of judgment, disappointment, frustration, and even anger and resentment.

Not only was I unconsciously mentally and emotionally abusing my immediate family, but also my striving to project a false image of perfection out of a desire to be loved and accepted by my wider family and community was creating the exact opposite result. I was being what Ram Dass termed as "phony holy." And again, Grace came in the form of a loved one, compassionately showing me what I needed to see.

While my and my sister Alyssa's families were gathering together one day, Alyssa mustered the courage to tell me a hard truth: I was doing such a good job of looking like I was "making it" in life that she was feeling like a failure. Considering how much I had been wishing for a close, authentic relationship with my sister all these years, it was a massive gut-punch to realize that my perfectionism was a primary obstacle to having that with her.

It was an unavoidable truth: my perfectionistic tendencies made me unrelatable and therefore a source of shame or unworthiness for those who could only see my highly veneered exterior. If I were to remain committed to liberation for all, then I had to take up the work yet again to transform my self-loathing to *radical self-love*—love that went all the way to the root of my being. The invitation before me was to risk being human. And the fruit of engaging that kind of courage was, beautifully, the possibility of authentic, deliciously-human, loving relationships—all that I ever really wanted in the first place.

Hindsight Wisdom

We are here to learn and grow, not to perform. There is no finish line, unless you count death (which I don't). So, let's learn together to embrace our skills and talents as well as our shortcomings. You never know what kind of beauty might unfold.

Conscious Conception and Birthing Autonomy

Although we had planned for each of our children's births up to this point, our son's conception was altogether different from our daughters'. When Elaina and Nolani were conceived, Paulo and I were still in our early stages of marriage; we were young, enthusiastically in love, and eager to use our love to create more love. Now in our mid-thirties, we had a lot of justified concerns as well as worn-out stories that needed to be examined before we were ready to begin this journey of parenthood again.

Nolani's wish for a younger sibling reignited a longing in each of us that demanded to be reconsidered. But having only recently emerged from the darkness of Paulo's addiction and my thoughts of divorce, we spent the next eighteen months talking about and praying about whether or not to bring another child into this world.

At times, I would imagine the joy a child would bring and the sense of responsibility and selflessness they would require. With the benefit of personal experience, I knew that I had the wisdom, patience, and resources to be even more the mom that I always strived to be for Elaina and Nolani. And now, working part-time from home, I would be able to be present for the miracle of watching a life unfold in a way that I was not always capable of when the girls were little.

At other times, the real possibility of Paulo's relapse or death or our separation would send waves of fear rippling across my mind; what if I ended up having to raise this child alone? I'd cry at the thought of it, but it was a possibility I needed to face. And then there were all of my fears around being too old and too poor, having such a significant age gap between the girls and this new child, and how I would have to once again adjust how I spend my days. I would need to share my body, my energy, and my time again, signing up for all of the agonizing uncertainty that accompanies raising children.

When Paulo and I came together to share how we felt, however, all of those worries began to melt away. "I always thought we'd have a break between children and grandchildren," I challenged.

"Why do we need a gap in between? We love raising children! The more, the merrier," he replied.

"But I'm thirty-five. That would make this a geriatric pregnancy. What if something goes wrong?" I asked.

"Jeni, you're in the best health of your life. And whoever and however this child is, we will love and care for them. They will be a part of our family."

I realized, too, that I was holding onto a narrative handed down to my mother from hers, one in which children impeded one's freedom. When I told my grandma that I was pregnant with Elaina, for example, she responded with, "Why would you want to do something stupid like that?" The story that I had been told was that the birth of a child began an eighteen-year-long countdown to a return to freedom when the child theoretically leaves the nest. It seemed hard for my mother not to resent the premature loss of her own young adulthood due to her having me at a younger age.

This storyline did not belong to me; my children were not an inconvenience or a burden to me. They were a blessing and a joy to take care of and shower with love and affection. I now know how to identify my own needs and make sure they're fulfilled. I know the importance of maintaining my self-identity beyond "mom" and to ask for help when I need it. I believed in the power of Paulo's and my love to see us through any obstacle or fire. And most crucially, I had a deep faith that whatever was meant to happen was already unfolding.

I visited my doula/Reiki/yoga/wild soul sister friend Danielle to share with her our intention to consciously conceive another child. We wanted to approach it in a more intentional way, which made the entire experience feel sacred. She offered a Reiki session for me and made a few recommendations of mantras, mudras, teas, and rituals. She encouraged Paulo and me to create a sacred space on the next new moon and take some time to lie in bed together with our hands on my womb, praying to the stars that if there was a soul who wanted to join our family, we would open our hearts and my body to them.

A Shaky Yes is Still a Yes

This one small decision to consciously conceive a child, though large in its scope of ramifications, made a potent energy accessible for other changes to occur as well. I envisioned my body as a reflection of Mother Earth, and I felt that just as we attend to the soil before planting seeds for a garden, I would want to take care of my body and prepare it for the life that it would create and nourish. I committed to going 100% alcohol-free, inspired to do a 30-day alcohol-free experiment by author Annie Grace (check out her free program at thisnakedmind.com), and was pleasantly surprised to observe that the craving for alcohol did not return this time. I was feeling more settled as a "non-drinker" as opposed to identifying as a "recovering alcoholic" or someone who's "trying to get sober." I realize that the distinction might seem insignificant, but to me it was a profound shift.

> "People are capable, at any time in their lives, of doing what they dream of."
>
> —Paulo Coelho

My acceptance of the unknown future momentarily unlocked my mind from its rigid structures enough to let me dream some more. In imagining my future becoming, the spontaneous thought arose that I want more live music in my life. I've always loved music, and there's something magical about the energy of experiencing music directly and not through the intermediary of a device. I was craving the pleasure of sharing a concert experience with Paulo, so I decided to get out of my comfort zone and purchase some concert tickets for us.

The first band we saw was Nahko and Medicine for the People. They weren't new to the music scene, but they were new to us. I discovered their song "We Are On Time" when I was internally agonizing about whether or not to stay in my marriage, and the message that came through this beautiful song made my heart crack right open. I don't know how to explain it, but this song helped me fall in love with Paulo all over again. So, I thought, what better band to kick off our new concert-going hobby with?

At first, I was a little nervous about attending a concert sober. Large crowds can pique my anxiety and, historically, alcohol was one of the ways I'd calm down enough to enjoy myself while in a sea of people. But the music this band played was quite different from the concerts I'd attended in the past. And although there was no shortage of electrifying energy and dance-worthy beats, my mind was calm and my heart was on fire the whole night. I danced, sang, cried, and swayed, all with full presence and such delight to experience it without some obscuration of my consciousness. We floated on a cloud right out of the concert and felt high for days afterward.

Paulo and me at the Nahko and Medicine for the People concert

The following Sunday was Father's Day and a full moon. Paulo and I decided to create another small ritual to give gratitude to Spirit for the abundance of blessings coming into our lives. We already had tickets for our next concert (Mike Love and the Full Circle) later in the summer, and I interviewed for and accepted a temporary job as a freelance writer for website content. No matter whether our little family was meant to expand or not, there was no questioning the expansion within ourselves and our relationship. And everywhere we directed our attention, the most beautiful synchronicities occurred.

Later that week, I taught a Summer Solstice class at the studio. Only one student showed up, a new student to me, so we got to play around with our practice in a curious and joyful way. After teaching my class of one, I went to the convenience store and bought a two-pack of pregnancy tests. When Paulo awoke to pee at midnight, I followed him downstairs to try one. The test line appeared immediately, but in a sleepy fog, we could not decipher but a ghost of a line for confirmation. Back to bed we went.

At 5:20 a.m. we awoke again, this time armed with a digital read-out test. We patiently waited the three minutes until Paulo looked down and saw, "Yes+!" Our baby Garuda had chosen us and was on the way into this world. Garuda is the name of a mythic eagle in Hinduism. Throughout our experience of conscious conception, imagery of eagles continued to come through. During my Reiki session with Danielle, she had encouraged me to practice Garuda *mudra* (a sacred symbolic gesture done with the hands). Before we named our child, we took to referring to them as "baby Garuda."

On the longest, most light-filled day of the year, our whole lives changed course.

Having accumulated more wisdom since my last pregnancy, I appreciated the importance of maintaining a healthy diet, ample movement and rest, and low stress levels during pregnancy. I continued attending Behnje's yoga classes up until my ninth month, and I taught classes as well until the studio permanently closed that fall. I was grateful for the opportunity to attend the final class at The Studio Yoga, taught by the wonderful Jennephyr, and in the company of so many long-time students. She even invited me to guide the class in a final meditation before we concluded. I felt both humbled and honored, and it was such a beautiful ending to an important chapter of my life.

After the studio closed, several of my students and friends began asking me where I would teach next. There were plenty of local yoga studios to apply to, but something about seeking a new teaching gig felt off to me. The only reason I even began teaching at The Studio Yoga was because I was invited. I didn't feel connected to any of the other studios besides my own teacher's Center, so I decided to take a break from offering public classes.

One of the gifts of teaching, however, was how it required me to engage consistently with my practices. In regular day-to-day life, it can be more than a little challenging to access the willpower needed to engage continually in formal practice. And if I'm not regularly stepping onto my mat with a sincere intention to explore my yoga practice and allow for spontaneous creativity to arise, my offering as a teacher will be dry and lack integration. I still longed for that reciprocal gift of teaching and to be a part of a spiritual community. So, I chose to lean on the wise advice from my teacher and follow my own heart's pull instead.

"Practice what you enjoy, teach what you practice."
—Behnje Masson

The truth was, ever since I returned from Maui, I had been contemplating leading a Ram Dass meetup. Although I regularly practiced hatha yoga to keep my body in good working order, my favorite practices were kirtan (chanting), self-study, contemplation, and dharma talks. And since this was what I practiced, this was what I desired to teach. I had gone as far as joining the ambassador group on social media and downloading some toolkits they offered for hosts, but it wasn't until the studio closed that I finally mustered the courage to go for it.

I created an online event invitation and shared it on my social media platforms. I held the gathering in my living room on a Sunday afternoon. Six people attended, including a childhood friend of mine, a couple of my yoga students, and a few new faces, too. After we all introduced ourselves and settled in, I led us in a brief yoga stretch followed by a guided meditation. We then listened to a Ram Dass lecture for which I had already prepared some follow-up inquiry questions. We engaged in a thoughtful conversation after the talk and concluded with a Krishna Das chant and a potluck.

The entire experience was so enlivening! There was a sacred authenticity and vulnerability to our conversation, even though no one knew each other well. Personal truths were willingly and lovingly shared for the benefit of the group, and everyone seemed to walk away from the Satsang a bit lighter and more open.

Despite that cherished first gathering, my confidence was not yet strong enough to keep it going. I could sense a natural pull to go inward for the coming winter months and the final trimester of my pregnancy. It was enough for me, for now, to know that it could be done and that there were others ready and willing to walk alongside me on this spiritual path.

The Grand Perfection (Completion) Of It All

It's interesting to me how in the West, we have culturally redefined our shared definition of perfection to something very Christian and "without sin" or pure. But if you were to contemplate that sterile, "all light, no dark" kind of perfection, you might begin to notice how this cannot be true. Without darkness, there can be no light. And without light, no darkness. We couldn't know "hot" without the contrast of "cold," nor what "up" is if we didn't sometimes experience "down."

It is through the experience of contrast that we come to understand extremes and reconcile them, experiencing the peacefulness of the totality, the grand perfection.

Forest fires, though disruptive and chaotic, turn the trees into ash, which nourishes the earth, creating a fertile space for new life to spring from. Fruit nourishes a pregnant woman's unborn child, who will be born, grow, and die, and whose corpse will feed the worms who will till and feed the soil for new fruit trees to feed new children. We have been trained to view birth and growth as perfection, and decay and death as failure/error/disgusting. And because we are zoomed in too close to see the much larger connections, cycles, and symbiosis, we cannot easily recognize that each part supports the whole. Indeed, far beyond these two simplified examples, an unfathomable play of interconnection and interdependence weaves together all threads in the tapestry of existence.

Completeness implies the inclusion of the totality of experience. It denies nothing; instead, it says, "Yes, and this too." This radical acceptance of our direct, felt experience is *The Big Yes* from which all wisdom flows. As there is smoke in the fire, there will always be some pain in the growth. The inflammation is the catalyst for healing. And without it, we remain trapped in a state of dull ache with scar tissue building up around the wounds we are too afraid to heal.

If we were all to wait until we're fully pure and without shadow to do our sacred work in life, the world and all its inhabitants would suffer and perish. We are invited to accept the reality that there will always be light *and* darkness, joy *and* sorrow, love *and* grief, peace *and* discord so long as we are on this plane of consciousness. And when we accept the truth of that, and we keep showing up anyway, quantum shifts occur.

> "I form the light, and create darkness: I make peace, and create evil: I the Lord do all these things."
> —Isaiah 45:7

11

Boundaries, Proximity, and Standing Alone

A friend once shared a joke about the fundamental difference between Democrats and Republicans: Republicans are primarily concerned about the well-being of their immediate families at the exclusion of the rest of the world, while Democrats are primarily concerned about the well-being of the rest of the world at the exclusion of their immediate families. While an obviously satirical oversimplification of the vast spectrum of values and political ideology in our country, I couldn't help but relate to it a little when I considered a particular family member's and my own political views.

If there is one aspect of my personality that this person seems most frustrated by, it's in the arena of politics. I don't think either of us prefers to be categorized as Democrat or Republican, yet we each maintain some strong opinions that tend to heap us into one group over the other. And although during this time his modus operandi was to speak the same litany of talking points in hopes that I'd have a coming-to-Trump moment, there was a time during the Obama administration when we tried to have a sincere dialogue to better understand our differing viewpoints.

Our country was in the midst of the "War on Terror" in Afghanistan and Iraq, and thanks to heavy propaganda and racism, Islamophobia was deeply embedded in certain cultural subgroups of the U.S. This family member and I agreed to meet at a local sports bar to have a "meeting of the minds" over a beer or two. As was common, he dominated the conversation, seeming to believe that maybe if he explained things to me *one more time*, I would come to my senses and agree with him. But when he started to explain how the "war" could be won if we, as a country, simply bombed any country that posed a threat to us, I could no longer tolerate his paranoid rhetoric.

"I need to stop you there," I interjected. "Being the biggest bully on the block will never bring peace, and we need to understand this. Let me give you an example: Suppose you lived on a cul-de-sac in one of those subdivisions with a homeowner's association, and there are ten families in total. Now imagine that one of the families is really different from everyone else; a totally different religious and ethnic background, different culture, different language… and this difference makes another family feel unsafe," I said.

I continued, "So in response to their unsubstantiated fear, this family manages to convince the other eight families that to keep everyone else safe, the mysterious, 'strange' family needs to be murdered. And since everyone else is now convinced of the danger this family poses, they go along with the plan."

"Except once the family in question is murdered, the eight families who acquiesced to the paranoid family now know what this dominant family is capable of. And in response, one of the eight families now decides that the ninth family, the one who suggested murder in the first place, needs to die too, for the remaining eight to be safe. Now, there's a slippery slope forming. Each time the once-united families witness how easy it is for the others to turn on each other, the paranoia takes deeper root, and someone else becomes a potential enemy that must be vanquished. And so it goes, each group of families turning on the others, until only two families, and then one, remain," I said, hoping he'd understand this analogy.

I added, "In this context, it's easy to see how a tiny seed of fear can grow into an unwieldy, highly contagious paranoia that consumes everyone's thoughts and diminishes our capacity for connection, which ironically, is what leads to actual—versus imagined—safety."

As I finished my story, a smile spread across his face. And with more condescension than tenderness, he said, "Jeni, I see what you're saying, but it's an oversimplification. We need a strong military so that everyone knows what we're capable of and they won't dare to start a fight with us."

My heart dropped; what I had thought would be an "aha!" moment for him was not. He didn't have the ears to hear what I was saying, so it didn't matter what I said or how I said it. He was afraid, and more than anything, he wanted himself and his family to be safe. His fear occluded from his vision the many billions of other human beings who also longed for safety, resources, and peace. And my frustration and impatience with his viewpoint provoked a self-righteousness in my young mind that made it tantalizing to concern myself with the billions of faceless others while utterly disregarding the sincere albeit misinformed dread that existed within the human being sitting in front of me.

> "It is always the case that both victim and perpetrator suffer the consequences of any acts of violence, oppression, or brutality. For what you do to others, you do to yourself... There is only one perpetrator of evil on the planet: human unconsciousness."
>
> —Eckhart Tolle, *A New Earth*

Alas, there must be another way. Because it is not so different if you were to imagine the entire world as that neighborhood. If the internet, all the wars, COVID-19, and climate change have taught us anything, it's that what happens over there does not stay over there. And in this precarious time during which we are living, it is critically important that we don't allow ourselves to be lured by paranoia. The only way for us to survive and ultimately thrive will be found by identifying our common humanity and striving toward deep compassion mixed with firm boundaries over what is moral and humane.

Hindsight Wisdom

Be wary of any belief that creates a sense of separateness, of Us versus Them. Truly, your eyes have never seen another individual who is not part of your family. That statement might taste metallic to you, and perhaps even fill you with outrage or defensiveness. That's okay. There are people in my family with whom I fundamentally disagree and therefore have had to create a strong boundary regarding what I will and will not accept. Yet, when I rest in the space in my heart where it's all One, I can recognize that same space inside of them, underneath all the armor and pain. I can feel a connection of warmth, love, and compassion for them while maintaining a firm stance against their outward behaviors. Reject the behavior, not the being.

As the Indian poet Kabir once said, "Do what you do with another human being, but never put anyone out of your heart." I once heard that a therapist added to this: "You might put them out of your life but never put them out of your heart."

Death, Birth, and COVID-19

Ram Dass died on the Winter Solstice, December 22, 2019. We were in Florida visiting my mother when it happened. I was eight months pregnant, and we spent Christmas together. When I heard the news, I wept quietly and briefly, and then I practiced yoga, meditated, and took a special bath offered to me by my mother. Warmth and tenderness saturated my being as I realized this meant that his essence was now everywhere, no longer limited to time and space. I was also overcome with profound gratitude for the Grace to have met him only twelve months prior.

We welcomed our *son*shine, Quauhtli, into the world a little over two months later on February 27th. Paulo's childhood friend, and now my sister-friend and doula, Élan, was a hero for me that day. She showed up at our door equipped with hot and cold compresses, a birthing ball, hand massagers, and support materials, and she applied counter pressure to my sacrum through every single contraction from the moment she arrived until I was preparing to push. Élan offered words of encouragement and essential oil massage, and she helped me find different positions to help progress my labor.

Hindsight Wisdom

It's amazing to me that before I was pregnant with Quauhtli, I didn't even really understand what a doula did. Now I feel very strongly that every birthing person deserves to have a doula's support and wisdom to guide them through pregnancy, labor, delivery, and even through the postpartum period.

As I had planned throughout my pregnancy, Quauhtli's birth was attended to by a midwife instead of an obstetrician, and I labored and delivered without an epidural. With my yoga, pranayama, and meditation practices, I felt confident that I could meet the experience of childbirth with the necessary strength. It was important to me to do this as a way of honoring my maternal ancestors and all the birthing people before me who were taught to trust the awesome strength and capacity of their bodies to create and birth life.

I was determined to reclaim my autonomy as a birthing woman this time. I would demand that my consent be honored for any and every intervention for me and my baby. I refused to be checked for dilation upon arrival, and I did not allow my water to be broken until there was evidence of meconium in my amniotic fluid. A large part of Élan's role as my doula was to be my advocate if and when any medical professionals were talking over me and to ensure that my birth plan was followed whenever possible.

Because I wasn't hooked up to an IV, I had the freedom to stand, walk, squat, and use a birthing ball to help me work through each increasingly painful contraction. Alyssa called my phone at one point, but I was too deep in the process to be able to hold a conversation. She talked to Paulo, asking if she should come to the hospital. Had I been able to speak on it, I would've told her no because it was so intense. But by Grace, my sister instead let Paulo know that she was on her way to help however she could.

By the time Alyssa got to the hospital, I was lying naked in the bathtub while Élan directed a warm water jet to my lower back. I had one leg draped over the side of the tub and both arms wrapped around a waterproof pillow. The lights were off as various Sanskrit chants reverberated from my portable speaker against the walls. I was moaning in pain with each wave of contraction. Alyssa immediately kneeled by my side, grabbed my hand, and spoke love into me. It was so sweet, and I was instantly grateful to have her there.

Paulo, Élan, and Alyssa were amazing supports as I growled, swayed, and squatted my way through almost seven more hours of contractions. At one point, I was kneeling naked on the L-shaped maternity bed, facing the wall, practically crawling up the bed with every contraction. I glanced over at the computer screen, and noticing how long it had been, a deeper voice arose from within me: "Jeni, you're bracing against the pain. If you do not move toward it soon, Quauhtli may become distressed, and you will need an emergency C-section. It's time to do what you're here to do."

At that same moment, my midwife came into the room and, looking into my eyes, tenderly said, "I know you think that lying on your back will be too painful, but if you will try, I think we might be able to deliver him now."

I silently nodded as Élan and Paulo helped me shift to my back. With each of them holding a leg, I began to bear down and growl with the ferocity of a wild animal. Feeling his head crown was intense, and I was about to make another massive push when my midwife's eyes locked onto mine as she said, "WAIT." It took everything in me to heed her command. And as soon as she said, "NOW," something happened that my words will surely fall short of describing.

In that moment, who I thought I was on that bed went offline. My consciousness was instantaneously transported to what I can only explain as velvety black darkness with shimmering lights. It felt as if I were in outer space. And in that timeless moment of utter nothingness, deep from within my body, I could feel the length of my son's body easily slide through my vagina. Painless, exquisite, inexplicable peace spread all over my being.

And no sooner did I have that sensation than my awareness came back into my body, my eyes taking in the scene before me. I was completely dazed as they placed Quauhtli on my chest. My mind couldn't quite register what was happening, and as I looked over to Paulo, I read in his eyes that this was cause for concern.

I heard someone comment that I was still bleeding heavily, and my midwife told me that they were going to need to give me an IV bag of Pitocin to help my blood start clotting. Thankfully, it did the trick, and no infusions or other treatments were needed. But now that I was handled, I realized that my baby was in the corner of the room being suctioned repeatedly, as many people began gathering around him.

I pushed Quauhtli into the world in only ten minutes, which meant that he didn't get a strong enough chest compression on the way out to remove all the amniotic fluid from his lungs. He screamed upon exiting, but had a wet kind of wheeze that gave the NICU team pause. I found out later they had been bedside for his birth due to the meconium present in my waters. The team immediately put him on a CPAP as they cleaned him up. After thirty-five minutes of sucking fluid out, they were starting to think he might need to go to the NICU.

With a stern mother lion voice, I said, "Quauhtli! Do you want to stay with your mother, or do you want to go with them? You better clear those lungs!"

Within minutes, he made a dramatic recovery; so much so that the NICU team laughed and said, "Well I guess he wanted to prove us wrong!" He was strong and ready to be in his new world.

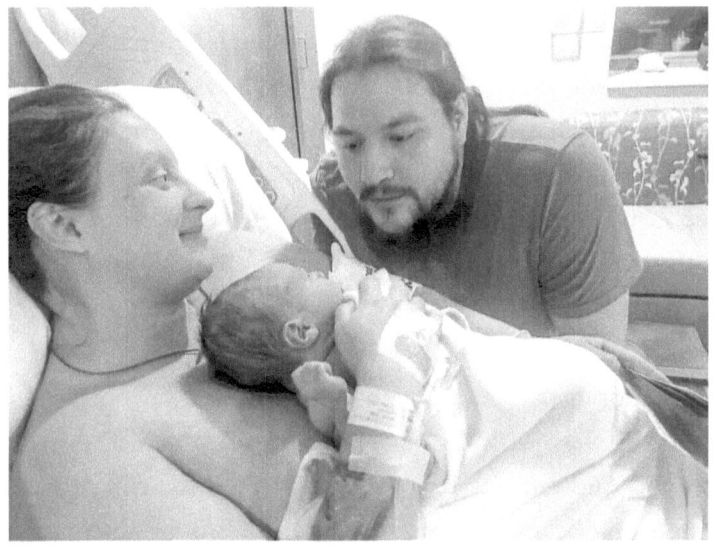

Quauhtli's birth

The first week was a wild ride. Paulo stayed home to care for the girls and me. It was so lovely to be together, just the five of us. Everyone would pile into bed with the baby and me after school and linger into the evening. I didn't leave my bedroom cocoon and upstairs bathroom for the first five days. I hardly even dressed myself, either; between nursing and pumping, there was no point in wearing a shirt, and with hemorrhoids and a giant pad, I lived in the mesh underwear for a few days before transitioning back to my own.

Thankfully, when my midwife had urgently instructed me to WAIT, it was so she could slide the last lip of my cervix out of the way before I pushed Quauhtli's shoulders through. I managed to need no stitches, and my postpartum healing was infinitely easier than it was with the girls, thanks to the body awareness I was able to maintain during my labor and delivery. Even so, I was in an utter daze that first week, marathon nursing all night and hardly getting more than ninety minutes of sleep at a time.

My mom came into town from Florida to help us when Paulo had to go back to work the second week after Quauhtli was born. While she understandably wanted to be present for his birth, she respected my request for space by agreeing to wait until after we had a week to adjust before visiting. She assured me that she'd be there for me, however I needed her. For that whole second week, my mom took the girls to and from school, cooked endlessly, and shopped many days in a row, making sure that we would be fully stocked before she left to go back home.

I cannot dismiss how deeply appreciative I was of her help at that time. The way she kept our house running and clean and fed was heroic. And yet, I can't help but wonder if I would have received a purer form of generosity and support from my friend circle if she were not emitting such a strong "Grannie time only" vibe. As we have done so many visits since her return from England, she and I trod the ground around each other lightly, ever conscious of the potential for emotionally triggering one another, along with the explosive reactivity that would inevitably follow.

I was weepy, hormonal, and exhausted, and I felt very much that this little baby and my body were still one; our moves and facial expressions mirrored each other, even twitching simultaneously at times. It was very hard to let anyone else hold him—even Paulo! But

I had a feeling that all my mom wanted was to sprinkle a little love on us and snuggle her grandbaby, so I did my best to hold my tongue and give some space while she was here.

Little did we know that her fifth day here, Friday, March 13th, would be a day that changed everything. It became the end of the school year as we knew it for all the children in Michigan and in many other states and countries across the world due to the spread of a novel virus, COVID-19. First popping up in China in October 2019, it made its way to the United States by January but was completely downplayed by then-President Trump until March, when everything across the country began locking down.

We didn't know how the virus was transmitted, how to properly treat it, or how to safely conduct business without risking our lives. Panic, paranoia, and medical system/economic collapse unfolded daily. A shelter-in-place order meant that all non-essential businesses were to shutter their doors, and we were all told to stay at least six feet away from anyone not in our immediate household. Unemployment spiked as millions of people were laid off, and thousands of people were dying as many went without food, the support of family, and medical care.

With the emergence of COVID-19, everything "normal" got flipped upside-down. It exposed massive disparities between white and non-white communities concerning appropriate and accessible medical care, remote employment opportunities, internet access, and quality of education. It illuminated fragile and illogical global supply chain systems, and it disproportionately affected countries already overwhelmed by poverty, political corruption, terrorism, and the climate crisis. The inflammation of white nationalism sparked an unprecedented number of hate crimes against Asian-Americans, and addiction, abuse, and suicide rates dramatically increased.

I don't have to tell you how the rest played out. Unless it's the year 2120, you probably lived through the pandemic, too. It was a worldwide traumatic event that immediately revealed all the weaknesses of our so-called modern society. The murders of Ahmaud Arbery at the hands of white vigilantes in February 2020, of Breonna Taylor by police as she lay asleep in bed in March 2020, and of George Floyd at the hands of Minneapolis police officers in May 2020 poured gasoline on the dumpster fire of coronavirus. The summer was filled with protests all across the world, with people declaring that Black lives matter and demanding an immediate end to state-sanctioned violence in all forms against people of the global majority.

The Juarez Family Does Homeschool

For years, the girls asked me to homeschool them, but I always responded that I wasn't qualified—not patient enough, not smart enough, not organized enough, not enough, not enough... But deep in my heart was a yearning to explore the possibilities of having sovereignty over my children's education. I would dream about a curriculum that included emotional intelligence and resilience, mindfulness and yoga, more outdoor time, creative arts, in-depth conversations around challenging topics, antiracist education, and wisdom teachings.

My interest in exploring a new educational model was first piqued after reading *Autobiography of a Yogi* by Paramahansa Yogananda. He spoke of the schools he built, fashioned around a yogic lifestyle and practical life skills, and I thought, "Wow! What a different world it would be if all of our children were being taught like this." But it still wasn't enough to make me want to pull them from their well-loved school, couched in the familiar traditions of an outdated system.

However, with so many unknowns surrounding the coronavirus, I was struggling to imagine sending the girls back to in-person school. While the case numbers had largely been controlled and even slightly decreased over that first summer, I worried that once cold and flu season hit, all bets would be off. I knew that there would be a slew of new hygiene and sanitization standards to follow at school; a confusing hybrid in-person/online schedule, mandated masks, frequent contact surface sanitizing, no physical contact between friends, no sharing supplies or food, no sports, no assemblies, no field trips, no parent volunteers... The teachers really had an uphill battle to make the school environment lighthearted and joyful.

I talked with Paulo and some of my mom-friends all summer long about my concerns and my dreams of a new framework for education. My mind vacillated between the girls' need for social connection and their need for tenderness and grounding during this highly destabilizing and traumatic time. While many children rely on our school system to provide them with meals, structure, security, and social-emotional support, my kids had the benefit of a parent at home who could offer all of those things while facilitating homeschooling. They didn't struggle with learning disabilities, food insecurity, or an abusive home. I didn't want them to increase the risk of transmission to children who depended on the services that the school offered as much as I didn't want my own children to face the stressors of the new mandates. And so, the conversations around homeschooling started to become more realistic.

Thankfully, a friend of mine who had been homeschooling for years shared some resources with me. I began my research into Michigan's education laws and contemplated our options. But it wasn't until twelve hours before the first day of school that I wrote an email to the school administrators expressing my intent to formally withdraw Elaina and Nolani from the school. What a scary moment! I felt both exhilarated by the possibilities ahead and grief-stricken by the letting go of the friends, teachers, and routines my girls had grown accustomed to.

The first several weeks were very interesting when I looked at them all together. Many nights ended with one or more of us experiencing an angry outburst, tears, or utter confusion, and sometimes all of the above in the same evening. Trying to balance homeschooling, caring for Quauhtli, and doing my job felt clunky and heavy. I had to change my priority list so many times, continually letting go of ideas, plans, and expectations. My priority list was short:

- Family/House
- School
- Work

Acknowledging this, I realized that all of those things took place in the same space, and more importantly, I wasn't on the list. It was a signal to me that I was operating in default mode. The increase in stress had brought me back to autopilot, because that's my home base.

And although it was familiar to feel like I was running all day long but getting nowhere, having more on my to-do list than I could possibly accomplish, it was also deeply uncomfortable. Actually, it was agonizing. I didn't like snapping at the people I love. I didn't like having to remember to breathe because I was holding my breath so much. I didn't like feeling achy and sore because I was too enthralled with my endless thought stream to take a few moments to be with the felt sense of my body.

But breakthroughs of consciousness can come in the most unexpected ways. And this particular one came because there was a work project that I was totally procrastinating on. It got to the point that I had no choice but to work through several weekends to get it done on time. And while I was holed up in my office for hours, I came across a note from a few months back: Elaina's list of preferred electives for seventh grade.

My heart sank. This was supposed to be the year that Elaina got to start exploring her own interests; that she could break away from the rigid class subject structure she'd come to know over the past several years. And here I was, leaning on my trusty, old standby: Perfectionism.

I had created a tight schedule of four different online classes, only augmented with some early morning reading, a leisurely lunch, a shorter day, and a sprinkling of art. We were already getting into a rut five weeks in. No wonder I was feeling snappy, tired, and overwhelmed. I was disconnected from what was happening in the moment because I was living in my head all day long.

It was in that recognition that my intuitive voice spoke to me: There is no right way. Only *our* way. This is our freedom—our freedom to create the kind of learning adventure that we want. Nowhere does it say how many chapters we need to complete or at what pace; only that we are *learning* and engaging. There is room for electives. Room for creativity. Room for exploration. I set the pace, and I create the map. The destination is a mystery, but the journey can be whatever we can imagine.

I let the girls know that starting the following Monday, we would cut our workload to two activities per subject, and after lunch, we would incorporate different materials. This included trips to the library, collaging, painting, and other expressions of art, conversations around fierce compassion and fighting oppression, baking, letter-writing, trips to the lakeshore, and cuddling on the couch while watching documentaries about social and racial justice, ancient and recent history, politics, and current events.

What I witnessed in my daughters over the remainder of the school year was nothing short of miraculous. First, the slower pace and spaciousness invited them to cultivate some self-care practices. They attended to their bodies and minds in more compassionate ways, such as healthy meals, personal hygiene, special baths, and journaling. Being in such a transitional season of their lives as preteens, it felt auspicious that they'd have this extra space for self-care and self-inquiry.

They also discovered what kinds of creative expression they were each drawn to. Nolani endeavored to add color to her world by painting light switch plates, tables, and anything else that could stand a little brightening. She discovered a love of aesthetics, and so she worked to create a peaceful environment in her bedroom where she could practice nail art designs, hairstyles, and skincare routines. Nolani expanded her cooking and baking skills with new techniques and experimented with food plating and food art.

Elaina pulled out her old sketchbooks and committed many hours to honing her drawing skills. The results were astounding! We all watched with awe as her skills expanded and sharpened dramatically in such a short time. She is truly a gifted artist, and it has brought her so much joy to get lost in the flow of her creation.

This time of recalibration also allowed their love of reading to blossom. No longer forced to read the required titles, Elaina and Nolani were free to let their interests and curiosities guide their book choices. They naturally gravitated toward diverse authors and challenging themes, which spurred many interesting and intellectually complex conversations among the three of us. Bearing witness to their explosion of awareness, confidence, and expression by far overshadowed the grief and sorrow that this time conjured for me.

You see, I had imagined during my pregnancy that Quauhtli and I would have an abundance of one-on-one time together spent playing at museums and parks, libraries, and play dates. Instead, he got to experience waking up to his older siblings each day with ample time at home to establish reliable, supportive routines of eating, playing, and sleeping according to his inner clock. I had imagined weekly visits from friends and family eager to get their baby fix, but instead, we spent Quauhtli's first year largely alone, except for blessed visits from my sister Alyssa and her daughter Lillian who was born five months after Quauhtli.

Life is sometimes like a hurricane. I feel like I'm blowing around, grasping for stability, and finding none. And then Grace steps in, flips on the light switch, and reminds me to practice; to find my inner groundedness, the only place I can ever truly stand.

I waste so much time and energy *thinking* I can't do something, only to discover that it takes much less time and energy to simply *do it*, even if I can't do it perfectly. And with humility and self-compassion, I accept that I'm learning as I go and no step on the path is ever wasted.

I still don't know if I made the best choice with homeschooling. But it's the choice that we made, and I'm grateful to have had the resources, ability, and courage to make it. I know that every family has tough decisions to make every day, global pandemic or not. And my heart aches for those who seem to have no freedom of choice when things already feel so out of control. We are all doing the best we can at any given moment. And through Grace, may our children be better off when all is said and done.

Reclaiming My Power

As I continued to curate a vigorous and expansive curriculum for my daughters' school year, I decided to take advantage of the synchronicity of it also being a presidential election year. Together we learned about and discussed our rights and duties as citizens, the theoretical basis for and actual structure of our democratic government, and the processes of pursuing candidacy and conducting free and fair elections.

In addition to their online civics and social studies course, we watched and reflected on documentaries like *All In: the Fight for Democracy*, about Stacey Abrams and the history of voter suppression in the U.S., *Knock Down the House* on Alexandra Ocasio Cortez, Cori Bush, Amy Vilela, and Paula Jean Swearengin and their 2018 grassroots campaigns for the House of Representatives, and *RBG* on Ruth Bader Ginsberg and her pivotal role in securing women's rights as a lawyer and Supreme Court Justice. A year later, I learned that non-binary Black lawyer, activist, and poet Pauli Murray was a powerful influence on Ruth Bader Ginsberg's passion for women's rights. Unfortunately, their powerful contributions and sacrifices have gone largely unrecognized, as is all too common for Black, Indigenous, and women of color, and especially those who are also queer or gender-nonconforming. There is a great documentary about them as well, called *My Name is Pauli Murray*.

We also learned about the major political parties of the United States and their platforms, and we took the opportunity to create a mock ballot, research the candidates and proposals for 2020, and "vote" our choices to see if they'd win in real life.

Of course, after enduring four years of increased political polarization under the Trump presidency, I was not naive to how important and intense the 2020 election cycle would be. Out of morbid curiosity, I would occasionally watch competing news channels (Think CNN vs. FOX) only to be startled by almost comically alternative versions of the same story. Never before had I encountered such demonstrable evidence that we each live in our own version of reality. How we each view the world is almost entirely dependent on intersecting variables such as age, class, race, gender, sexuality, religion, culture, ethnicity, familial history and political affiliation, education, geographic location, life experiences, and more.

With all the division, I couldn't help but feel like I was supposed to "pick a side" among the many conflicting viewpoints, but it became increasingly difficult to know where to stand. As the co-occurring pandemics of coronavirus and politically motivated disinformation raged on, nearly everyone began boxing themselves and each other into either/or categories of right/wrong, righteous/evil, smart/naive, and so on. But it doesn't take much contemplation to realize that we each tend to hold certain people and certain professions as more trustworthy and therefore a more reliable source of truth. A major challenge in this digital age is that I can conveniently find whatever "evidence" I need to reinforce my personal biases and make me "right," and then I simply need to place the opposition in the "wrong" category.

It was and continues to be painful to witness all the vain attempts at psychological reductionism. As humans, we long for things to be clean, clear, and simple. We want to reduce everything to "It's all because of X" or "If we'd only do Y." But that's not how life *is*. Life is full of complexities and paradoxes, whether that makes us comfortable or not.

Even at what seemed to be the height of controversy during Trump's first presidency (which, to my mind was the assault on the nation's capitol on January 6, 2021), I found myself reluctant to succumb to a politically driven Us vs. Them mentality. Although it seemed so appealing to belong to the group judging and hating Trump and all his supporters, it also felt untrue to lay blame for all that is wrong in this world at his feet. To be sure, he is a poignant archetypal embodiment of our collective shadow. He brings to light many of the darkest aspects of society and us that we'd rather not reckon with but must for our survival as a species. Clearly, there are plenty of folks disconnected enough from their hearts that they're willing to accept his narrative that a violent reckoning is the only way forward.

When we took a road trip up north a few months later to get a much-needed change of scenery, I considered why so many of those northern Michigan houses still had their Trump 2020 flags flying in their front yards. Perhaps the pandemic and the ensuing shutdowns devastated their livelihoods and their sense of self. Many had been separated from loved ones in nursing homes or other care facilities, and entire ways of living were abruptly changed with little support.

The world was changing, and they didn't like what they saw. And although they certainly weren't the only affected demographic, nor perhaps the most affected, their pain was no less valid. Businesses closed, homes abandoned, loved ones lost... These families were suffering and looking for two things: someone to blame and someone to save them. And as a brilliantly manipulative businessman, Trump knew all the right things to say to activate this wide swath of traumatized humans.

There would be times that I'd talk to friends about what was happening and I would share that I was practicing sending Metta (loving-kindness) to Donald Trump. I wished for him to be happy and at peace so he would stop feeling compelled to violence and subjugation. Without exception, I was met with looks of shock and sometimes horror and disgust as well. I was astounded to observe folks I'd generally consider intelligent, compassionate, and non-violent become so deeply entrenched in their political identities that they were at risk of becoming that which they were vilifying. It reminded me of the *Hunger Games* trilogy in which the working class militarized itself to overthrow a violent dictator, only to nearly replace the reviled president with an equally corrupt, power-hungry leader.

> "Peacemaking doesn't mean passivity. It is the act of interrupting injustice without mirroring injustice, the act of disarming evil without destroying the evildoer, the act of finding a third way that is neither fight nor flight but the careful, arduous pursuit of reconciliation and justice. It is about a revolution of love that is big enough to set both the oppressed and the oppressors free."
>
> —Enuma Okoro, Shane Claiborne, and Jonathan Wilson-Hartgrove, "Common Prayer: A Liturgy for Ordinary Radicals"

I found myself explaining to them that if only he would approach the podium and apologize with great humility and sincerity for all the ways that he's caused harm, that I would forgive him *if* the apology were paired with authentic penitence, restorative justice, and a dramatic shift in behavior. I realize that someone like Trump is unlikely to ever do such a thing, but isn't that what we all want? The space and safety to admit our faults and misdeeds without fear of shame and retribution? To be given a fresh chance to do better, be better, and show up differently in the world?

If I want that for myself, if I want people to stop packaging and labeling me as who they think I am, then I must be prepared to give that same spaciousness of love and compassion to those whom I would so readily box up. But let me be abundantly clear: unconditional love does not equal unconditional tolerance. And just because I have the capacity to forgive does not mean someone else has unbridled freedom to act in heinous, barbaric ways.

Shifting Perspectives, Shifting Relationships

We were a full year into the ongoing crisis of COVID-19, so out of necessity, I had gained a certain measure of comfort and confidence in expressing my boundaries and saying "No" as a complete sentence. I was letting go of my people-pleaser tendencies and rebuilding a trusting relationship with my body's signs and signals of discomfort. When friends and family wanted to visit unmasked, I mustered the courage to let them know that if they wanted to come into our house, they had to wear a mask. When I received an invitation to a large gathering, I realized that I had the right to graciously decline. This groundwork and space allowed me the opportunity to reclaim my sovereignty and my right to decide which relationships I wanted to invest my time and energy into.

"You are the company you keep, so keep good company."
—Douglas Brooks

I began to notice how some of my relationships with friends and family members were quite one-sided. While I was always ready and eager to show up and offer support when my people were experiencing challenges or hardship, many were conspicuously absent when the tables were turned. There was little to no reciprocity. I also realized that while I was steeped in my journey of self-discovery and healing, many others were not ready or wanting to self-reflect, learn, and grow. If I were to challenge their opinions or perspectives, I was met with defensiveness, circular arguments, and drama. It's not that I expected them to be anything other than who they were. It's that I understood that I had choices to make.

By continually pouring into relationships that were no longer aligned with who I was or where I wanted to go in life, I was exhausting myself. I was easily sucked in to other people's narratives and finding it difficult to maintain the habit changes I had worked so hard to establish. There was no possibility of gathering and redirecting my attention and passion toward something creative if I was going to let myself become drained in this way. I needed to enact boundaries for my own well-being.

And while my mind and heart (and my therapist) affirmed that enacting these boundaries was a wise decision, it was jarring and painful to watch some of my oldest connections begin to crumble under the weight of sincere, healthy conflict. Decades-long relationships quietly ended as I stopped saying yes when I meant no and pouring into people who did not match my energy.

Hindsight Wisdom

When we grow up learning to be people pleasers, we can struggle to learn how to set boundaries in our relationships as adults. And if we do, we tend to swing from one extreme to the other. In my own experience, my boundaries went from non-existent to harsh. I became intolerant toward anyone who didn't share the same viewpoints or values as me instead of being curious about why they saw life the way they did. I burned a lot of bridges before finding the middle way of calmly articulating boundaries and following through with them without hostility.

"The only people who get upset about you setting boundaries are the ones who were benefiting from you having none."

—unknown

It was becoming clear that while many of my friendships had been rooted in common traumas, shared history, or mutual leisure activities, it was time to create and cultivate friendships that were instead rooted in common goals, shared values, and mutual respect. Thankfully, I already had many such friendships, and now I began appreciating them much, much more. Where I hit my next wall, however, was when it came to assessing the level of common goals, shared values, and mutual respect concerning my parents and extended family.

Around this time, I had a very vulnerable conversation with my brother-in-law about traumatic childhood experiences and how they have shaped how we relate to our parents as adults. We talked about the paradox of being able to recognize unhealthy relationship patterns in our parents and family members now that we're older and also being subconsciously impacted by the continued emotional and mental abuse despite our awareness of it.

In other words, just because I can see that their reckless speech and behavior have a root cause in their own childhood traumas—and seeing that, I feel compassion for them—does not mean that I'm immune to the damaging effects of manipulation, passive aggression, judgment, and criticisms. I can use my brain to try to think my way out of having hurt feelings, but the wound from feeling abandoned, abused, and emotionally neglected is so deep that no amount of cognition is going to heal what hurts me *to my bones.*

Hearing my brother-in-law talk about his sense of familial loyalty and responsibility to help those who won't help themselves, the painfully obvious realization hit me: when we let ourselves believe that we have to engage continually with people who hurt us—emotionally, psychologically, sexually, or physically—in essence we have decided that we don't deserve to live our lives. We willingly throw away our dreams, our goals, our values, and our self-respect because we have somehow decided that another person's life is more important than our own.

I immediately recognized the scalable wisdom from this microcosmic relationship: When I think of my own children, I think about how my function as their parent needs to grow and change as they grow and change. They won't need me in the same way at twenty-one or thirty-five as they did at three or eleven. And even though this seems pretty obvious, there are a whole lot of parents out there trying to punish and reward, criticize and praise their adult children into becoming the version of "child" they always wished their children would have been, instead of loving and appreciating them exactly how they *are* right *now.*

When I call my adult children someday in the future, I don't want them to send me directly to voicemail or block me on social media out of a need to protect themselves psychologically. *I want them to want to talk to me!* Hell, maybe they even want to call *me* first! I want to be invited occasionally to come drink coffee and chat, go out to lunch, or watch a movie with them. Maybe my parents wish for that with me, too. But because they're so over-identified with their *roles* as "parents," they've missed the part where their *function* needed to change as I became an adult. They've also failed to realize that we are never done growing up, that we each have a responsibility to stretch ourselves continually to be and do better as we age.

As I was speaking with my brother-in-law, all of this awareness flooded into my brain simultaneously. I looked him dead in the eye and said, "Brother, I want my kids to want me in their lives when they become adults. And that means I need to be the kind of person that they want to be around—authentic, considerate, and loving. I need to respect their boundaries, their opinions, and their right to express themselves and pursue their passions regardless of my feelings about it. I need to be trustworthy and compassionate without enabling them or throwing my own life away in favor of theirs. I need to uplift, support, and encourage them, taking a sincere interest in what brings them joy. In other words, I have choices to make, and those choices will determine whether or not I'm worthy of having a relationship with them. And those choices are my responsibility alone."

Speaking this out loud, it was as if an opaque curtain was temporarily lifted from my inner gaze. I could see that my parents also had these same choices; that even if they were *unconsciously* trampling my personal boundaries, disrespecting and talking down to me, or manipulating and guilt-tripping me, they had the capacity to notice and acknowledge their harmful behaviors and work to show up in a different way, if it mattered enough to them to do it. When I finally had the awareness, language, and courage to tell them that they were hurting me, if they still chose not to reflect upon this new information, then that was a clear indication that protecting their ego was more important to them than healing our relationship.

Make no mistake: realizing how we've caused harm and suffering for the people we love is a painful blow to our ego. When someone we care about tells us that we've hurt them, we generally have one of two responses: "No I didn't" or "I didn't mean to." Sometimes people will deflect responsibility so much that they'll throw it back on the person who's calling them out: "You're being too sensitive," "You're attacking me," or "You do it, too." Shame is quite possibly one of the most uncomfortable human emotions. We don't even like talking about it passively.

But again, if something matters enough to us, then we will do whatever it takes to make things right. We'll even wade through the stinky tarpit of shame to notice our behavior patterns and the effects they have on the people whom we care about most. I say this with authority because it's exactly what I've had to do. I continue to peel back layers of grief, shame, and trauma, excavating the scar tissue and taking tender care to heal the deep, infected wounds that continue to influence my current relationships negatively. I'm cleaning out and tending these wounds so they can heal properly this time.

It's ugly, hard, painful work and it'll probably take the rest of my life. But the potential reward of healing this attachment trauma and rebuilding my self-respect is exhilarating to imagine: a life filled with relationships rooted in mutual respect, authenticity, vulnerability, trust, and compassion; a life in which love and generosity are freely given and gratefully received.

We all have such capacity for growth and change, if only we value curiosity and learning over being "right." We can't make other people be how we *think* they should be, and we shouldn't want to. Who are we to decide that? But we *can* decide how much time and energy we want to invest in any particular relationship. We can own our personal power and our human capacity to evolve so that others can see and imagine the possibility for themselves. We always have a choice.

Hindsight Wisdom

Maybe this resonates with you and the work you've been doing, too. Or maybe this is all new and uncomfortable. To get a better reading of where you presently are with this work, here are some questions to contemplate:

- Do you have any relationships (parents, relatives, lovers, friends, colleagues, children) that drain your energy and ruin your mood?
- Are you in relationships with people who make you feel bad about yourself, who envy your success, who lie to you, publicly shame you, or reinforce an old version of "you" that no longer exists?
- If yes, why? Is it because you have a common history, common trauma, or common interests? Do you believe that you can say or do something that will change them?
- Are you obligated to maintain this relationship?
- Are you speaking your truth when someone hurts you? Why or why not?

These are hard questions to ask, but as you begin to notice how you've subconsciously given certain people permission to abuse you, you can begin to revoke that permission and instead establish appropriate boundaries that respect your intrinsic worth, dignity, and rights.

"We must be the change we wish to see in the world."
—Mahatma Gandhi

It used to be that I'd say my parents had to die before I could write this book. As it turns out, that was true. The storyline in my head of who *I thought* my mom and dad were, including their personalities and roles, had to die. I ultimately had no choice but to let go of my mental construct of who they were to see the perfection of who *they are* and free us all from our mental imprisonment.

As long as I was clinging to my beliefs that they—or anyone else—were the gatekeepers of my power, my resources, and my self-expression, I would be trapped in a small, helpless, voiceless version of myself. And the All that lives within me could no longer tolerate being held back; the time had come to break free.

Permission to Take Up Space

Despite the progress I had made over the years with learning about holistic health and taking kind care of myself, there was still a shadow of self-rejection that loomed over my thoughts. I will never forget the moment that my heart cracked open in despair over my deeply rooted body hatred.

I had been concealing from Paulo an ingrown hair on my belly roll above my pubic area, which had become quite irritated and painful. It was in an area that, as a fat woman, was not so easy for me to see and attend to; I needed his help. This wasn't *the* moment; after eighteen years and three children together, I was slightly embarrassed but still comfortable asking him to help me tend to the wound.

What broke me was how, once the wound had been attended to, I couldn't bring myself to let it air out by wearing my form-fitting yoga pants underneath my belly. There I was, sitting in the comfort of my own living room, among the four people who love me and make me feel the safest, and the tyranny of fat phobia was preventing me from seeking relief from my pain. The thought that was looping in my head was: "No one should have to be subjected to the sight of my disgusting body." And although this cruel, shadowy mantra has been running low-key on repeat in the background of my mind for my *entire life*, this time, I *heard* it, and my heart shattered.

A voice arose from a deeper space inside me, softly whispering: *"Sweetheart, why do you speak to yourself in such a way? This is your home! This is your family! You deserve to be in comfort. This self-hatred is abuse and it's not true."*

This recognition of such a long-standing storyline (that had been passed on to me from others who had been likewise programmed) made room for a new layer of understanding to emerge. While I had abandoned my efforts to lose weight for the sake of conditional self-acceptance, I had yet to do any work toward unconditionally *loving* my body.

As had happened so many times before, Grace came to me in the form of a book. I was wandering around the bookstore with my daughters one afternoon when we were feeling particularly restless from social distancing. As I scanned the shelves of the self-transformation section, my eyes landed on a book with an exquisite photo of a Black, fat, bald, *radiantly beautiful* woman on the cover, entirely naked save for some strategically placed flowers, framed by multi-colored butterfly wings, and crowned by a sunflower. The title was *The Body is Not an Apology*, and the image was of the author, Ms. Sonya Renee Taylor. I snagged it excitedly and purchased it along with a couple of books for the girls.

Despite my initial enthusiasm, I avoided reading the book for a few weeks. When I finally did crack it open to read the dedication poem, I burst into tears. In it, Sonya describes the fat, cake batter-like belly of her momma and how much she delighted in kneading her tiny hands into her belly as a child; how she longed for the familiarity of that belly after her mother's death. I cried and cried, moaning between sobs, grieving for my unsatiated longing to feel such a depth of awe and honoring of my own belly.

It took time for me to work my way through that revolutionary book, but it initiated a healing process for which I will forever be grateful. There was a pivotal moment when, while sitting in the backyard and soaking in the warmth of the springtime sun, I abruptly stopped reading, flipped to the back cover, and wrote in yellow highlighter the following:

Can I ask you a question?

Do I belong to you? No.

Do I owe you something? No.

Okay. Then stop treating me as if I do.

I still don't know who this elusive "you" was that I addressed. Perhaps my parents? Perhaps society as a whole? But the clarity resulting from the questions and answers was profound. I am not property; my body does not belong to anyone but myself. I do not owe thinness or attractiveness to anyone. It's not my job to make other people comfortable with my body by adhering to beauty culture's ridiculous standards. This was the moment that I, too, decided to stop apologizing for my body.

When Paulo came home from work that afternoon, he joined me in the backyard. "From now on, I give myself permission to take up space," I excitedly declared to him.

Confused by my cryptic statement, he tentatively responded, "Okay…"

"What I mean is, I'm not apologizing for my body and the space it takes up anymore. I'm not going to dress according to some misogynistic, fat-phobic rules anymore. When the weather turns hot, I'm going to wear shorts and tank tops. I don't care if my stretch marks, fat rolls, or veins disgust other people. I don't care that there will be people body-shaming me for wearing a bathing suit at the beach. I don't care if my back fat hangs over my bra or my belly bulges over my pants when I sit down. I declare my right to exist."

"I deserve to dress weather-appropriate," I continued. "I deserve to feel comfortable in my skin and to be freed from shame. I deserve to be fully embodied and to radically love myself, to love myself to my *root*."

As I made this declaration, the confusion melted away from Paulo's face and was replaced with a look of affection mixed with pride. "Good. That's how it should be."

He hugged me close, and I felt such a release of contracted energy. Freedom. Space. Sovereignty. It was as if I had unbound myself from the invisible shackles of toxic beauty culture with a key that had always been in my back pocket, simply waiting to be used.

This didn't mean that I was going to forever abandon my efforts toward optimal health and physical fitness. What it *did* mean was that my motivation would never again be to achieve the impossible, oppressive beauty standards of a society ruled by white supremacist, heteropatriarchal norms. If I wanted to get my nails, hair, and makeup done, great! If I didn't, great! The scale doesn't rule my life, and neither does the billion-dollar beauty industry. The way I choose to show up in my body is my choice and mine alone.

Having let go of that futile fight, I now had access to liberated time and energy that could be directed and focused on much more important things, like dismantling those systems of power that had kept me imprisoned within my own body for so much of my life. I vowed to myself that I would commit to this work for the benefit of the countless others who remain trapped in an endless cycle of self-flagellation. To create a society rooted in radical self-love, compassion, and justice, we need all hands on deck.

Photo of me wearing a bikini at the beach for the first time in my entire life at age 38

12

Coming Home to Myself

This naturally originating inner radiance, uncreated from the very beginning,

> *Is the parentless child of awareness—how amazing!*
>
> *It is the naturally originating pristine cognition, uncreated by anyone—how amazing!*
>
> *[This radiant awareness] has never been born and will never die— how amazing!*
>
> *Though manifestly radiant, it lacks an [extraneous] perceiver— how amazing!*
>
> *Though it has roamed throughout cyclic existence, it does not degenerate—how amazing!*
>
> *Though it has seen Buddhahood itself, it does not improve—how amazing!*
>
> *Though it is present in everyone, it remains unrecognized—how amazing!*
>
> *Still, one hopes for some attainment other than this— how amazing!*
>
> *Though it is present within oneself, one continues to seek it elsewhere—how amazing!*
>
> —Excerpt from the *Tibetan Book of the Dead*

Freedom of Path, Necessity of Practice

Back when I was periodically doing rounds of Whole30, friends would ask why I kept coming back to it. I'd explain to them that each time I engaged my willpower in service of my well-being, I would not only learn something deeper about myself, but I would become stronger and more resilient when in high-stress or painful seasons of life, when I was most likely to turn to food for comfort. I came up with a little story that I'd share as an analogy:

It's as if I have been walking this same circular path all my life, following the rhythm of trigger-behavior-reward-shame-repeat, until my faithful feet began to dig a trench in the ground. I was on this continual circuit, and the more I walked it, the deeper the trench got. Eventually, I had dug down so far that I was trapped in it, or so I thought.

Committing sincerely to eating only whole foods for thirty days was, for me, the equivalent of someone sending me down a ladder so I could finally climb out. Once out, my self-discipline was like dirt that I was tossing into the trench as I walked along the perimeter. However, eventually I would get bored or distracted or significantly overwhelmed, and I would trip back into the trench, once again following the well-worn path.

Except this time, the trench wasn't as deep, thanks to the little bit of fresh dirt I'd tossed in, and I still had the ladder. I would begin again by climbing out and continuing to fill the trench slowly with dirt as I walked the perimeter. Over time, the fruits of my fervent consistency became more visible: the trench was now more like a modest dip in the ground. I would occasionally trip and fall back into the sunken path, but this time I could simply step back out onto the ground whenever I chose to.

The well-trodden path was still there, but I now had the resources I needed to recover. While I would inevitably go through periods of depression, grief, and anxiousness, I wouldn't go down as deeply or for as long. Over time, I let go of Whole30 as a practice because I understood that until I attended to the root cause of my using food as a coping strategy, there would be subtle harm incurred by being overly strict with my eating.

Still, I consider my experience with Whole30 to be a beneficial sadhana. I turned to the program when I was most in despair over my health, and it demanded that I really dig in and commit myself completely to what I set out to do. Similarly, my yoga practice came to me when I was in great mental, emotional, and spiritual despair. That deep ache, mixed with inarticulable longing, propelled me into a resoluteness to learn, practice, learn more, and practice more.

Hindsight Wisdom

It seems that yoga and mindfulness as practices have all but lost their meanings nowadays, thanks to the watered-down, capitalism- and aesthetic-driven value systems of the West. For those who even have the resources and luxury of time to attend classes, yoga and mindfulness tend to be framed more as self-soothing, exercise, or performance enhancement, with many teachers using the practice as a way to bolster their egos.

But truly, these are scientific systems that have been in use for over 5,000 years as methods for learning about oneself and living one's life in the most peaceful, skillful way possible. They reside in a space that I have always been delighted to occupy: the space where science meets spirit. These practices are meant to challenge us to uncover the answers to the questions that have echoed throughout the halls of human evolution: Who am I? Why am I here? What is it that I *really* want?

Anything done with *ekāgratā,* or one-pointed concentration, can become a practice. It might lead to an end result or be entirely purposeless. But initially, the point is to strengthen our muscles of attention. Some other examples might include:

- Gardening
- Knitting
- Reading
- Cooking
- Cleaning
- Creating art
- Braiding, beading, or weaving
- Walking
- Singing
- Playing an instrument

What makes an action mindful is the quality of attention. In Zen Buddhism, it is taught that when one is eating, one should simply eat; when one is walking, one should simply walk; when one is washing the dishes, one should simply wash the dishes. This teaching contains an important kernel of wisdom: do what you are doing fully, for the sake of doing it, and not "in order to…"

We might be washing the dishes hurriedly while thinking about what we'll do next. Or we might eat while watching TV or scrolling on our phones, completely detached from the sight, smell, texture, and taste of our food. Notice how easily the mind wanders like a toddler or a puppy.

The practice is to respond to this natural occurrence of wandering mind with the same gentleness as we might use with redirecting the toddler or training the puppy, kindly bringing the mind back to what is being done in the here and now, with patience and compassion.

Once we've strengthened our capacity for attention a bit, it's wise to add a layer of practice devoted to *tapasya,* or purification by heat/friction. What I mean by purification is an intentional engagement with a system of living that clears away or transforms habits of mind and body that prevent us from progressing in our sadhana. It's much like the ancient goldsmith who subjects the impure ore to intensely high heat until the gold is liquified and the impurities rise to the surface to be skimmed off. Once the goldsmith can see her reflection perfectly, she knows the gold has been purified.

Whole30 was tapasya for me. So was yoga teacher training, therapy, and even writing this book. If you feel called to bring curiosity to your own automatic patterns and work with them, there are multiple systems available depending on your resonance. This could include psychotherapy, body-based therapies like EMDR, or the yamas and niyamas of the Ashtanga school of Yoga. Or perhaps you feel drawn to the precepts of Taoism and of Buddhism or to the core values of Christ. Your ancestral culture may have a traditional system, or you could create your own. This is an important part of the practice because it builds self-discipline and refines our habitual tendencies so they're more aligned with our highest aspirations.

For this reason, I have found it highly beneficial to have a teacher, therapist, or spiritual guide. In my personal experience, and I'm pretty sure the data would back me up on this, humans do not typically make sincere commitments to habit change unless they *must*. It's often a despair-filled, do-or-die vulnerability that compels us to turn toward our longing for unfathomable love and wholeness. As we already know, no one is coming to save us and no one can do the work *for* us; if we wish for our lives to change, we must allow life to change us.

A teacher helps us remain steadfast, humble, and heart-centered even as we access deeper reserves of strength, courage, and wisdom. Practice is not always enjoyable; in fact, there were many times that I had to push through impulses to skip a class because I was tired, lazy, or wanted to do something else. But because I had invested money and intention into it, I showed up anyway. And I never—*not once*—regretted going to class. The fruit of my self-discipline was always greater freedom in my body/mind.

When we disregard this important aspect of sadhana, we do ourselves a great disservice. It becomes much easier to succumb to spiritual materialism, fluttering about from experience to experience without fully integrating the teachings. Or worse, we jump ahead to advanced practices without setting the foundation properly and we risk creating more harm than benefit in the world because of our arrogance. It's best to move from a space of humility and curiosity, striving to maintain a beginner's mind regardless of the progress we make.

> "In the beginner's mind there are many possibilities, but in the expert's, there are few."
> —Shunryu Suzuki, Zen Master

While this process of refinement is never-ending, we do eventually reach a point where it requires less effort. Our practice begins to shift from method to goal. Whereas at first, we commit to sitting in meditation, practicing yoga, reading sacred texts, praying, attending therapy, volunteering, or whatever our formal sadhana is, over time, our practice becomes our haven. It becomes a form of sanctuary, a cave in our spiritual heart that we can take refuge in, regardless of what we're up against in life.

It used to be that silence terrified me, but now I yearn for it. The opportunities that I find to settle back into the breath and give myself over fully to my experience are more precious than any material object I could obtain.

As we engage in self-discipline to cultivate what my teacher's teacher describes as a strong body, clear mind, and open heart, spiritual practice also becomes a form of exaltation or celebration. Our sadhana then manifests as spontaneous creativity and joy. Behnje would often communicate this as boundaries leading to freedom. We gather our *shakti*, our creative energy, into the core of our being until it can't help but extend out in all directions as an exquisite expression of *shri*, or auspicious splendor.

If you wonder how this can be true, consider how a pianist commits to practice until the music flows naturally from their fingertips. Or how a dancer faithfully attends classes, exercises, and cares for their body in a way that allows them to glide across the floor with such elegance and poise. Self-discipline, when done with sincerity and compassion, leads us inexorably to freedom.

But what kind of freedom? I'm not suggesting that if you work hard enough, you can become perfect, never make another mistake, and never fall into autopilot again. I hate to break it to us, but that's not real life.

While I may still fall into self-defeating habits of behavior or thought from time to time, I'm no longer imprisoned by them, either. I can see them now, and their roots, and I love myself anyway. I know that when I'm afraid of change, it's my ego that's doing the talking. My soul is wild and free, capable of meeting any moment with skill and wisdom. Through a dynamic balance of self-effort and surrender to Grace, my eyes have been opened to an infinite number of winding paths that have always been available to me, even though I did not know it.

My lineage is love. My practice is life. My path is limitless.

My Imaginal Friend

Ram Dass explains the method of the guru (*guru kripa*) in his book, *Polishing the Mirror*: "[It] is the particular form of bhakti yoga that focuses on the guru and on the guru's blessings or grace (kripa). Most of the time I'm just hanging out with my guru, even though he's no longer in the body. The thoughts and remembrances of him come up a thousand times a day. I may be sitting with someone, and they turn into my guru—over and over again... The essence of a relationship with the guru or spiritual teacher is love. The guru awakens incredible love in us, then uses that love to help us out of the illusion of duality." (Dass, 2014, pg. 22)

I know that "guru" is quite a loaded word in the West, but in Eastern religious philosophy, guru is the remover of darkness or ignorance (in Sanskrit, *gu* is darkness and *ru* is light). The guru is a perfect mirror in that the guru shows us where we're not, where we are still attached or confused, and in this way guides us back to our Source.

Hindsight Wisdom

This "illusion of duality" points to the incomplete knowledge of our interconnection and interdependence. Quantum physics demonstrates the truth of this non-distinction in that all matter is composed of an indestructible primordial energy that vibrates and coheres in accordance with natural law to create what we understand as objects. Although we are made of the same material, albeit in infinitely unique and ever-changing formations, we continually separate ourselves from everything "not us" in a subject/object relationship. This fundamental misunderstanding and imagined separation are the cause of much, if not all, of our suffering.

Following the *upaya* or "skillful means" of guru kripa has been a natural and delightful unfolding for me. Considering that Maharajji died before I was born, my experience of him as an embodiment or avatar of Love has come through the wisdom teachings of his *chelas* or devotees and the retelling of their stories of being with Maharajji. My connection to the guru also comes from the study and contemplation of other great beings and saints, including Christ and Buddha, and their teachings. Although I've never met him in the body, he is still a very real energy in my life, offering encouragement and guidance from dimensions beyond this one.

I honor Maharajji's teaching of "Love Everyone, Serve Everyone, Remember God" by embodying Hanuman's servant heart and devotion to Rām. Hanuman and Rām are beings from the Hindu tradition who are so irrevocably connected that you cannot talk about one without the other. Their story is beautifully illustrated in the Indian epic *Ramayana*. To love everyone, I practice seeing all human beings, animals, and nature itself as embodiments of the Divine. When I look into the eyes of another being or creature, I see God. While I am a meat-eater, I strive to source my meat from conscious farmers, and I give thanks to the animals and plants who sacrifice their own life force to sustain mine. When I become unreasonably frustrated or incensed by another person, I work to interrupt my self-righteousness by viewing it as teaching from God to let go of my attachments.

To serve everyone, I practice service (karma yoga) to God in the form of the world whenever and however I can, within the realistic limitations of my capacity. This has often been in the form of preparing food for friends, family, and those who are ill or struggling emotionally. Because our financial resources have always been limited, I have at times felt impotent or that I am not doing *enough*. That pervasive not-good-enoughness is a difficult belief to rewrite! But then I remind myself of Mother Teresa's wise encouragement: "Not all of us can do great things, but we can do small things with great love."

To remember God, I do my practices. Maharajji is believed to be a reincarnation of Hanuman, and he taught that *"Ram naam karne se sab pura ho jata hai"* (from continually repeating the names of God, everything is accomplished). I practice japa with my mala (prayer beads), and I chant and sing prayers, including the Hanuman Chalisa, a 40-verse prayer in praise of Hanuman. I savor moments of deep presence within nature by appreciating, even for a moment, the exquisite phenomena of plants growing and decaying, insects toiling, birds flying, clouds floating across the sky, and any other subtle miracles my senses perceive. I remember God by opening my heart to the immense, ecstatic love that flows between me and my children and my Beloved. There are moments in which I steal a glance of their precious essence, and my heart swells with bliss so much that I weep.

For me, guru kripa is a way of living that sees all experiences as teachings, blessings, or both. It's a way of living that sees each expression of life, whether a person, plant, creature, or otherwise, as Love in form. The inner dialogues I have with Maharajji and the Divine Mother are a beautiful interplay of my imagination and my direct experience. Although I use archetypal figures as a point of focus in my practice, I understand that I'm actually praying to the deepest part of myself, to my own soul, which is connected to the Soul of the World.

While I accept the teacher in all forms, and I am particularly drawn to certain teachers and methods over others, I do not submit to the authority of those teachers; I defer to it. I am grateful for this teaching from Professor Douglas Brooks who taught to, "defer, but do not submit" to those who appear to have more credentials or qualifications in a particular matter than you. I don't deify human beings, as all human beings possess fallibility and shadow. Through my own experiences, I have concluded that there is a razor-sharp edge between honoring the boundless wisdom that emerges from the soul of a being and the very problematic, unwise, and downright violent behaviors that can come forth from the bounded, ego-driven aspect of that same being.

A true guru—a *Sat Guru*—does not need a body to do their work. To paraphrase Ram Dass, if you're going to follow the path of the guru, a dead one is a great guru to have. There is no fear-mongering propaganda or anyone demanding any money or actions out of me. No one is manipulating my neuroses as a method for controlling me, making me afraid to be curious or making me feel guilty for questioning the status quo. These are real risks that arise from following self-proclaimed gurus in this day and age.

Instead, I am continually reminded of Ram Dass's guidance that if any spiritual path or method is truly successful, it eventually self-destructs. We do not practice yoga to become perfect yogis, nor do we meditate to become expert meditators. Likewise, the guru is a method to go beyond the guru; at a certain point, the devotee and the Beloved merge to become One.

> "The Guru is both 'external' and 'internal.' From the 'exterior' he gives a push to the mind to turn inward; from the 'interior' he pulls the mind towards the Self and helps in the quieting of the mind. That is Guru's grace. There is no difference between God, Guru and the Self."
>
> —Sri Ramana Maharshi

And through this framework, each moment becomes consecrated; sacred and meaningful. Nothing is by accident, and nothing goes to waste. Truth becomes immediately understood as paradox: that we are each both/and; unique and the same; individual and collective; form and formless. I come to understand that I am both an important character with unique gifts to offer in the play of humanity, and I am but a flicker of a point of energy within time and space; another wave in the ocean who believes they are separate when they only exist as a momentary expression of an infinitely larger source.

Self-Forgiveness and Self-Responsibility

Throughout my entire journey toward self-realization thus far, there have been many difficult pills to swallow: I see in others what exists within myself; everything on this plane of consciousness exists in polarity (duality); life lessons are recursive until we learn them; the true cause of suffering is our straining; and we are the only ones capable of removing our suffering. However, the toughest pill for me to swallow thus far has been that I am not responsible for what I did when I wasn't self-aware, but now that I *am* self-aware, I'm responsible for what I do from now on.

What this means is that a part of my healing journey is to *forgive myself* for the horrible things I did, said, thought, or let happen when I was numbed out, self-absorbed, and afraid for my safety. And secondly, I must make it a priority to pay attention to my **full experience**—including myself in a much larger perspective—and *take personal responsibility* for my intentions, attitudes, and actions from now on.

My inner knowing has been watching all along, but I wasn't tuned into that channel; I was too focused on being the doer-of-all-the-things. And from that first-person point of view, I am a victim of my life, and I am reluctant to acknowledge the ways in which I harm others. But as I hone my sensitivity and my attention, I am better able to access the inner observer, giving me a more accurate, less defensive or self-protective understanding of what's going on within and around me. This naturally leads to greater integrity and moral uprightness, because I now call *myself* out on my bullshit.

On the surface, this might seem logical enough, but scratching right beneath the surface reveals much more complexity than that, especially when brought into a larger context: Other people are also not responsible for what *they* do before *they* are self-aware. YUCK. That kind of pill is the large one without the gel coating that tastes like a mix between baking soda and Vitamin C tablets. Why? Because it takes away the source of my self-righteous indignation and resentment of "The Other."

Because as I go deeper and deeper into that contemplation, I realize that they are not all that different from me, except *maybe* I am a little more down the path of evolution than they are. But not by much! It really wasn't that long ago that I was judgmental, callous, condescending, sarcastic, and petty. And that's putting it mildly; add in manipulative, self-serving, racist, homophobic, xenophobic, gossiping, and <fill in the blank>.

It's much easier to practice this compassionate forgiveness with my children, close friends, strangers, and people in the outer rings of my social circles. It gets quite a bit harder with my spouse, siblings, and extended family. And it feels nearly impossible at times with my parents. Why? Because they were my fundamental connection to this earth; the ones whom I most needed to attune to. But their own childhood wounds prevented them from connecting with me.

This is the oldest and deepest wound in my heart—the first separation, which initiated the second: my separation from myself. Since I am now fiercely committed to my own peace and wholeness for the sake of everyone else's peace and wholeness, I choose to walk directly into the fire of the greatest challenge.

Hindsight Wisdom

I am instantly humbled when I consider how often I would engage in or be a bystander to gossip as a primary form of bonding and of entertainment among friends. I see now that it was a projection of my own self-rejection, a feeble attempt to make myself superior by categorizing others as inferior. It is self-protective and small-minded to avoid discussing oneself by speaking instead about the shortcomings of others. We are all invited to discover vulnerability as a superpower that heals hidden wounds and reconnects us to ourselves and each other.

"For what is laid down first in the incarnation is the last to go in the spiritual journey, for it is the deepest."

—Ram Dass

Coming to a place where I could forgive and unconditionally love my parents demanded that I first acknowledge the pain that this insecure *attachment* wound had caused me. Attachment Theory (first published by psychoanalytic writer John Bowlby in the 1950s and furthered by Mary Ainsworth and others) seeks to understand and explain the connection between early childhood attachment to primary and secondary caregivers and mental/physical/social health later on in adolescence and adulthood. I needed to see and validate my own grief, and developing the courage to do so took a while. This compassionate *being with* my grief is a cyclical process that I know will take time. It is not a one-and-done kind of healing; it's heavy lifting, but it's unbelievably rewarding.

Allowing my heart to become tender has also strengthened it. From this perspective, I appreciate that my parents have always been *the perfect parents for me.* They loved, supported, challenged, and hurt me in all the most perfect ways to help me along my life path, and for that I am deeply grateful to them.

The deeper truth of forgiveness is that it is a gift we give ourselves. It is permission to release the burden we've carried as a result of the injuries we've experienced. What we often fail to realize is that a refusal to forgive—or at least energetically release ourselves from—those who've harmed us does not have any impact on the perpetrators. They're not losing sleep over our hurt feelings (especially because, in some instances, they are unaware of our hurt feelings in the first place). And in holding this contracted feeling toward them in our bodies, we become "stuck" in a way that limits our access to our confidence and power.

By separating the being from the behavior, we create the inner safety and space to offer forgiveness to the *being* while maintaining outer safety from the *behavior* through appropriate boundaries. This becomes a reclamation of our personal power because we *choose* if and when we're ready to forgive, and we *choose* to not be imprisoned by the storyline that casts us as "victim." Instead, we become a *survivor* and experience liberation from the experience as we integrate it into our wholeness.

It becomes clear to me over and over again through little signposts and symbols that I have been gently guided and redirected throughout my lifetime. It's as if some mysterious being or energy has patiently held my hand as I suffered and struggled and kicked and screamed, resisting the path my entire life, wanting to double down on my giant ego and my ability to FORCE life to be what I wanted it to be. Maintaining the false belief that, "If I work hard enough..."

But no, that's not how it was at all. I was simply learning lessons, some easier, some much more difficult and painful, but all were necessary keys slowly unlocking the most tender and powerful part of me: my unarmored heart. As I slowly burned away my karmic sludge, my habit energy, more of my true nature was being revealed—the playful, creative, joyous, kind, compassionate, wise essence of my Self—emerging from behind all the armor and storylines.

And while the transformations have occurred slowly and almost imperceptibly, when taken in from a distance, it's astounding to see how much my life and my beingness in the world has changed in the past decade and a half. It's now been fifteen years since my grandfather died, and so much has happened since then. It humbles me and brings tears to my eyes because I immediately apprehend that none of this was done *because of me*; I was not the Doer. This was done *through* me, just as soon and as often as I was able to *get out of the way* and *let Life happen.*

Integrity > Fitting In

The wise words of my many teachers string together like prayer beads, becoming more meaningful each time I contemplate them. My connection to the bigger energy through my experience of Divine Love has grown into this exquisite, wordless compendium of soulfulness and wisdom. My personal experiences with the world around me become the fabric of space in which my understandings roll around like raw gemstones, crashing into one another, smoothing out the rough edges. Instead of resisting or bracing against discomfort or conflict, I work to remain strong in my roots and flexible in my branches like that of a mighty yet humble willow tree.

Cultivating steady groundedness and spaciousness of mind, body, and heart creates the "set and setting" for sincere self-reflection, leading to an outward creative expression that serves all of humanity. We plunge into an endless energetic cycle of receiving and giving, which was never created and will never be destroyed. "Set and setting" is a term coined by Ram Dass and Timothy Leary back when, as Harvard professors, they did research on the use of psychedelics. "Set" refers to the mindset of the study participant and "setting" refers to the environment in which the study is conducted. Indigenous communities naturally honor the set and setting in their ceremonial use of plant medicine, taking great care to respect the plant and thank it for its medicine.

How do I cultivate grounded spaciousness? What practices, values, and attitudes help me feel embodied and present as well as open and curious? What false beliefs and unhelpful habits represent obstacles to this aim and need to be released? When I sat in contemplation of this inquiry, here's what came through for me:

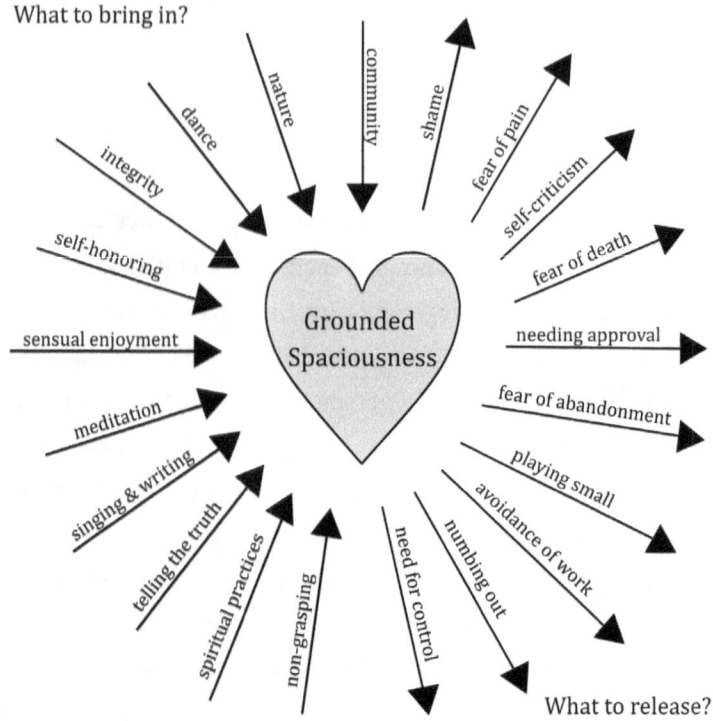

What to bring in?

community
nature
dance
integrity
self-honoring
sensual enjoyment
meditation
singing & writing
telling the truth
spiritual practices
non-grasping

Grounded
Spaciousness

shame
fear of pain
self-criticism
fear of death
needing approval
fear of abandonment
playing small
avoidance of work
numbing out
need for control

What to release?

Everyone has their unique way through this incarnation. I have a life path that belongs only to me. So although mine is entangled and interdependent upon everyone else's life path, I cannot live according to anyone's vision but my own.

A significant teaching I received from my relationship with my parents was to let go of my need for validation from others. Seeking external validation of my internal experience is pointless. My heart bears witness to my own journey. My story may be relative and incomplete, but it *is* valid. And it's mine to tell, should I choose to do so. Each of us has a story and a perspective that matters and deserves to be witnessed.

I've always said I was a born rebel, and yet I spent the majority of my young life trying to comply and fit in. Now I understand that

I was not created to fit in. My naturally rebellious behavior is not a defect; it is a counterbalance to an extreme expression of fear, greed, and desire for power. My aim is the middle way—to intentionally act against a delusional status quo in service of my highest aspirations. It is the path of the spiritual warrior, where living in integrity needs to matter more than fitting in.

"My commitment is to truth, not to consistency."

—Mahatma Gandhi

When I first deviated from my life plan by quitting my "big job," the way forward was full of uncertainty and aloneness. It was uncharted water, and I leaned heavily on my newly-rediscovered-but-quivery faith. Throughout that process, pockets of joy and connection and wonder began to make themselves known. I could see the exquisite beauty in the mundane and my life became so much richer. I contemplate death daily and hold life tenderly, with great appreciation. I understand now that the purpose of life is to live it, and it will only have meaning if I create it.

I still struggle. I overextend myself and get depressed. I take things personally and become resentful. I lose my inner groundedness and fall victim to my emotions, impulsively reacting in hurtful ways. I'm no less neurotic than I was before, and fear is an ever-present companion. However, what's different now is how I relate to myself. I see the precious child within me who is afraid and thinks she's never going to be enough. I hold her close to me, tenderly, and I tell her, "I know that you're afraid, and that's okay. But you're also very brave. And you've always been enough. You can do this."

No matter how many times I stumble, I can and will get back up and keep going. What else is there to do? Giving up is as much of a choice as persevering is. Just like you, I have a 100% success rate of overcoming every single thing that has ever tried to destroy me in this life. I choose daily to step into my creative power, and I invite you to do the same.

You might wonder why I'm focusing so much on courage and creative power. The reason is, in part, because my teachers have told me all along that the two highest purposes for practicing yoga are self-knowledge and creative expression; practice is about discovering who you truly are, including your unique gifts, talents, and abilities, and putting them to good use for the world around you. I've also been taught that creativity keeps us out of boredom and depression as much as it keeps us out of narcissism and nihilism. Creativity keeps us *moving*.

But it's more than that. Look around and you can take your pick of crises to get lost in: ecological collapse, human trafficking, pedophilia, governmental corruption, the rise of authoritarianism and fascism, runaway capitalism, cultural and ethnic genocide, homophobia, racism, and all the violence perpetuated by white supremacy and religious wars. There has, of course, never been a shortage of suffering. But if we spend all of our time and energy focusing on the suffering, exactly at what point do we begin to actively dissolve the old systems while simultaneously creating new systems in their place?

"When the crowded Vietnamese refugee boats met with storms or pirates, if everyone panicked all would be lost. But if even one person on the boat remained calm and centered, it was enough. It showed the way for everyone to survive."

—Vietnamese Buddhist master and
peace activist Thich Nhat Hanh

When we reclaim our authorship and our sovereignty, we recognize our inherent value; we're worthy of happiness and peace because we exist. We're all meant to find our way through the suffering to our contentment. We're allowed to dream big knowing that we can achieve those dreams because nothing is off limits when we believe in ourselves and show up for the work. The Divine Mother wants to see us succeed; She is always opening doors and lighting up pathways and whispering to us in our hearts, if we can get quiet enough to notice and brave enough to listen.

Reverse-Engineering Happiness

We spend so much time wanting to be happy, all the while believing that we don't deserve it. You might read that and think, "No! I really do want to be happy, and I deserve it!" Stay with me here ...

If you believed you deserved to be happy right now, in this moment and exactly as you are, then every choice you make moment-to-moment would be in service to your happiness. How long you choose to sleep, how you eat, how you move your body, what you do with your time, who you spend it with would all be in alignment with your highest potential for joy and peace of mind.

So, what gets in the way? There's a lot of complexity that goes into the "what," but the "why" is universal and straightforward: we think we don't deserve it.

The only person who has kept tally of every single kind, generous, selfish, cruel, heroic, malicious thing we've ever done or thought is us. Our minds have kept track and our inner judge is ruthless and unforgiving. We might not even recognize our inner judge's voice until we spend quite a bit of time meditating and self-reflecting, but I promise you, it's there. It might sound like your mom or dad, or maybe a boss or teacher... It might even sound like you, but it is *not* the real you. And it's what is getting in the way of you living your best life.

My teacher's teacher always told her, "Take a decades-long view," so let's pan back a moment. Imagine you are an eagle flying high above the timeline of your life, and you're reviewing everything that has happened from the moment of your conception to now. You see the good, the bad, and the ugly. The ebbs and flows of joyfulness, contentment, depression, and utter despair. Since we're so high above the timeline, let's also take advantage of the opportunity to see what lies ahead. Take a peek into your future through the lens of your imagination. If you were the author of your life, how old would you be when you die? What would you die from? What would your funeral be like? What would be your legacy? That is to say, what would people remember you for? What would be their final memories of you?

In the years right before your death, would you be in a relationship? If so, with whom? Where would you live and what would your house look like? What would your friends be like; do you recognize them from childhood or young adulthood, or are they new friends? Do you have children? What would your relationship to your children be? What would you do for a living and how much money would you make? What kind of foods would you eat, and what kind of health would you be in? What would you do for fun? What are your hobbies and favorite vacation spots?

As you reflect through these inquiries—and I hope you take at least a breath or two to sit with each of them separately—do you notice a theme of love, contentment, peace of mind, compassion, and wisdom? Or do you notice a theme of suffering, scarcity, disappointment, fear, and loneliness? How deep does your sense of "not-good-enoughness" go? If you find that it's more depressing than inspiring, walk around the room or step outside, shake it off, and try again. See if you can go through the series of inquiries and imagine the best possible end of your life, the best life you could ever dream of for yourself. Don't keep reading until you've done this…

Okay, welcome back.

Now that we have this eagle's vision of the end of our lives, let's begin to fly a little lower so we can see a slightly more detailed view. Let's begin the process of reverse engineering. Here's an example:

Suppose one of the details of the end of your life is that traveling around the world is one of your favorite hobbies, and your most enjoyed vacation spot is in another country. One of the places I've always wanted to visit is Greece. What would I need to do to make that a reality? Most of the time, people immediately say "time and money." That's true, but it's also vague. Let's go a little deeper. If I want to visit Greece, first I need a passport. To get a passport, I need to print off an application, complete it, return it and pay the fee, have my picture taken, and wait to receive it in the mail. After that, I need to research places in Greece that I would like to visit, where I would want to stay, how to get there through various flights, how much money I would need to have available for travel, lodging, food, and pleasure. I would need to save that amount of money diligently over a period of time, arrange the vacation time, book the lodging and flight, schedule a cat-sitter, pack my bags, and rideshare to the airport.

Suddenly, what seems so impossible—a lifelong dream trip to Greece—is now not only possible, but fairly straightforward to achieve. There's a series of logical, chronological steps to take, and BOOM: dream actualized.

But what if what I'm envisioning in my future is more complicated? What if I'm dreaming of still being married to Paulo and having a strong, loving relationship with my children, friends, and family? Again, it's about reverse engineering and breaking things down into the smallest steps. Being in strong, loving relationships with my husband, children, and other loved ones means remaining authentic, honest, compassionate, and committed to conflict resolution, healthy boundaries, and personal growth. Are there little things that I can do every day that will slowly walk me toward these ideals? Of course there are!

I can pray, meditate, take classes, read books, see a therapist, journal, and prioritize my closest relationships over relationships with acquaintances or strangers. There is no "one thing" that will guarantee a healthy, long-term relationship, but in observing ourselves and others, we can see that it requires persistence and fortitude. We have to keep showing up, keep trying again when we slip into unconscious behaviors, and keep remembering our "why."

Let's apply this to a desire for good health and physical independence at the end of our lives. What does that look like when we pan back to right now, in this moment? Well, I'll tell you what it *doesn't* look like: a violent, forceful changing of every unhealthy habit all at once, with an all-or-nothing attitude. *That* is a recipe for failure.

We have accumulated **so** many coping strategies from over-sleeping to overworking, from alcohol to drugs, from shopping to food, from sex to sports teams to exercise regimens, from numbing to paranoia to outrage, from unhealthy relationships to self-harming... Life is not without hardship, and we each have our "favorite" go-to's on how to cope. What we have in common, however, is that most of our coping strategies *do not work*, and they **definitely** *do not get us to where we want to go.*

So if we can't (and don't want to) violently rip away every unhealthy coping strategy we've ever accumulated, then what do we do? The first step is to keep doing them, but with awareness. It's only when we can observe our tendencies with non-judgmental curiosity that we can begin to notice what is triggering them and why, and what instead will serve our highest aspirations. This is a patience and compassion game; we can't rush it, we can't avoid it, and we can't hate it. It's only by unquestioning acceptance and compassion for ourselves as we are in this moment that we can begin to have a choice about where we are headed next and how.

It's about slow, steady, incremental shifts in habit energy. You pan out to check in with your decades-long view, then you zoom back in to the next breath and the next choice. It's holding both views simultaneously so that you can ask yourself moment-to-moment, "Is this life-enhancing? Or life-diminishing?" This is one of the highest pieces of wisdom my teacher Behnje ever offered me. It's no longer about good vs. bad or right vs. wrong; it's a straightforward question of, is this leading me toward my dreams or away from them?

Some examples of self-sabotage:

- I don't have the time or energy to work out, but I have time for happy hour and binge-watching TV
- I don't know how to cook healthy food, but I can learn how to use my new phone
- I have too much going on in my life right now, but I'll have time later (Will you? Will life ever stop offering challenges?)
- I can't afford to take vacations, but I can afford a bottle of wine and eating out once or twice a week
- I'm not smart enough to learn a new skill, but I was able to learn my job responsibilities when I was first hired
- I don't have room in my week for getting together with my spouse or friends, but I have a few hours to comment back-and-forth with them on social media

Listen, I'm not saying you can snap your fingers and make your life perfect tomorrow. And I'm not saying it's a walk in the park to rewrite decades of habits and coping strategies; most of us are contending with complex developmental trauma on top of generational trauma, and meanwhile, the world seems like a giant dumpster fire.

And yet, and yet... Would you rather spend every day of the rest of your life waking up, going to work, coming home to scroll social media, eat dinner, watch TV, go to bed, and repeat? Would you rather keep filling your life with useless material items that translate to more mess, more cleaning, more trips to the dump or thrift store? Would you rather connect with your community via memes online instead of fits of laughter and vulnerable conversation over a cup of tea or a nourishing meal? What are we really meant to be doing here?

Nowadays, you can take a high-quality course on pretty much any subject online, whenever you want to. You don't need to limit your learning to seven hours a day, Monday through Friday, and only until your eighteenth birthday. There is no rule that says you aren't allowed to pursue your interests on weekday evenings or on the weekend; how you spend your time is up to you.

And no matter how random and disparate your interests may seem, I promise you that nothing goes to waste. There are no mistakes on this path; everything informs a future becoming of you, whether you realize it or not. Even if you do something that you end up completely hating, at least now you know that that's not meant for you. It will amaze you when your talents and skills begin to coalesce with your attention and willpower. When this happens, even when you encounter inevitable challenges, your entire life will be infused with adventure and delight. All built by the power of indescribable Love.

Hindsight Wisdom

If you're already feeling pulled by your heart to certain desires, ask yourself, What is something I could do *today* that will guide me in the direction of these dreams? Is there a phrase or word, a business or organization I could look up? Do I know someone who knows someone in a job or company or place like this that I could reach out to? This becomes the guiding question for each day: *What is something I can do today that will guide me in the direction of these dreams?* Each baby step, each thought, each time you speak it out loud to a journal or a friend, you are drawing yourself nearer to the story of your dreams.

As Maharajji once said to Krishna Das, "Courage is a really big thing." We need to be brave with our lives, because we deserve to live curiously and creatively. Who knows? Maybe you'll become wildly successful, work at a pace that serves your health, and end up leading some powerful humanitarian effort that ends oppression or hunger. Maybe your art or creative expression saves someone's life or inspires them to follow their dreams. Maybe you'll end up living an intentionally simple life spent doing what you love with who you love every day until your last breath. Wouldn't you like to try? Sweetheart, you deserve it.

Repeat this practice of inquiry and imagination as often as you'd like and notice how what's important to you changes over time. This is the natural evolution of Life! Allow your path to wind over hillsides and down valleys, twisting and turning in a never-ending expression of love and celebration.

> "We only regret the chances we didn't take, the relationships we were afraid to have, and the decisions we waited too long to make."
>
> —Lewis Caroll

Generosity and Abundance Go Hand-in-Hand

If the idea of wishing yourself well still feels like an impossible task, perhaps it might be more accessible to begin with cultivating a generous spirit. How do we cultivate such a spirit? For me, the entry point was gratitude practice. And while I have come to use this practice regularly upon waking and at bedtime (and as often as I can remember throughout the day, too), my gratitude practice had a very sweet and memorable beginning.

Many years ago, my stepmom gave me a beautiful pink glass jar that closed with an oversized cork, along with a little tin box for Christmas. The tin box had a sticker on the lid with the word "Prayers" written in script. Inside was a stack of colorful slips of paper and a miniature pencil. The purpose was for me to write prayers or intentions on the paper, then fold them and place them in the jar. I *loved* this gift! I loved it so much that I created prayer jars for Elaina and Nolani and a couple of my nieces, too.

The prayer jar

As often as we could remember, the girls and I would retreat to the yoga room to jot down prayers, intentions, and acknowledgments of gratitude for the abundance in our lives. We decided to create a ritual on New Year's Eve during which we'd silently read and burn the slips of paper in a fire, releasing to the universe all that came to pass and all that did not. It was a tangible way of letting go of the previous year in order to make space for the year to come. And I was often delighted to note how many of my intentions had come to fruition.

Over time, however, I slowly stopped asking for situations to manifest in a particular way. It felt strange to ask the universe to unfold according to my absurdly limited perspective and fleeting desires. I mean, how do I know what's supposed to happen? I could sense the ego in it, and I noted the humor of my propitiating to God as though Grace is something that can be bought with good behavior, well-spoken prayers, or stylized ritual. So instead of wishing or hoping for what I didn't already have, I prayed that I might be content with my life exactly as it is. Eventually, my only prayer became "Thank you."

> "What I have is enough. What I am is enough. What I do is enough. "
>
> —Behnje Masson

What I discovered was that when I tap into a sense of gratitude and appreciation for the abundance that already exists in my life, a spontaneous desire to share arises. When fear makes me forget or minimize that abundance, however, it becomes all too easy to slip into a scarcity mindset. If I let myself believe that I am in perpetual lack and that everyone else is a threat to what little I *do* have, then I act from a space of fear, greed, and paranoia. From this mindset, I prioritize my own safety and comfort over that of anyone else's.

Because we have each been harmed by trauma, oppression, scarcity, and fear of death somewhere in our genetic and spiritual lineage, it is only natural that we cycle between generosity, greed, and everything in between. So, when we're discussing generosity, volunteerism, caregiving, philanthropy, and the like, it's important to self-reflect on two critical factors: the intent behind the offering and the bestower's current state of inner abundance.

"In considering generosity, ask where the purity is."

—Sharon Salzberg

The intent behind the offering provides us with information about the purity of the generosity. If we're giving something to someone out of obligation, coercion, or for our own benefit, then the offering is impure. While not at all uncommon, this impure transaction is energy-depleting. The subtle harm caused by giving or receiving "in order to" fractures our wholeness by way of diminishing authentic connection. When I speak of the bestower's state of inner abundance, I am referring to their willingness to access an abiding sense of gratitude and appreciation. I am speaking of a profound sense of inner stability, a weightiness of faith borne from personal experience which affirms that, no matter what is going on in the world, I am okay.

Carol taught me to practice being grateful for little things like breathing, or toilet paper, or coffee. By refining my gratitude to accommodate more subtle blessings, my mind becomes peaceful and the energy of grasping or fearing is freed up for other things.

Notably, as I have practiced tapping into this state of inner abundance, external abundance has begun to manifest as well. This is not to say that our family has amassed large sums of money or that we can make anything we want appear at the snap of a finger. Actually, we still live paycheck-to-paycheck as we always have, and we are not without a sizable amount of debt. And yet, we have never not been able to eat. We have always had clothes to wear, personal transportation, and at least one income within our household.

Not only have our basic needs been consistently met throughout our lifetimes, but also we've been lucky enough to travel, to purchase our own home, to take family vacations, and to buy Christmas and birthday gifts. These are luxuries that are not guaranteed to all people, and certainly not in the same context and manner, regardless of their work ethic. There are many folks who've hardly worked a day in their lives and yet they have access to copious resources, including quality education and medical care, safe housing, clean drinking water, nutritious food, clean air, community support, and, of course, gainful employment and money. However, there are many more folks who do not have access to those same life-giving resources despite having sacrificed to the very last drop of themselves.

I pray that you, the reader, will give some time to contemplate what I've said and what it brings up for you. If you are in safety, lean into any sensations or emotions that arise and consider how these insights might guide you in how you perceive and live your life. But before we move forward, I'd like to share two of the highest teachings I've received thus far with regard to generosity and abundance.

First is the understanding that all transactions are an exchange of energy. Whether that energy takes the form of time, money, services, or goods, it's all energy passing between parties. And it needs to keep *moving*. Fanatically accumulating and hoarding energy in the form of goods or money is no less unhealthy and stagnating than binge eating at every meal. While we each need to determine what "enough" looks like to us, I do believe we are each capable of discerning between enough and too much.

My personal practice is to intuitively share a portion each time I receive an abundance of energy. I call my practice of this reciprocity intuitive because I do not have a predetermined percentage to share, nor do I have a predetermined recipient in mind. I simply feel into the needs of those within my awareness, and trust where and how my heart is pulled. Sometimes I contribute money to a person or cause, sometimes a meal. Sometimes I share my resources with a company or organization whose work I believe in, or I give of my time and physical energy to a friend who is suffering. Part of my practice is to remain anonymous whenever possible and to refrain from the egoic desire to receive credit. In truth, I am perfectly okay with dissolving completely into anonymity. It's enough for me to plant seeds that I may never live to see bear fruit.

The second high teaching I'd like to pass on to you is with regard to spontaneous generosity. This is something I learned from meditation teacher Sharon Salzberg while at the Ram Dass retreat in Maui. During one of her dharma talks, she discussed this notion of trusting the clarity of the first instinct to give. Sharon challenged us to consider how, oftentimes, a spontaneous desire to give something is overshadowed by an almost immediate next thought of, "No! You can't give that away!" This second voice is typically the fear-focused ego that I mentioned before, the part of us that thinks we're deficient and living in scarcity. Sharon went on to encourage the balancing effect of discriminative discernment. "Don't give away your rent-controlled apartment in New York City," she teased. But outside of such obvious boundaries, if the thought arises to give something, simply do it and notice your experience. I have put her teachings into practice many times since that day, and I have yet to regret a single instance.

This unconditional, unrestrained generosity creates abundance in all directions. It becomes a joyful expression of an endless dance of moving energy. And each such exchange of energy fosters a love and connection that makes the whole web brighter and more exquisite.

> "In the practice of generosity, there is nothing too small and nothing too big. Don't let society's norms limit you. See what happens."
>
> —Sharon Salzberg

Having Compassion for Others' Journeys

As we become less self-focused, energetic boundaries become an important piece of the work we do within our interpersonal relationships. One of the insights I have gleaned from my practice is that, because I'm a deeply feeling person, I oftentimes get really uncomfortable when the people around me are uncomfortable. In other words, the boundary between their suffering and mine tends to be blurred unless I notice that the unpleasant emotions I'm feeling do not belong to me. So, when I'm on autopilot (which is like ninety-five percent of the day), I'm eager to "make the bad feelings go away" for them so that *I* can get back to feeling comfortable.

This is problematic for several reasons, including the fact that the world does not revolve around my personal level of comfort. And since I cannot truly know someone else's internal experience, why do I think that I know what's going to make it better? I have no mental grasp of the complexity of the circumstances, so what makes me think that I, alone, can magically solve someone else's problems? In fact, engaging in a situation with an intention to "rescue" someone from adversity might cause more harm than good by virtue of my actions containing a victim/savior value judgment.

What I'm saying might seem paradoxical at first; let me clarify that I'm not suggesting you merely smile and shrug your shoulders when you see that someone is having a hard time. What I'm saying is that "helping" someone else from a position of self-righteous superiority renders the action full of ego and is likely disconnected from the heart. It separates us from each other instead of bringing us together.

Hindsight Wisdom

If this line of reasoning feels confusing to you, let me offer an example. In 1231, the Church formally began an Inquisition into anyone accused of heresy, or holding a belief or opinion contrary to orthodox religious

(Catholic) doctrine. For over 500 years, in an effort to consolidate and maintain power over the peasants, church leaders united with the royal and military classes to suppress such freedom of thought by invading neighboring lands, burning books, destroying temples and artifacts, and torturing, imprisoning, and murdering anyone who threatened that consolidation of power. Once imprisoned or killed, the land and property of the accused were confiscated by the church.

While it was clearly a land-, money-, and power-grab by corrupt individuals holding the highest offices, the Inquisition was framed to everyone else as an attempt to save the souls of those who had strayed from God's Will. It was a supposedly compassionate attempt to force their confession, religious conversion, and therefore salvation from eternal damnation in hell. All under the guise of *saving* the peasants from their long-held and deeply personal spiritual beliefs.

When I simply start by listening, validating, and honoring another person's experience instead of jumping into "fixer mode," the energy of contraction that they're holding begins to soften. There is a wonderful quote by David Augsburger that says, "Being heard is so close to being loved that for the average person, they are almost indistinguishable."

Do not underestimate the power of being present with someone; by doing so, you become a container in which they might feel safe to explore their own experience. Safe space allows for the possibility of meaningful insights to surface naturally within this inner exploration. In other words, they discover intuitive answers to their own questions instead of relying on someone else for them. Ram Dass often joked about how one of the worst traps to arise out of our practices is our attempts to "do good." (See the last note for reference!)

The cosmic humor lies in the fact that we often are unaware of the underlying motives of stroking our egos or making ourselves more comfortable when we decide to "help." I notice that when I react to situations with indignation and reprehension, my rage becomes destructive in the most unhelpful of ways. I react with extreme defensiveness because my ego feels under attack.

And of course, there have been plenty of times I've reacted in the opposite way: by spiritually bypassing other people's suffering, taking no action to help, with the motivation of extricating myself from the pains of living. This underscores the cruciality of building our ability to tolerate and hold space for our own emotional responses. The space I aim to occupy is the here and now, where I can maintain both the doing and the being in a dynamic, balanced way, where I intuitively know when to act and when to rest.

There's so much confusion, anxiety, and rage bubbling up all around us that unless you're living under a rock, you or someone you love is having a really hard time at any given moment. It's normal to want to help—compassion is a natural attitude. Let's each take up the work required to be effective agents of compassion, including learning when to offer what my dear friend Meg refers to as "practical support" in the form of time, money, or effort, and when to offer a listening ear and a heartfelt hug or word of encouragement instead.

And even when faced with people whom you vehemently disagree with, there is an opportunity to extend compassion. They, like you, long to be free from suffering. They experience pain, injury, illness, loss, and grief just like you. They desire to be happy, safe, loved, and cared for, just like you. Perhaps for a very good reason, you do not feel called to help them by way of your time, space, or energy right now. And that's okay. There's enough room for that.

"Boundaries are the distance at which I can love you and me simultaneously."

—Prentice Hemphill, founder of
The Embodiment Institute

What is needed most right now is for each of us to become a container for our own grief as well as the grief of others, and to be moved to live in a way that works to heal that collective grief. We must learn how to hold space for one another. The key to our being in the world optimally is directly related to our ability to pay attention to the present moment with curiosity, non-judgment, and kindness, as well as our courage to speak and act from our hearts. That ability is accessible to every single one of us if we look for it.

This Will Be Interesting!

As I completed the writing of this book, we were days away from beginning the 2021-2022 school year. Although COVID-19 continued to rage on with the dramatic surge of the delta variant, my daughters began sixth and eighth grade in person at our local public school. They have transitioned beautifully and are now in their sophomore and senior years of high school. Together, we have done so much social-emotional learning and healing, particularly since Quauhtli's birth. I am proud of my children and how they show up in the world, and I am honored to have the privilege of watching them grow.

When Paulo and I celebrated our fifteenth wedding anniversary in 2021, I surprised him with a proposal in front of our closest family and friends at the same place where he lost his ring nine years ago. It took us a long time to afford a replacement ring, and I was delighted to have the opportunity to "choose" Paulo again and ask him if he was willing to choose me again, too. Our wedding invitations had a quote on the back which read, "I love you not only for who you are, but for who I am when I am with you." Those words still ring true, and I am so grateful to have such a partner to grow through life with.

Paulo and I welcomed another child, our sweet son Ocelot, into the world on June 25, 2023. Through the surprise blessing of his birth, we learned our answer about whether or not Quauhtli would be an "only child." Now all of our children have the gift of a best friend to grow up with, and our family finally feels complete.

Baby Ocelot

As with millions of others around the world, my job was affected by the coronavirus. Eighteen months into the pandemic, the GR Center for Mindfulness was facing financial peril. Carol and I agreed that it was in the company's best interest to lay me off. Having worked for the past twenty summers of my life, I was actually pretty excited to let go of that responsibility for a while.

The freedom in my schedule has allowed me to be even more present to my children's needs while also nurturing my creative expression and exploring what work I'd truly like to do in the world. Since then, I reimagined the Ram Dass meet-up into what I now call Sacred Rhythms Fellowship. We meet at each turn of the season according to the wheel of the year, and I teach yoga, meditation, pranayama, and then offer a dharma talk followed by community discussion. It has been such a beautiful unfolding, and the relationships that I've created along the way mean everything to me.

I also tried my hand at podcasting under the title *Tending to Change with Jeni Juarez*. Learning and experimenting with these new platforms for teaching has been challenging but fulfilling. I don't know where this path will take me, but I finally feel like I'm doing what I'm here to do. Interestingly, I'm not afraid of the uncertainty! I'm curious, but my practice is to relax into the mystery and trust my intuition of what to do next. Instead of praying for particular outcomes, I pray for the clarity to see the next step and for the courage needed to take it. I trust that whatever comes next is what's meant for me. I neither force nor avoid.

The life that I'm meant to live is the one that I am living. And for these past five years, life has invited me to embrace my calling as a mother and wife. Although our society would have me believe that these roles are a given, inconsequential, I find the opposite to be true. My experience of raising children and nurturing my marriage is equal parts purification and medicine, a fire that both burns and soothes.

"What if your dharma is just to be a really good mother?"
—Behnje Masson

Things are still not great between my parents and me, but the quality of the relationship has shifted. Writing this book retriggered a lot of unresolved wounds that I had to work through. Out of necessity of my mental health, I went low- and no-contact with both of my parents for quite a while. To support my healing, I started with a year of talk therapy before switching to a more body-based therapeutic approach called Eye Movement Desensitization and Reprocessing (EMDR).

My experience with EMDR was life-changing. I began with the goal of letting go of the anger I held toward my parents. But what I came out with was so much more. I was able to integrate and reframe some of the oldest, deepest wounds from my childhood as well as sexual assault as a teen. It helped me better understand some of the challenges my parents faced as they grew up and raised me, and it deepened my compassion and gratitude for them.

I had to unlearn and relearn what it means to be in a healthy relationship, including setting and maintaining appropriate boundaries, taking personal responsibility, and how to repair a relationship after conflict or rupture. This has been immensely helpful within the context of my marriage and close friendships.

There's a hard truth here, however. While taking the time and space I needed to work through my wounding, I hurt my relationship with my parents in the process. We love each other dearly, and they have demonstrated time and again that when shit hits the fan, they will be there. But trust in both directions is deeply eroded, and we still haven't learned how to communicate well with each other in an authentic, vulnerable way. Perhaps naively, I will never give up hope on reconciliation. All I ever wanted was a healthy, secure relationship with them. And until we can work through the challenges that prevent that outcome, I continue to wish them a peaceful, happy, and healthy life. My work is to meet them where they're at, keep my heart tender and open, and operate from the highest level of integrity that I can.

Since writing this book, I also came out to the world as bisexual. I have known this about myself for as long as I have been conscious of my sexuality. But because I witnessed the church and my own family shun and excommunicate anyone who did not uphold their view of "normal," I tragically suppressed my body's wisdom, thus becoming my own oppressor in a way.

Even so, I have always loved women. Not necessarily sexually or romantically, but cosmically. I love women for all that we are as creators and containers of life and beauty, as carriers of culture and wisdom. I had to overcome a lot of fear, shame, and codependency to be brave enough to declare my love of women in public.

Not that my sexuality is anyone's damn business, thankyouverymuch. I am monogamous and deeply in love with Paulo. But I viewed my coming out as a personal step of voluntarily releasing some of the unearned privileges and power that come with being seen as heterosexual in this current cultural narrative. Coming out was about me releasing my shame, speaking my truth, and demanding that all beings, regardless of any aspect of their identity, be treated with love, respect, and dignity. It was also an offering to folks within my friend and family circle who might also be a part of the LGBTQ+ community but, for whatever reason, have not felt safe to be themselves, out loud. I wanted to create a safe space for them to rest by declaring to the world that they are not alone.

Hindsight Wisdom

It is not with any underestimation that I say we stand on the shoulders of giants. When I think of all the fierce, unrelenting women who insisted on not just surviving, but *thriving* in a world set on their destruction, I am moved to tears. Not only tears of gratitude, but also tears of sacred rage; there are still so many places where women continue to be abused, mutilated, restrained, exploited, shamed, and murdered.

Our rights as women—rights that we take for granted, such as the ability to work, get an education, take out a loan, buy property, own a business, and decide our reproductive fate—are young and fragile. The work of dismantling the systems that suppress and oppress women and girls is not done, and we are at an inflection point. The questions being asked of us are, are we brave enough to do the work before us? And, how beautiful are we willing to imagine it?

I also continue to examine how white supremacy and patriarchy live in me and guide my unconscious attitudes and behaviors. This part of my practice still feels heavy, but no less important. While my natural tendencies are now recalibrated toward kindness, connection, and curiosity, I am not perfect. There are times when I slip below consciousness and then later have to reckon with the ways in which I caused harm to those around me as well as to myself.

I have come to appreciate that although I am owning up to my "sins" or unskillful behaviors ("sin," etymologically speaking, actually translates as "missing the mark"; it's not some original, shameful deficiency, but rather, as Krishna Das puts it, "bad aim."), it does *not* mean that:

- The people whom I have harmed are required to forgive me.
- I'm magically healed from ever perpetrating violence unconsciously again.

The whole process requires my sincere commitment to monitor my behavior and thoughts continuously. The depth of practices I've done over the past several years does not mean I no longer react to intense emotions and self-righteousness from time to time. But I appreciate how my way of being has evolved from flat-out refusing to take accountability for my actions to maybe holding a grudge for a little while and then apologizing, to apologizing immediately afterward, to catching myself mid-action. Of course, my desire is to simply *not* do or say the hurtful things at all, but hey, I'll get there eventually. For now, my work is to take responsibility and accept accountability for *adharmic* or inharmonious actions and beliefs as they inevitably arise.

It is my experience that once one has integrated even a modest understanding of the ecosystem of humanity and our interconnection to the world around us, we don't need as much external authority in terms of skillful and unskillful behavior. It becomes self-evident that to harm another is to harm oneself, so I don't need laws or commandments to remind me not to harm other beings. My moral compass must be guided by my integrity and humility. If I rely on how others perceive me as evidence of my "goodness," I can be easily led astray by those who wish to manipulate me. The ego-demolishing truth is that I will never be liked, accepted, loved, or valued by *everyone*, especially when it comes to those who cannot consider a perspective other than their own.

When I'm faced with new information that conflicts with my current framework of reality, my practice is to breathe a little space around any tightening that arises and allow for alternate viewpoints and experiences. I don't immediately abandon my understanding, but I offer an attitude of curiosity and openness. Perhaps what is being presented is more accurate than what I previously believed; perhaps not. But one thing I know for sure, being at peace is more important to me than being right.

"This is what I think, but I'm prepared to be surprised."
—Pema Chödrön

It has taken me years of intentionality, practice, and the support of innumerable friends, teachers, and guides to consider more than *my* perspective of reality. But I have tasted enough nectar to appreciate the feeling of ease and peace of mind that arises from living with an open heart and a curious mind. When I can simply *be* in the moment without labeling it, clinging to it, or pushing it away, I somehow end up taking the next right step, and things flow together in a beautifully poignant way. It feels like an unfolding process or the turning of a page in a story instead of an overwhelming barrage of random events.

The gift of this attitude is the peace of letting go of always wondering, worrying, and preparing for some imagined future. Instead, I allow myself to imagine a million different potential futures that I would be delighted to live in. And then I release the dreams like a giant bunch of colorful balloons into the sky, accepting that where I am right now is exactly perfect. And where I am in the next moment will be exactly perfect, too, for infinite moments.

No matter what lies ahead, as long as I am paying attention, it will be interesting!

Our little family in 2025

Now, the Exposition of Yoga Begins

Chögyam Trungpa Rinpoche once said, "Enlightenment is ego's ultimate disappointment." While I am by no means an enlightened being, I'm beginning to appreciate the wisdom of this teaching. It reminds me of something I once told my daughters: "I spent the first ten years of your life telling you how special, important, and unique you are. And now, I'll spend the next ten years explaining to you that so is everyone else, which is to say, you're not special at all."

This might seem harsh but take a breath and read it again. Each human being, each form of life, is a child of the Divine Mother—one of the many that is One. We are distinct human beings with distinct experiences, and yet we can only survive as a species if we co-operate; if we operate together. So, when I consider how we *seekers* (of Truth or God or Creator or Source) do all of this striving and straining and fighting to "achieve enlightenment," I can't help but recognize that even if there is an "end" to the seeking, that end would be the realization that each life form before our eyes is but another version of us. Each one of us, at the core of our beings—our *atman* or individual soul—is longing to come back home to our original Self, to our primordial source.

Until then, here we are. There's no use in rushing. Pushing someone else to "wake up" seems inevitably to result in some form of violence. We can let go of aggressive self-improvement, too. Everything we are is everything we need for this journey; we do not need to get rid of or add anything to ourselves. If certain habits, beliefs, or relationships must fall away, it will be like the snake shedding its skin. As my mother often said, "Always in perfect time and proper order." There's nothing to acquire, like a secret mantra or talisman, and there's nothing you have to make happen through complicated rituals or extreme practices. *What* we do isn't nearly as important as *why* we're doing it.

Our intention is what matters most. Aspire to have your thoughts, words, and actions be in harmony with whatever is needed in the present moment. Trust that the only reason you've even stepped a foot onto the path in search of something is because what you're seeking has been calling out to you. Grace is the word I happen to use for that "something," but you're welcome to label it however it comes through for you. The label is ultimately irrelevant since it is simply a beacon that brings you back to your Self.

> "Before Enlightenment, chop wood, carry water. After Enlightenment, chop wood, carry water."
> —Zen Proverb

When I am peaceful but engaged, instead of avoiding or disconnecting from life, I can hear what resonates as true for me, and I do not need to rely on some external source to tell me what to believe. It's something I feel *to my bones*. And when I act from that space, I trust that the action I take is always in harmony with Life. I aim to *work with,* not force, the energy all around me.

By rediscovering this deep source of self-reliance, I worry less about what other people think about me. I and the Divine Mother know my heart, my intention, and that's good enough for me. I know that at any given moment, I'm operating from the highest level of integrity that I can. And I'm not too proud to hear when there's another opportunity for me to learn and be better. In fact, I welcome those opportunities, because that's where the magic of life is.

Enjoying our lives is our sacred right. We are each invited to do what we love, simultaneously recognizing that if our joy requires the suffering of another form of Life, that this joy will always be incomplete and rife with fear and disequilibrium. If, however, we can navigate a dynamic, ever-changing landscape while savoring and appreciating joy in its countless forms, then an abiding inner peacefulness and sense of wholeness will naturally blossom.

I can't help but wonder what type of future we could collectively co-create if we each rediscovered our capacity for compassionate, skillful action, if instead of being weighed down by regret, anger, or fear, we were each tapped into our innately visionary, collaborative, courageous selves. I wonder if we'll ever be willing to let go of "normal," of expectation, of control, and instead let love build a life that is more exquisite than our wildest dreams. May we each come home to ourselves and delight in our united multiplicity.

I'm up for it. Are you?

Epilogue

What a gift it is to recognize all at once the beginning and end of the path. The beginning is chaotic noise—dysregulation; disharmony; confusion; going through life as a bystander or as a constant victim; feeling as if life is happening *to you,* like you're thrashing about in the waves and, every once in a while, there's a break in the endless storm. It is a tunnel vision view of life taken in through your own eyes, a story in which you think you're the main character and everything is viewed through the very blurred lens of your narrow life experience.

When there is a *break in the mental storm,* you experience moments of sweetness, of true connection and belonging, moments of *flow* in which you're joyful, light, playful, happy. But you don't fully appreciate it, at least not until it's gone. Or you worry that it will soon be gone.

Then something miraculous happens. Grace happens. Grace is when you notice that you're noticing; you begin to "see" yourself living the experiences of your life. And as soon as that happens once, you have begun to awaken. You have pulled back the curtain and you saw what you were seeing, saying, doing. You began to observe your life *as you were living it,* and that moment changed everything.

It changes everything because when you're fully present, you relate directly to your experience instead of through the intermediary of mental concepts colored by your memories and emotions. There is a sort of figure/ground reversal in which what used to be background (the unfolding of the universe and its infinite interconnections) becomes foreground (you are now aware of how much you aren't aware of). And what was foreground (you as the main character) becomes background ("you" as one of infinite characters).

From this moment, your new journey begins. This is the journey that follows your longing—the longing for true connection, for authentic living, for remaining ever balanced in an inherently unbalanced world. You've tasted the sweet nectar of that connection and now your heart pines for it, but not only for yourself anymore; now you wish for everyone else to come along with you. Because you can see how they too are feeling victimized by life, insecure and uncertain of their worthiness, unsafe to express themselves freely and joyfully like a child. And because you want that for them, the work becomes work on yourself.

But how can that be true? How can you need to work on yourself for other people? Because the only thing you can truly do for another person is to be an environment for them to feel safe, to be seen and heard from a space of vulnerability, of open-heartedness, of pure love.

Most of us have not been taught that such an ability to "notice the noticing" exists inside of us, let alone how to tap into it or operate in the world while maintaining it. But someone who can and does can be a powerful teacher for those who've yet to experience it for themselves. It's possible to ignite that recognition in others because it is a reflection of a space within that exists in every single one of us.

We all experienced the intrinsic state of absolute joy, absolute love, and absolute freedom naturally as young children. Babies come into the world free of cognitive frameworks for their experiences. Everything they experience is full of wonder and bliss because they don't ruminate over their memories or project fearfully into the future. Even when babies encounter pain, overwhelm, or frustration, they allow themselves full, unobstructed expression of those emotions, and so the emotions quickly pass. Babies and young children are deeply interconnected with their world, and to them, life is resplendent and awe-inspiring.

But somewhere along our individual paths of social programming and personal traumas, we forgot. Because of our complete reliance on our caregivers, we were subtly taught that other people knew what was best for us and that we should trust them more than ourselves. We were taught to betray ourselves, often as a matter of survival, and it caused us to lose touch with our deep inner knowing, our intuition or bodily wisdom. And when the pain of that fragmentation becomes discernible, our journey back to ourselves begins.

So, you practice. You clear away the mental confusion layer by layer, and you work to reintegrate mind, body, and heart. You "begin again" a million times and then a million more, because now that you've begun to wake up, there is no going back to sleep. You can try all you want, but the truth is that an inevitable process has already begun. You don't want to suffer, and you don't want to create suffering. So, you keep engaging in your life in a way that honors all people and situations as a blessing or a teaching or both. You maintain your ability to stay present as well as discern what contributes to your ability to maintain presence and what detracts from your ability to do so.

I long for us all to feel connected to our hearts and empowered to choose how we move through our lives, both as individuals and as an inextricably interconnected organism. I want all of our needs to be met and for all of our suffering to work itself out until there is no more functionality behind it, and therefore it ceases to exist. So please join me in committing again and again to this sacred work in ourselves for the benefit of all sentient beings.

With deep love and respect,
Jeni

Prayer of St. Francis of Assisi

Lord make me an instrument of Your peace.

Where there is hatred, let me sow love.

Where there is injury, pardon.

Where there is doubt, faith.

Where there is despair, hope.

Where there is darkness, light.

Where there is sadness, joy.

O Divine Master, grant that I may not so

Much seek to be consoled as to console;

To be understood as to understand,

To be loved as to love;

For it is in giving that we receive.

It is in pardoning that we are pardoned,

And it is in dying that we are

Born into eternal life.

Acknowledgments

To my Beloved, Paulo. How many times would I have given up on this project if it weren't for you? You are my best friend, my rock, and my safe space. I love you not only for who you are, but for who I am when I'm with you.

To my husband and children, for your unyielding love and the gift of your beingness. Thank you for teaching me, for believing in me, for walking this journey with me. My life is duly blessed because you are in it.

To my ancestors who have offered up all of their wisdom and life experiences, who have suffered and persevered, who have laid the framework on which I now stand. I honor your love and sacrifices by carrying on your noble work.

To my teachers, who come to me in innumerable forms. For your grace, wisdom, patience, and love for me, I offer up my heart and sincere gratitude. To shine light into darkness, to bring illumination through self-inquiry, to restrain oneself to only offer just enough to empower the student, is such a beautiful, selfless gift. May I honor your dedication by sharing this gift in the same Spirit.

To all my dear friends who supported, uplifted, and encouraged me during the writing of this book. Julie and Meg, you were there from the start. Thank you for nudging me for greater detail, Julie, and to you, Meg, for helping me hone my grammar. To Sue, Karen, and Carol for beta-reading my rough drafts and encouraging me to continue forward. To Rachel, for providing a much-needed eye for revisions.

To my editor and mentor, Parvati, for your graciousness and patience. I am profoundly grateful for Maharajji's Grace leading me to you. You helped me shape this into an actual book and provided invaluable guidance for my path as an author. This would not be what it is today without you. Thank you.

To all lineage holders of the sacred traditions. For your fortitude and commitment to liberation for all, I honor your solemn vows and abiding faith. Thank you for keeping alive these eternal truths for the sake of humanity and the whole of life.

For the teachings that rest in my past, for the blessed opportunities that await in my future, for the love, peace, and contentment that embrace me in the here and now, thank you.

References

Centers for Disease Control and Prevention. (021, April 6). *About the CDC-Kaiser ACE Study |Violence Prevention|Injury Center.* CDC. Retrieved February 20, 2021, from https://www.cdc.gov/violenceprevention/aces/about.html

Claiborne, S., Wilson-Hartgrove, J., & Okoro, E. (2010). *Common Prayer: A Liturgy for Ordinary Radicals.* Zondervan.

Cohen, J., & West, B. (Directors). (2021). *My Name Is Pauli Murray* [Film]. Participant; Storyville Films; Drexler Films.

Cortés, L., & Garbus, L. (Directors). (2020). *All In: The Fight for Democracy* [Film]. Story Syndicate.

Dass, R. (2014). *Polishing the Mirror: How to Live from Your Spiritual Heart.* Sounds True.

Ferriss, T. (2009). *The 4-Hour Workweek.* Crown Publishers.

Hartwig, M., & Hartwig, D. (2014). *It Starts With Food: Discover the Whole30 and Change Your Life in Unexpected Ways.* Victory Belt Publishing.

Kendi, I. X. (2019). *How to Be an Antiracist.* Random House Publishing Group.

Kiloby, S. (2017). *Natural Rest for Addiction: A Radical Approach to Recovery Through Mindfulness and Awareness.* New Harbinger Publications.

Lears, R. (Director). (2019). *Knock Down the House* [Film]. Jubilee Films; Atlas Films; Artemis Rising.

Markus, P. (2015). *Love Everyone: The Transcendent Wisdom of Neem Karoli Baba Told Through the Stories of the Westerners Whose Lives He Transformed.* HarperCollins.

Mascaró, J. (Ed.). (2003). *The Bhagavad Gita* (J. Mascaró, Trans.). Penguin Publishing Group.

Menakem, R. (2017). *My Grandmother's Hands: Racialized Trauma and the Pathway to Mending Our Hearts and Bodies*. Central Recovery Press.

Millman, D. (1999). *Everyday Enlightenment: The Twelve Gateways to Personal Growth*. Grand Central Publishing.

O'Connor, J., & Seymour, J. (2011). *Introducing NLP: Psychological Skills for Understanding and Influencing People*. Red Wheel Weiser.

Salzberg, S. (2013). *Real Happiness at Work: Meditations for Accomplishment, Achievement, and Peace*. Workman Publishing Company.

Taylor, S. R. (2018). *The Body is Not an Apology: The Power of Radical Self-love*. Berrett-Koehler Publishers.

Trungpa, C. (2002). *Cutting through spiritual materialism*. Shambhala.

Welwood, J. (2002). *Toward a Psychology of Awakening: Buddhism, Psychotherapy, and the Path of Personal and Spiritual Transformation*. Shambhala.

West, B., & Cohen, J. (Directors). (2018). *RBG* [Film]. no production company listed.

Yogananda, Paramhansa, *Autobiography of a Yogi* (W. Y. Evans-Wentz, Trans.). (1993). Self-Realization Fellowship.

About the Author

Jeni is a 500-hour Registered Yoga Teacher, podcast host of Tending to Change with Jeni Juarez, a mother of four, and a dedicated student on the path of the heart. She offers public classes as well as personal sessions designed to inspire and empower others to reclaim their wholeness and sovereignty, for the benefit of all beings. She is excited to be actively working to bring forth the value of emotional resilience and peace of mind. Learn more about her offerings at www.jenijuarez.com

www.ingramcontent.com/pod-product-compliance
Lightning Source LLC
Chambersburg PA
CBHW030908120626
46554CB00001B/65